DEVELOPING TOGETHER

Developing Together challenges systematic biases that have long plagued research with marginalized populations of children. It traces the unexamined assumptions guiding such research to definitions of subjectivity and the psyche based in Western cultural norms.

The book provides alternative paradigms, applying a comprehensive methodology to two unique schooling contexts. Through this new approach children's development can be seen as an interactive, collaborative process.

The chapters highlight how theoretical assumptions directly influence research methods and, in turn, affect educational practices. Unique in its provision of a detailed alternative method for conducting research with children, the book explains how the study of collaborative competence would influence education and applied fields. It is an essential resource for researchers in developmental psychology, educators, and policymakers alike.

REBECCA R. GARTE is Professor of Teacher Education at the City University of New York (CUNY), and she has published extensively in the areas of developmental psychology and teacher education. As a recipient of a large-scale grant from the W. K. Kellogg Foundation, she led the Comprehensive Educator Empowerment Program, a multiyear research practice partnership with New York City public schools.

DEVELOPING TOGETHER

Understanding Children through Collaborative Competence

REBECCA R. GARTE

City University of New York

Shaftesbury Road, Cambridge CB2 8EA, United Kingdom

One Liberty Plaza, 20th Floor, New York, NY 10006, USA

477 Williamstown Road, Port Melbourne, VIC 3207, Australia

314–321, 3rd Floor, Plot 3, Splendor Forum, Jasola District Centre, New Delhi – 110025, India

103 Penang Road, #05–06/07, Visioncrest Commercial, Singapore 238467

Cambridge University Press is part of Cambridge University Press & Assessment, a department of the University of Cambridge.

We share the University's mission to contribute to society through the pursuit of education, learning and research at the highest international levels of excellence.

www.cambridge.org
Information on this title: www.cambridge.org/9781009446662
DOI: 10.1017/9781009446686

© Rebecca R. Garte 2024

This publication is in copyright. Subject to statutory exception and to the provisions of relevant collective licensing agreements, no reproduction of any part may take place without the written permission of Cambridge University Press & Assessment.

First published 2024
First paperback edition 2025

A catalogue record for this publication is available from the British Library

ISBN 978-1-009-44669-3 Hardback
ISBN 978-1-009-44666-2 Paperback

Cambridge University Press & Assessment has no responsibility for the persistence or accuracy of URLs for external or third-party internet websites referred to in this publication and does not guarantee that any content on such websites is, or will remain, accurate or appropriate.

I dedicate this book to my children and all children who want to be seen for their full selves.

Contents

List of Figures	*page* ix
List of Tables	x
Preface	xi
Acknowledgments	xvi

PART I COLLABORATIVE COMPETENCE: IN PURSUIT OF A CULTURALLY VALID ACCOUNT OF SOCIAL DEVELOPMENT

1 Why a New Direction Is Necessary — 3

2 Can the Self Be Relational? Culture at the Root of Psychology — 26

PART II ELEMENTS OF COLLABORATIVE COMPETENCE: EXPANDING ON PRIOR RESEARCH

3 Redefining Subjectivity and Intersubjectivity for a New Method — 47

4 Framing Intersubjectivity during Children's Interactions: A Critical Examination of Theories and Methods — 64

5 What Makes for "High-Quality" Interactions at Home and School? — 85

6 Collaborative Competence: A New Model of Development — 97

PART III A NEW THEORY AND METHOD FOR ASSESSING DEVELOPMENT VIA COLLABORATIVE COMPETENCE

7 Capturing the Complexity of Collaborations in Varied Settings — 113

8 Principles for a Developmentally and Culturally Valid Methodology — 137

Contents

9 Analyzing Components of Collaborative Competence during Preschooler Free Play — 156

10 Collaborative Competence during Early Elementary Playful Learning Activities — 177

PART IV IMPLICATIONS FOR THEORY, RESEARCH, AND PRACTICE

11 Making the Shift to Interactivity in Education and Psychology — 209

12 A Theoretical Home for the Role of Collaborative Competence in Education — 221

References — 233
Index — 260

Figures

3.1	Constructs of intersubjectivity according to the domain, theory, and operationalization that are the focuses of each.	page 50
4.1	The theorized relationship between the elements of intersubjectivity.	66
7.1	Dialogue codes as they occurred over the course of a playful learning episode.	133
7.2	Intersubjectivity codes as they occurred over the course of a playful learning episode.	134
7.3	All interactive codes across an episode of playful learning collaboration.	135
10.1	Teacher A's Activity A1 – frequency of dialogue.	189
10.2	Teacher A's Activity A2 – frequency of dialogue.	189
10.3	Teacher B's activity – frequency of dialogue.	198
10.4	Coding of Teacher A's Activity A1.	199
10.5	Coding of Teacher A's Activity A2.	201
10.6	Coding of Teacher B's activity.	203

Tables

7.1	Codebook for early elementary collaborative competence.	*page* 125
8.1	Demographic variables of children and teachers by classroom.	143
8.2	Inter-rater agreement of the intersubjectivity measure across item and score.	150
8.3	Inter-rater reliability for collaboration measure by item.	152
8.4	Cross-tabulation of collaboration scores between two raters.	153
8.5	Number, flexibility, and reliability of activity areas (n = 38) by classroom and percentage of scores given for flexibility across all activity areas and classrooms.	154
9.1	Group characteristics and structural features of interaction episodes.	163
9.2	Descriptive statistics of predictor and outcome variables.	164
9.3	Multivariate analysis of covariance effects of contextual variables nested within classrooms on intersubjectivity and collaboration variables.	165
9.4	Nested regressions for interaction variables by classroom characteristics.	167
9.5	Two-level model of the effect of activity area variables on interaction variables.	168
10.1	Teacher talk directly preceding child response, comparing Teacher A and Teacher B activities.	195
10.2	Forms of dialogue that included references to internal states by teacher.	197

Preface

My first job working with children was at a day care center in Philadelphia. I was an assistant teacher in a three-year-old room and had just begun to study psychology after having been an English literature major. There was a boy named Stephen in that room. He flapped his arms wildly all day and only spoke in a way that I later learned was termed "echolalia" due to its echoing and apparently meaningless nature. He almost never made eye contact. Shortly after he joined our class, I noticed Stephen bouncing and chasing a red ball on the rug. I decided I would get him to play with me. I caught the ball he had thrown, held it up to him to make sure he was watching it, then threw it in his direction. Each time I grasped the ball he would squeal with delight and flap his arms, jumping with anticipation before running for it. At first Stephen would only glance fleetingly at me and watch the ball, but after about a month of daily ball games he began to sustain eye contact, adjust his placement on the rug according to my position, and move in anticipation of my movements. My initial goal had been eye contact, but then Stephen uttered his first noncholalic word "more" while looking directly at me and beaming. I knew instinctively that if I could achieve with Stephen what his classmates exhibited automatically – driving cars over their heads in tandem while making *vrrrmm* sounds, passing pretend tea back and forth in the dramatic play area, jumping into puddles together and laughing at the splashes – an entire world would open up for him, one that included language, but beyond that one in which meanings could be shared – the world of intersubjectivity.

Years later I taught four- to eight-year-old children at a high-poverty public school – the younger prekindergarteners during the day and the six- to eight-year-old children as part of a program for students deemed "at risk" for literacy failure in the late afternoon. I became intimately acquainted with how schools are microcosms of society and how oppression and social injustice, including structural and interpersonal racism, misogyny, and xenophobia, play out at every level of human interaction. The macro-context of those years of teaching was an endless avalanche of injustices that comprised the overarching situation in which my students and their families lived. Yet, in the foreground, the micro-interactions between my students and their classmates, myself, their families, the educational assistants, and certain colleagues created an opposing context – that of an intersubjective world that was based in empathy, curiosity, and shared creativity. This intersubjective space of thousands of collaborative interactions and moments of shared meaning-making served as an implicit form of resistance to the oppressive forces of racism and savage capitalism surrounding us all.

I recall so many moments that transcended the oppressive mundanity of what one might expect life in an urban school to be like. There was the time when my first and second graders shared their final stories after multiple drafts, with every one of their classmates listening to their fellow authors with rapt attention before providing insightful critiques one by one without needing any prompting by myself – the teacher. Or there was the day when my most emotionally challenging four-year-old student decided to measure the entire classroom with Unifix cubes. All of his classmates, enthralled with his endeavor, pitched in by moving aside furniture, reattaching Unifix sections that had come apart, and helping record the mathematical findings once each section was completed.

These moments proved that classrooms can be spaces of transformation and that the human capacity for shared meaning-making has the power to transcend everything that oppresses. I knew that trauma and disconnection – a lack of trust – created a barrier to many students' ability to learn in school. I knew that social hegemonies prevented families from feeling that they had a place within the school, and that so many complex cultural historical dynamics bred hostility among the adults that trickled down into the children. And yet, those intersubjective experiences – those times when each of the children was productively engaged in sharing materials and exchanging dialogue, when parents began to trust the safety of the classroom and share in the community it represented – continued to occur regardless of the oppressive realities that formed the backdrop of the school community.

Since entering academia, I have been committed to spotlighting the everyday brilliance of children like the ones I taught, who demonstrate their tremendous capacities for intersubjectivity and sophisticated collaboration out of their own drive to engage in shared meaning-making with their peers. I have also been committed to recognizing these capacities more formally through the concepts and definitions that structure theories and research within psychology and education. Celebrating cultural diversity is not just about recognizing and appreciating differences but about realizing that all our assumed ways of thinking about human behavior are culturally grounded, and that the culture that looms largest in the Western social sciences and in American social institutions, like schools, is that of Anglo-European heritage.

There are status and power differentials between what is represented by schooling (its norms, subjects, and methods) and students – their cultures, languages, and family histories. The former becomes the entrenched representation of what is aspired toward, while the latter become subsumed beneath the goal and promise of adopting the former. This striving toward the school – representing power, opportunity, and prosperity – is contingent on a simultaneous striving away from everything that is not school: family, community, culture, and language of origin. Only now, over 100 years since the assimilationist goals of the American classroom were clearly articulated by the founders of American public schools, are education scholars taking seriously the benefits of maintaining students' native languages, even when those languages are associated with nations considered less powerful or prosperous or with races that had been deemed inferior for most of American history.

However, despite some critiques of Eurocentric approaches to education, the central premises and assumptions of American education remained unchanged. The values and norms embedded within white middle-class culture are seamlessly incorporated into the functioning of schools and classrooms by the 90 percent of American schoolteachers who are from white middle-class family backgrounds. Teacher training programs within departments of teacher education in university schools of education are similarly almost entirely composed of white middle-class faculty. It is almost impossible to look critically at the norms of a culture that one is entirely entrenched within and when most of one's professional relationships are with people entrenched in that same culture. Enacting one's own cultural norms just feels right, whereas attempting to understand norms that conflict with one's own culture feels awkward and foreign.

Criticisms of Eurocentric societal functioning that marginalize, disenfranchise, and disproportionately incarcerate people whose speaking styles, interactive norms, and relationships to American institutions derive from distinct historical and sociocultural experiences have been acknowledged recently among American progressives and considered within academic institutions. The historical and contemporary oppressions and violations of the human rights of many have, after decades of effort, become impossible for the mainstream American society to ignore. However, in the classrooms where young children seek to engage in collective meaning-making with their peers and teachers, they often find themselves misunderstood, misrepresented, ignored, or even vilified. There is enough research to show the extensive implicit biases of educators toward students based on race, ethnicity, gender, and social class. Yet there is no clear method for addressing them.

This book lays out the multilayered complexity of what might comprise an education based on the strengths that have been shown to predominate among minoritized children in the United States. Education would begin with supporting and facilitating collaborative competencies and the development of intersubjectivity with peers and teachers rather than with the false promise of meritocracy. Rather than organizing schools according to hierarchies of individuals, they would be organized into teams of those who share common goals and whose skills complement one another's. Each child's unique set of abilities would not be ranked according to relative degrees of inferiority and superiority as compared to their classmates, but rather children's sets of skills would be recognized holistically, and they would be grouped with peers who would fill one another's skill gaps to create a well-rounded team. Assessments would no longer be based on the false pretense that it is possible to extract the mind from the social world wherein all meaning is created and functions, but instead assessments would keep track of the learning, creativity, and problem-solving among groups of children and adults working together to solve authentic social problems.

This hypothetical redesign of schooling would ensure that the transformative intersubjective moments that defined the true meaning of education in my classroom and in many others were consistently placed at the center of education rather than the periphery. Children should not have to wait until recess to engage in joyful, collaborative, meaningful shared activities with their peers. Rather than separating the concerns of children and adults, multiaged groups should work together to collectively solve the problems that affect their lives. In so doing, the social hierarchies that have long plagued American society and education will no longer define schooling and classrooms. The power of intersubjective interactions to breed joy, empathy, and shared knowledge creation will become primary, allowing all members of the classroom community to participate equally.

This book reviews a wide variety of research findings in developmental psychology and education to provide both an argument and a method for making such changes to how children learn in American schools in concrete terms. In addition, new questions for psychological and educational researchers are raised by the proposal of new methods for capturing collaborative competence. At the same time, preexisting psychological theories of the past decade that offer pathways for expanding the focus on human experience as inherently collaborative and transformative are reviewed. This book aims to serve both educational and psychological practitioners, policymakers, researchers, and theorizers. By presenting practical methods of assessing and structuring learning activities and providing a trajectory for supporting the development of collaborative competence throughout childhood, the hope is that new concepts that take such interaction seriously as a primary unit of analysis will be spawned.

Acknowledgments

The first impetus for this book came from the children who shared their brilliance with me and showed me that there was so much more to their development than the research was showing. Their families and the educators who continue to work in classrooms while advocating for holistic forms of education also inform this work. I am grateful to the scholars in the Department of Human Development within the Graduate Center of the City University of New York who first introduced me to concepts like distributed cognition and interobjectivity, freeing me to pursue new models of development. Chief among them is Anna Stetsenko, my doctoral advisor, whose work continues to inspire and shape my own. I thank my colleagues Jeremy Sawyer and Jennifer Gilken for their thoughtful feedback on earlier drafts of this manuscript and the ideas behind it. I am grateful to Yolanda Medina and Cara Kronen for their continuous support of my research and teaching. Finally, I thank my husband, Jocelyn Azandossessi, whose insights have pushed me to decenter aspects of Eurocentrism that I could not have perceived on my own.

I am also very appreciative of the editorial team at Cambridge University Press for all their assistance in preparing this book for publication.

PART I
Collaborative Competence
In Pursuit of a Culturally Valid Account of Social Development

CHAPTER I

Why a New Direction Is Necessary

Developmental Psychology in the Lives of Children Classified as "At Risk"

Today's developmental psychologists are continuing the tradition begun with the child study movement of using science to better the lives of society's most vulnerable children and families (e.g., Lee et al., 2022; McTavish et al., 2022; Reynolds, 2021). In today's context, those most in need are the children who are subject to the deleterious effects of "cumulative risk" (CR; Burlaka et al., 2015; Evans et al., 2013). The concept of CR was introduced to developmental psychology in 1978 by Rutter (1978). This enabled a new way of classifying children according to how poverty and other adverse experiences of their birth and later years predicted long-term negative outcomes throughout their lifespan. The seminal research on CR shows that each component of social vulnerability that is present at birth (e.g., poverty, single parenthood) increases the likelihood that additional negative environmental factors will affect a child as they continue through development. For example, children born to impoverished parents are more likely to attend overcrowded schools, to witness violence in the home and community, and to be undernourished.

Members of the "at-risk" population have since become research subjects for a vast literature that encompasses much of developmental psychology. While "basic research" in developmental psychology seeks to discover the origins of human capacities and describe universal norms and sequences of skills and abilities as they develop during infancy and childhood, "applied research" is mostly focused on understanding and addressing deficiencies that occur because of suboptimal early experiences. This applied literature can be categorized according to (1) studies that model the effects of broad environmental risk factors such as poverty on equally broad indicators of maladaptive functioning during childhood and

(2) studies that focus on more proximal relationships, including how deficits in one developmental domain affect other domains.

The first research track contrasts various statistical models of how multiple risk factors intersect using the concept of CR. Outcome variables include acute developmental damage such as failure to thrive and the standard assessments of child maladaptive functioning developed by Achenbach (1966). These child behavior checklists (CBCLs) provide an overview of internalizing and externalizing psychological and developmental pathology during childhood. Such studies mirror medical research on the adverse effects of various conditions, treating factors such as poverty and violence as environmental "toxins," with problematic behavior and delayed development as the symptoms. Some interventions aimed at reducing poverty and child maltreatment reference this literature and use similar outcome variables.

The second line of research provides a more fine-grained analysis of how specific aspects of parenting, the home environment, and school-based interventions impact areas of cognitive, social, and language development among the "at-risk" child population. This literature has been largely centered on early childhood. Rather than what could be seen as the "medical model" of the CR literature, the early childhood-focused research provides what could be considered a psychological model. Accordingly there is a bidirectional relationship implied between innate characteristics of individual children and the impacts of various risks on their development. This allows researchers to test for individual differences among children experiencing similar environmental risk factors. The CR literature takes as a given that harmful conditions have detrimental effects on children's well-being and aims to provide accurate models that depict this unidirectional relationship with precision for the purpose of targeting social interventions. By contrast, the "psychological model" examines individual differences among the at-risk population to identify protective factors that enable resilience and even resistance to the negative effects of adversity.

While many studies in basic developmental science are focused on the cognitive domain – addressing questions like whether humans are innately wired to understand mathematical concepts, for example – the applied research is heavily focused on the social domain. "Social competence" is listed as a key outcome in most studies of children who are at risk. The foundational assumption guiding applied developmental psychology is that children placed at risk tend to develop deficiencies in multiple domains of functioning over time (e.g., Atkinson et al., 2015). The results from studies showing how risk factors affect early childhood development set the groundwork for research on elementary and adolescent at-risk populations. Therefore, negative effects early in development are added into models of longer-term impacts demonstrating unique and cumulative effects of adverse early experiences on later childhood, adolescence, and adulthood (Evans et al., 2013).

The early childhood studies that focused on children aged two to five years departed from examining specific environmental effects on children and instead used children's behaviors, capacities, and skills as both explanatory and outcome variables. For example, rather than studying the effects of low family income and living in a neighborhood with high crime statistics on children's self-regulation, the early childhood literature would examine the effects of children placed at risk's own self-regulation skills on their school readiness. While the CR literature has social policy implications, including for interventions, much of the psychological early childhood literature seems to suggest that the key to improving child outcomes is to target specific areas of children's skills for improvement, with the expectation that this will in turn improve related areas of child functioning (e.g., Bulotsky-Sheerer et al., 2020; McDermott et al., 2022).

Conceptualizing Risk

The shorthand "at risk" has been widely applied to children at all stages of development and in a variety of contexts. The latest iteration refers to children "placed at risk" to signify that the risk is not a characteristic of the child themselves but rather a circumstance that affects them. Despite this rhetorical intention, the idea that individual children may be differentially impacted by the same risk factors suggests that they do contribute in varied ways to their own developmental responses to adverse experiences.

The framing and results of much research designed to understand the deleterious effects of "at-risk" status on children have led to a host of findings highlighting such children's developmental deficiencies in every domain. These include significant underdevelopment and/or delayed development of language, theory of mind, IQ, self-regulation, and executive functioning (Atkinson et al., 2015; Chang et al., 2012; Fernald et al., 2013; Finegood & Blair, 2020; Gilkerson et al., 2017; Gobeil-Bourdeau et al., 2022; Mistry et al., 2010). The culprits in these developmental disadvantages range from global factors like home environments to more micro-elements like the number of words spoken at home during the child's first years and the nature of parent–child interactions.

Missing from most research on children and risk is any critical evaluation of the methods and measures used to define either the explanatory variables – how risk factors are defined – or the outcome variables that measure aspects of children's development. Three nationwide US data collection clearinghouses have created a battery of assessments that serve as the standard for the field. These include the Head Start Family and Child Experiences Survey (FACES) and the Early Childhood Longitudinal Survey – Birth to Kindergarten (ECLS-B) and Kindergarten to 5th Grade (ECLS-K). Funded by the American federal government, these data collection initiatives conduct measures of national cohorts of children to enable research with both cross-sectional and longitudinal designs. The batteries of tests cover every developmental domain as well as assessing the contexts of children's lives and classrooms. Each dataset includes measures of basic cognition such as executive functioning along with school-based learning such as preliteracy and prenumeracy (FACES) or knowledge of the curriculum up to the 5th grade (ECLS-K). The dataset also includes measures of social and emotional development, specifically social skills and problem behaviors. There is extensive overlap between the CR, FACES, and ECLS datasets in terms of the constructs of interest, measures used, and tests of validity/reliability. A large percentage of published research within the field of developmental psychology is composed of secondary analyses drawn directly from these datasets – studies that build on their findings and use the measures and constructs as defined and validated by them. Therefore, the accepted standards for how to assess children's development with the greatest rigor and how both optimal and suboptimal developmental characteristics should be conceived within the field are highly influenced by these data clearinghouse.

Measuring Risk and Child Outcomes

Most studies using observations and other innovative methods are conducted with middle-class or mixed-income samples. For example, a recent study by Garner et al. (2021) considered racial congruence and emotion knowledge as variables impacting teacher–child relationships and school readiness. Their sample was composed of middle-class preschoolers from white and African American backgrounds. In this case, the teacher report measure asked teachers about their relationships with the children rather than asking them to objectively assess the children's behavior. The school readiness scale used in the study was specifically designed to be strength based, and the measure was triangulated by assistant teachers to increase the validity and limit the inherent bias associated with using a single rater. Finally, the construct of emotion knowledge was assessed via an emotion knowledge performance task conducted by the researchers. This study of preschoolers from middle-class backgrounds included measures and procedures designed to minimize bias. In addition, by including the impacts of teacher–child relationships and racial congruence, the study acknowledged the inherent influence of teachers' own potentially biased perceptions of children on their assessments of them.

Studies focusing specifically on the development of poor children are much more likely to make use of the standard assessments used in the national datasets than studies of middle-class children. Furthermore, uncritical use of teacher reports to determine children's deficiencies is common in studies in which the entire sample is composed of children from low-income families (Mason et al., 2014). A few studies of poor children do apply innovative methods developed specifically for the purpose of challenging assumptions. These studies may tease apart the nuances of what constitutes an adverse experience or an environmental risk factor; for example, involvement with children's protective services (CPS), maternal education level, and family income are often used as proxies for child neglect and maltreatment and impoverished home environments. However, involvement with CPS is not always an accurate indicator of neglect or maltreatment but might be rather an indicator of racial bias or other negative experiences (such as retaliation by relatives; Bostock & Koprowska, 2022; McTavish et al., 2022). Bostock and Koprowska (2022) analyzed transcripts of interactions between CPS workers and families that revealed racial bias and demonstrated how institutions such as schools and child welfare agencies used their privilege to assign and define risk in a way that did not match family experiences or perceptions.

Therefore, while risk factors associated with poverty and racial minority status have the potential to create adverse experiences for children and families, these might not occur through the same mechanism as child abuse or neglect by parents (McTavish et al., 2022). Similarly, neither poverty nor maternal education level alone explains negative child outcomes. Rather, associated factors such as stress and children's own traits such as temperament mediate the parent–child relationship (Chang et al., 2012; Gobeil-Bourdeau et al., 2022; Hill & Palacio, 2021; Mistry et al., 2010; Seay & Kohl, 2015; Washington et al., 2020). A scoping review found that household chaos as assessed primarily by parent report had a greater negative impact on child outcomes than a host of other risk factors, including poverty (Marsh et al., 2020).

Many studies have found differences between racial and ethnic groups in the ways environmental risk along with parent's stress, behaviors, and beliefs impact child outcomes (Cappa et al., 2011; Hyun et al., 2021; Knauer et al., 2019; Washington et al., 2020). For example, a study by Knauer et al. (2019) demonstrated that among low-income Mexican families parental warmth and nurturing during infancy predicted positive outcomes during preschool age, whereas parental "stimulation" did not. This study used the Home Observation for Measurement of the Environment (HOME) inventory, which assesses both parental responsiveness and emotional support along with North American middle-class ideals of an intellectually stimulating environment. Parenting behaviors that signified intellectual engagement during preschool age did relate to concurrent measures of child cognitive development, whereas items assessing educational materials in the home showed no such relationship. This is only one study among many that suggests that there are multifaceted, multidirectional influences between parenting behaviors, home environment, and specific child outcomes among families living in poverty and from different cultural backgrounds.

Defining and Measuring Poor Children's Development

Nonetheless, when taken on aggregate, the risk factors related to poverty are more likely than not to lead to negative child outcomes. Although the CR literature generally models population trends, the early childhood literature uses the FACES and ECLS constructs to parse how the same risk factors differentially affect individual children. However, the measures and study designs do not allow for consideration of how global risk factors might be differentially construed and experienced by individual families. By conceptualizing all risk as universally experienced, individual differences in children exposed to the same risk factors can only be explained by differences in child characteristics. The implication is that there is something special about the children who experience fewer negative effects rather than the reality that there are always multifaceted and multidirectional impacts of any common experience on children (e.g., Gobeil-Bourdeau et al., 2022). It is likely that large numbers of children living in poverty are protected by the unique characteristics of their families and immediate communities (e.g., Barajas-Gonzalez et al., 2022). Indeed, resilience considered as a group response to collective hardship and trauma has been demonstrated in various cultures (Chua et al., 2019; Diaz-Loving,

2005; Ebersöhn, 2019), yet communal forms of resilience are not considered in the at-risk literature.

The outcome variables used within the CR literature have been subjected to extensive psychometric testing and widespread use in varied fields, including child psychiatry. The CBCLs are the most common outcome measures. They indicate a wide array of behavioral symptoms categorized as either externalizing or internalizing pathologies that are assessed from early childhood through adolescence. However, some research has questioned the cross-cultural validity of these measures (Liu et al., 2011). In addition, the checklists are almost always completed by the child's primary caregiver and/or teacher rather than a clinician. There is rarely any observational protocol or data triangulation included in such studies to account for the potential biases of these secondhand raters. Nonetheless, given that the CBCLs assess the presence of extreme and developmentally atypical behavior, their convergent validity with other measures of pathology does support their general validity for determining population trends. However, their predictive and concurrent validity for psychopathology among preschoolers has been challenged (de la Osa et al., 2016).

The psychological early childhood literature, on the other hand, makes use of more fine-grained assessments of both explanatory and outcome variables. These include the quality of educational materials in the home, parenting styles, and the way in which adults speak to and around children. In doing so, this literature aims to delineate the mechanisms by which poverty affects children. However, by focusing on parenting behaviors it also shifts the blame from the structural issue of poverty (as defined in the CR literature) to the behaviors of individuals living in poverty. The measures used to assess such individual characteristics have been both widely lauded and critiqued. For example, the HOME inventory (Bradley & Caldwell, 1979) became such a standard proxy for the "quality" of poor children's home environments that it was used in virtually every study of early childhood development involving poor children in the decades following its development. However, cultural differences have been found in the meanings of the measure's items (Holding et al., 2011; Jones et al., 2017).

Similarly, the language deprivation found among children living in poverty permeated political discourse and spurred national movements for improving young children's early language exposure, such as home-visiting programs and curriculums targeting vocabulary at early learning centers (Fernald et al., 2013). This research has since been critiqued along similar lines to that leveled at the HOME survey (Sperry et al., 2019; Sugland et al., 1995).

Critiques of culturally biased methods for assessing the quality of poor maternal parenting exist, yet results from these measures are widely cited as justification for additional research designs that build upon them. The findings of research based on potentially biased measurement tools can create inaccurate assumptions within academia as well as unhelpful public policy and interventions.

While the explanatory variables described above are subject to questions regarding their validity, it is the conceptualization and measurement of the outcome variables used to assess poor children's development that are most prone to criticism. Within the cognitive domain these measures include IQ (most commonly assessed using the Peabody Picture Vocabulary Test), executive functioning (assessed using self-regulation, impulse, and attention control tasks), and theory of mind. Assessment of each of these constructs involves a procedure in which a researcher sits with a child apart from their classroom and administers a performance task. This procedure ignores the potential psychological impact on a three-, four-, or five-year-old of being separated from their classroom by a stranger and asked to complete something that requires focus and attention. The likelihood that the stress of such a "strange situation" (Ainsworth et al., 1970) might impact children's task performance is high given that stress has been shown to affect the cognitive performance of children as young as three (Ding et al., 2014; Zelazo & Lyons, 2012). The fact that these procedures do not include a measure of the child's affective state at the time of task completion raises concerns regarding their measurement validity. Nonetheless, these cognitive assessments have the benefit of allowing for direct observation of children's behavior.

Within the social/emotional domains, such measures are administered in a far less objective way. They often do not include any direct observation of child behavior and instead rely entirely on the secondhand reports mainly of early childhood teachers, with a smaller percentage of studies surveying parents. Although the race, class, gender, and other biases of teacher report – especially within early childhood classrooms – are well documented (Berg-Nielsen et al., 2012; Mason et al., 2014; Splett et al., 2020; Yates & Marcelo, 2014; Zulauf-McCurdy & Loomis, 2023), these measures persist as the most common means of assessing the social development of poor children. These vast differences in measurement procedures between the cognitive and social/emotional domains imply that cognition is too complex to assess via secondhand survey report alone, whereas social and emotional development is simple enough that preschool teachers, without any specific training in what constitutes social competence, are qualified to evaluate it among their entire class over the time it takes to complete a survey.

Head Start as Context for Applied Developmental Research

Parallel to the research demonstrating the exponential negative effects of poverty on young children, solutions in the form of social programs designed to ameliorate these effects have propagated. The largest of these is Head Start, an American federally funded preschool program that can begin to serve families through Early Head Start when the child is as young as two years old. Head Start programs thus provide a highly accessible and convenient site for collecting data on young children placed at risk given that all enrolled families live below the poverty line. This setting allows researchers to catalog the nature of various developmental deficits that disproportionately characterize these children and at the same time to test the impacts of specialized programs designed to improve their functioning.

Researchers have examined the impacts of the Head Start program itself, including its curriculum and teacher training, on indicators of child development such as cognitive, language, and social development following program participation. In addition, subprograms instituted within the standard Head Start curriculum have been developed by researchers to address specific areas of need (see Burchinal et al., 2016, for a review).

Within the Head Start literature, many studies forego the performance-based assessments of cognitive function in favor of the vaguely defined "school readiness" construct. These studies often ask teachers to assess children's social behavior in one survey and their "school readiness" behavior in another. Studies that test the relationship between a teacher's perception of a child's social competence and their perception of that same child's school readiness are common. Surveys items seem to suggest that both constructs refer to how well-behaved a child is according to a given teacher. Studies that use the same reporter for both explanatory and outcome variables are not generally considered rigorous or valid within psychological science, yet they comprise much of the research on children attending Head Start programs.

School Readiness

As mentioned earlier, the outcome variable applied most often in Head Start studies is "school readiness." The construct of school readiness reflects a mixture of governmental and Head Start policy along with teacher perceptions of which traits and skills predict long-term school achievement (Robinson & Diamond, 2014). From a cultural perspective, "school readiness" represents the extent to which a child has been socialized into the cultural norms of American schooling by the age of five (Cole, 2013). Although early academic skills have been found to be moderately predictive of later achievement (Rabiner et al., 2016), the Head Start research has focused most extensively on the social behaviors deemed necessary for success in kindergarten. The school readiness construct, with its combination of social, behavioral, and preacademic skills among children placed at risk, has taken precedence as a more precise predictor of school achievement than preliteracy and prenumeracy skills. The notion that self-control, compliance, and conformity to a given authority figure are conceptually equivalent to intellectual capacities for math and literacy learning suggests that "school readiness" may be more about teacher perceptions of poor children than about children's actual developmental skills (Kulkarni & Sullivan, 2022). Indeed, the Head Start studies make clear that what matters for the developmental outcomes of children placed at risk is the extent to which they can integrate seamlessly into American public school kindergarten classrooms (Robinson & Diamond, 2014).

Developmental psychologists have long conducted studies to improve our understanding of the complex factors that comprise social competence such as inhibitory control, emotion regulation, executive functioning, and sociocognitive skills among middle class children. The research defines these observable capacities in terms of the ability to delay gratification, read social and emotional cues, actively control impulsive social behavior, and self-soothe. Neurophysiological data indicate the neurobiological relationship between such behavioral skills and brain development during early childhood (Patrick et al., 2019; Perry et al., 2016). However, when applied to children who attend Head Start programs, these constructs have been redefined in teacher report items as sitting still, paying attention, following directions, and taking turns during classroom routines. The Head Start and high-poverty public school classrooms that serve as research contexts typically score lower on measures of classroom quality than private preschools or more affluent-serving early elementary schools (Fauth et al., 2019; Pianta et al., 2016). The laboratory research on middle-class children has given rise to complex developmental constructs describing typical development that portray there being that depict a mix of biopsychosocial factors in a constant state of flux during early and middle childhood. Unlike observational and physiological measures of social cognition, social competence measures applied to poor children are defined as simplistic nondevelopmental behaviors, so that teachers with no specialized training can easily recognize and rate them. The consequence of this research aimed at identifying the developmental deficits of children attending Head Start programs is that it shifts these programs' focus from their original emphasis on improving pedagogy for children placed at risk toward improving children's behavior to meet the requirements of kindergarten.

Today's developmental psychologists are exceptionally careful to remove any language from their reports that conveys a "deficit lens" regarding children placed at risk. This includes children living in poverty, those whose families are recent immigrants, and those who are learning English for the first time, as well as those belonging to a historically oppressed racial group. Occasionally, such studies disaggregate race/income/language/immigration status and parent education level. More often, low-income children from diverse racial backgrounds who attend Head Start programs are assessed as a single group and compared with predominantly white middle-class children attending a private or university preschool.

Despite the cautious use of language, the premise of most research on Head Start attendees is that by cataloging the developmental deficits that disproportionately characterize poor children researchers can identify protective factors that support some children for the purpose of cultivating these among all poor children. Accordingly, the social domain – encompassing the ways in which children react to situations behaviorally – has become the focus of much research on both Head Start attendees and children attending high-poverty public elementary schools in the US.

The Social Domain for Children Placed at Risk

The social domain has received extensive attention in Head Start research over the past decade. Originally conceptualized as "social competence" – a mix of peer interaction skills and responses to teachers – a recent reconceptualization termed "affective social competence" (ASC) has been developed to encompass social/interactive, emotional regulation, self-regulation /compliance, and sociocognitive skills (Halberstadt et al., 2001). Researchers argue that this new compilation of skills and traits signifies a more holistic understanding of young children's behavior that better predicts school readiness than measures that define skills like attention regulation, emotion regulation, and behavioral control separately (Eisenberg, 2001; Halberstadt et al., 2001). Although the original conceptualization of ASC is based on multi-faceted analysis of the ways that emotional knowledge and regulation function during social interactions, the applied version of the construct is often reduced to teacher perceptions of children's agreeability, especially when the population includes children placed at risk (e.g., Creavey et al., 2018; Jones et al., 2015). Indeed, research suggests that teacher reports of ASC are highly influenced by teacher characteristics and teacher–child relationships, and that those relationships are influenced in turn by teacher–child racial congruence (Garner & Mahatmya, 2015).

As developmental psychologists turn their focus to elementary school children, those classified as possessing low levels of ASC and school readiness during preschool are given the increasingly pathological label of Emotional Behavior Disorder (EBD) as they age. Similar to the constructs applied to Head Start attendees, the construct of EBD is not based on psychiatric assessment but rather is defined according to the demands of elementary public school classrooms (Gage et al., 2017). Accordingly, EBD is constituted by disruptive behavior, poor social skills, and poor academic skills. This classification does not exist within the Diagnostic and Statistical Manual of Mental Disorders (DSM) despite the term "disorder" but rather exists solely in the "at-risk" literature. As such, children attending high-poverty elementary schools are assessed for levels of EBD according to classroom-specific indicators such as low levels of on-task behavior and high avoidance of academic tasks. Research suggests that teacher ratings of EBD are impacted by teacher bias, particularly in relation to gender and race (Sheaffer et al., 2021). Despite evidence that elementary schoolteachers' perceptions of individual children are influenced by factors such as classroom composition, teacher characteristics, and the time of the school year when the assessment is completed (Buell et al., 2017; Sutton et al., 2021), teacher reports without controls for any of these variables are the most common assessment tool in research on children placed at risk in elementary school.

This distinction between how basic developmental research is conducted with middle-class children versus the classroom-specific applied research conducted with children placed at risk creates a dual track within developmental psychology. On the one hand, middle-class children are assessed as individuals in laboratories and homes. Measures of these children's functioning are designed to capture subtle differences between and within individuals. This approach to documenting individual differences leads to the unsurprising findings that contextual differences elicit differential functioning that reflect a unique combination of skills, challenges, and strengths. Alternatively, the measurement of poor children's development is subsumed within the demands of their schooling. Therefore, the well-known "uneven development" of children reflecting intraindividual variation is not accounted for in such studies. Rather, developmental assessment of children placed at risk is reduced to measures of the extent to which they please their teachers. Longitudinal research with children deemed "at risk" predicts increasingly negative lifelong consequences over time. Preschoolers with low ASC and school readiness become elementary children with EBD and adolescents showing antisocial behavior, delinquency, and a host of psychiatric symptoms. Left out of these studies are any measures of the quality of their schools, classrooms, or teachers.

By measuring only individual child behaviors without consideration of the impacts of context or of teacher report bias, the original purpose of studying CR – that social factors beyond children's control have negative effects on their development and therefore public policy must intervene – is no longer the underlying goal of such research. Instead, the focus shifts toward how the characteristics of the children themselves predict their own negative developmental outcomes.

A Circular Argument in Research on the Deficient At-Risk Child

The idea that an individual child's poor social skills "contaminate" all other areas of their development has been described as producing "spillover effects." This is the rationale for why research on poor children's social and emotional development includes behaviors such as "paying attention" that are generally considered within the cognitive domain, and why EBD – a measure of "emotional behavior" – includes items asking teachers about children's academic skills and attitudes toward classwork. Given that N. American teachers within the same school system generally reflect a similar set of values, cultural biases, and expectations regarding children's behavior, it is not surprising that teachers' assessments reflect a consistent perspective across separate developmental domains and even across multiple grade levels.

Therefore, rather than reporting on the development of children placed at risk, studies employing teacher report as the sole or primary measure demonstrate that this population of children is considered deficient in multiple areas by their teachers. As they move through different developmental stages and grade levels, the negative perceptions that their teachers hold of them, combined with various adverse experiences likely produce adolescents and adults who do exhibit pathological or substandard psychological functioning. However, these early measures provide no actionable insights for policymakers or practitioners because they do not present a nuanced or meaningful picture of such children's development. Instead, they simply document how teacher bias disproportionately affects children placed at risk.

Research on middle-class children's social development often considers their social skills within the context of social interactions (either using sociometric analysis or in conjunction with observations of peer interactions). On the other hand, the social skills of children placed at risk are often defined by survey items that ask teachers to report on general propensities without giving regard to any specific social interaction or context. Accordingly, a child who is rated as aggressive is assumed to behave aggressively regardless of the social situation in which they are engaged. This methodology locates social behavior discretely within the individual child. In such studies, the environmental factors that form the basis for the original designation of at-risk status (e.g., poverty, violence) are not investigated regarding their mechanisms of impact. The focus on how children placed at risk's behavior itself leads to their negative outcomes renders the term "at risk" merely a rhetorical device while the methods and results paint a picture of children who are inherently flawed.

The optimal and deficient social development of children placed at risk is defined according to behavioral expectations of N. American classrooms. This occurs despite the reality that, especially for children placed at risk, American classrooms may be experienced as hostile due to cultural mismatches and biases (Delpit, 2006, 2012). This way of defining developmental traits according to a highly culturally and institutionally specific social context – a classroom in a N. American school – serves to reify the social development of at-risk children as a specific type that exists solely within the cultural context of N. American schooling.

Problems with Validity and Reliability in Studies of Poor Children

Whether the focus is on school readiness, social competence, or EBD, the methods used to define the constructs create a closed feedback loop in which a narrow sociocultural perspective is used to define competence. Much like how children's risk is multiplied by each additional unfortunate life experience, their perceived deficits are compounded by each new measurement that builds upon prior overly narrow or biased measures.

Broad critiques of "developmental psychology" have centered on the absurdity of studying the human condition using methods from the natural sciences (Burman, 2017; Morss, 2024). Isolating discrete components of behavior like cells in a petri dish runs counter to holistic and systemic views of development (Burman, 2017; Morss, 2024). The notion that the human organism is infinitely complex considers behaviors, relationships, the physical environment, and many other factors to be functioning in a web of interconnected contingent responses. Using the example of motor development, dynamic systems theory has long demonstrated how something as apparently simple as a toddler navigating new terrain involves multiple series of contingent feedback loops. Thelen and Smith, (2006) describe how and communication between multimodal systems of the child's biology function in concert with the many factors present in their physical and relational context (Thelen & Smith, 2006).

Rather than looking holistically at the results of assessments of social and emotional functioning, in most studies of poor children's social competence each dimension is treated as a separate variable and then tested for correlations. This creates an artificial separation between knowledge, behavior, and skills, which are known to work in conjunction with each other during development. Measurement procedures reflect this atomistic extreme as well. The performance-based tasks described earlier ignore research showing that cognitive performance is highly influenced by the social and emotional aspects of context (see Monette et al., 2011) and assume that young children can perform at their fullest capacity under any circumstances simply by being prompted.

The composition of elementary school classrooms and the cultural responsiveness of the teacher impact children's behavior and academic achievement (Jensen et al., 2020; Sutton et al., 2021). Research in this area suggests that measuring individual children's "problem behaviors" will provide far less useful insights than attending to the relational dynamics among all members of a given class – especially those that occur between teachers and students. Excluding classroom factors that are known to shape children's behavior from performance task and teacher survey data decontextualizes the meaning of such results.

In addition to the face validity problems with secondhand reporting of complex psychological concepts, the general bias of such methods have been well documented. Research with a nationally representative sample of Head Start and low-income early elementary school attendees indicated that teacher ratings did not consistently predict children's problem social behavior (Hamre et al., 2008). Instead, teacher ratings of children's behaviors were more strongly related to teachers' own characteristics than independently observed child behavior (Hamre et al., 2008). In a study of teachers' perceptions of preschoolers' pretend play, a racially diverse sample of teachers attributed negative adjustment only to the Black preschoolers in their classes despite there being no difference between their play behavior and that of the white and Latinx children (Yates & Marcelo, 2014).

A recent study showed significant differences in ratings for assessing social skills between parents and teachers (Heyman et al., 2018). The biggest discrepancies were for low-income children because teachers gave much lower ratings of social skills to poor children than they did to middle-class children. Parents of both income groups rated their children higher than the teachers did. These findings point to issues with basic reliability in the use of such measures.

Temperament – a well-known determinant of behavior as originally reported by Kagan (1989) – has been shown in countless studies to impact the responses of people to the environment, especially to change. For young children, temperament affects the ease of transition between activities and participation in whole-group settings but is not associated with negative or positive outcomes on its own (Gobiel-Bourdeau et al., 2022; Kagan, 1989). However, along with other well-researched constructs that contribute to young children's behavior at school, temperament is often left out of the Head Start research. Yet differences in temperament along with many other factors not within a four-year-old's control explain individual differences in areas such as compliance, direction following, and participating during teacher-directed tasks. In addition to innate personality differences, the impacts of race, class, and gender on how teachers perceive, respond to, and thus shape children's responses to them have been widely demonstrated. For example, a study one study showed that among low-income preschoolers, those who had more negative perceptions of their teachers were also scored more negatively by those same teachers (Mantzicopoulos & Neuharth-Pritchett, 2003). The negative child perceptions of their teachers were also correlated with lower academic achievement scores. In addition, male African American children had the most negative perceptions of their teachers and were scored lowest on social skills and highest on problem behaviors by the same teachers (Mantzicopoulos & Neuharth-Pritchett, 2003).

These findings suggest that children as young as preschool age are aware of their teachers' perceptions of them, and more disturbingly that these negative perceptions and expectations influence how children behave socially and emotionally as well as academically. Given this, it is impossible to believe that teacher reports represent a neutral, objective system for rating children, especially those who are categorized as "at risk." Instead, such measures embed bias – especially toward low-income, African American, and male children – into studies that use them.

This methodological trap of atomism, decontextualization, and bias creates an endless loop wherein our biased notions of how children born into poverty and from historically oppressed racial backgrounds should behave inform the research design used to measure what it is we believe they should be able to do but can't because they are at risk. The concept of school readiness – that from under the oppressive heap of the multiplied risk that our society allows such children to experience they should, of their own accord, emerge ideally socialized via the sheer force of compliance with teachers in classrooms whose curriculum, environment, and activities may not be relevant to them – is a harmful farce that does nothing to address the needs of children and families. But this is not the only way to understand this population of children.

Another Way

Alternative methods must first detach from exclusive reliance on national data obtained from clearinghouses using flawed measures. Small-scale observations of children in context have provided holistic, contextualized, processual accounts of the development of children from various income backgrounds. Such studies provide sensitive observational schemes for understanding children from the "at-risk" population. Studies of children placed at risk must first seek to understand their development before assuming that they need to be fixed. An attitude of curiosity rather than judgment could allow methods designed to capture the widest range of variability among the population rather than focusing only on the most harmful effects of poverty on children. In addition, to conduct basic research on the social development of children placed at risk, it is necessary to redefine the social domain. As long as individual skills continue to comprise our notion of social development, researchers will continue to use the social skills of middle-class majority white samples of children as the metric for comparison. Racial and class biases are embedded in the way we assess and norm individual social behavior.

Using similar measures with slight changes will not create a culturally valid way of defining social development for all children. Instead, it is necessary to treat social development as innately social. Social interaction as a component of relationships within which children's social behavior has meaning can provide a lens on their competence that would be otherwise missed. Rather than a discrete skill, like the ability to hold a pencil, all children use social behavior to achieve goals, build connections, and make meaning. We must first discover the unique ways in which minoritized, culturally diverse children from low-income families with various national origins and languages demonstrate their social competence before assuming that they can be captured by the same indicators used for white middle-class children or defined by compliance with teachers. To provide this expansive lens for observing and capturing such development, we must shift the unit of analysis from the individual to the collective.

Collaborative Competence

The concept of collaborative competence at the center of this book has been developed for this purpose. Throughout, I argue that children's naturalistic collaborations with one another in school, beginning with those that occur during the free play periods of Head Start classrooms, offer an ideal context through which to understand development. This approach is holistic, contextualized, and process-based designed to highlights areas where so-called children placed at risk have been shown to be typically more advanced than their white middle-class counterparts.

Collaborative competence provides an alternative means of understanding and assessing children's development. The impetus for this concept is to provide a culturally valid way of describing and measuring the social behavior of children placed at risk. However, the collective lens for assessing social behavior offers new insights for understanding all children. By looking at how social behavior functions in dyads and small groups, numerous discoveries regarding young children's capacities become possible.

Although social competence and collaboration have been studied as separate concepts, connecting competence with collaboration signals a shift in both conceptualizations. Competence is typically assessed among individuals in relation to mastery. Once an individual has gained competence in a specific area, they are unlikely to lose it. This set of associations with the idea of competence is very much ingrained in Western psychology, philosophy, and values (Cole, 2013; Harkness & Super, 2020; Valsiner, 2017). These ideals conjure the image of the developing individual moving forward on a solitary path toward some clearly defined goal that represents individual achievement. This vision may appear triumphant, inspiring, and heroic or, alternatively, selfish, disconnected, and lonely depending on the cultural context within which it is viewed (Tobin et al., 1989, 2009).

Collaboration, on the other hand, automatically implies interaction. It is one of the few Western psychological concepts that does not have an individualistic definition (Cole, 2013; Valsiner, 2017). Collaboration has not been the focus of research within traditional developmental psychology to the same extent as related but more individualistic notions such as "social skills," "emotional regulation," and "perspective-taking". Collaboration describes an ideal form of social interaction, one in which interacting parties are mutually engaged and equally contributing to some shared endeavor.

Given the preceding descriptions, the concepts of "competence" and "collaboration" have been conceptually opposed within developmental psychology. The former reflects individualistic assumptions that guide standard assessment, whereas the latter is mainly found in approaches that challenge individualistic norms and assumptions. To investigate the process whereby collaborative competence develops during a real-time interaction, it is necessary to diverge from how standard assessments frame developmental achievements. The nature of collaboration as inherently interactive and irreducible to the individual is simultaneously in conflict with how most forms of "competence" are conceptualized. Therefore, the term "collaborative competence" on its face presents a tension with most assumptions of developmental psychology. However, the idea of competence is important if researchers and educators are to take collaboration seriously as a driver of development. The idea that collaborations can be assessed implies that, like individual skills, they vary in effectiveness and are influenced by factors that either support or detract from their efficacy.

The purpose of bringing these two ideas together is to provide a way of systematically documenting collaborative processes that develop between children. This method can be applied to a wide variety of interactive contexts that are valid across a variety of cultural norms. The goal of this book is to provide a methodology for both practitioners and researchers to capture the complexity and nuances of collaborations. Through assessing collaborative competence, those features of classrooms and relationships that are most conducive to supporting highly effective collaborations will also be identified. In this way, the concept offers practical information and serves as a critical alternative to more narrow conceptualizations of the role of interaction in development. Collaboration develops, functions, and ceases within the context of an ongoing interaction. Therefore, defining an ideal collaboration requires a notion of competence that is also inherently interactive.

Collaborative competence serves as a concept that can document children's growth and development within schools and classrooms over time. Documenting and assessing how children collaborate at different points in development, within different contexts, and for different purposes represent an alternative to the methodological trap that views children "placed at risk" through a deficit lens. Studying collaborative competence requires careful attention to the details of social interaction – to the ways that myriad components intersect to produce moment-by-moment change within a dyad or small group. This analysis can produce concrete implications for teachers. Introducing new material, changing interactive partners, or adding in a suggestion can change the flow of the collaboration. Although this does not provide a linear trajectory from one individual milestone to the next, it can reveal trends and patterns in how groups learn to work together over time. This set of patterns could be scaled with the potential to predict group outcomes from environmental factors, as well as to produce changes based on interventions to group work that shape collaboration experiences. Expert collaborators during free play in Head Start programs may become highly effective project team members in high school. Ideally, support provided during play to enhance creativity and interactive dynamics among group members can carry through into the collaborative activities of kindergarten and 1st grade classrooms. Children who experience such support will apply their collaborative skills together as they change developmentally over the course of their school careers.

It is tempting to include a depiction of how individual children internalize the collaborative skills that they then apply to future groups. However, the concept of collaborative competence offered here resists the tendency to individualize and maintains that even within the context of a developmental trajectory collaborative competence must be analyzed at the group level. Because moments of competence peak and wane over the course of an interaction according to emergent group dynamics, no one child can be deemed more or less "collaboratively competent" than another. However, longitudinal studies can investigate how collaborations change at different ages, controlling for the influence of individual differences. Studies can also investigate the impacts of familiarity and prior relationships on collaborative competence by following paired cohorts in which children remain in the same class over multiple time points. Thus, studies of collaborative competence can answer two related but distinct sets of questions that have not been addressed in the literature thus far.

One area of investigation seeks to discover and formalize descriptions of the process of how collaborative competence develops among different ages and within different contexts. The other investigates the impacts of various contextual factors on the quality and nature of collaborative competence. These factors include the social context of the interaction (prior relationships/familiarity, gender composition, size of the group and other group-level or relational components) defined at the group rather than individual level. For example, rather than asking about each participant's language status, measures would reflect the extent to which the group members share the same first language. The social context might also include the institutional context in which the interaction occurs, such as school, playground, or home, as well as the adults and other children present in the larger space where the interaction occurs. Similarly, materials and space may be analyzed on two levels: firstly, the most proximal materials that are used during the interaction and the space in which it occurs; and secondly, the more distal forms of space and materials that characterize the broader environment surrounding the interaction. Through this approach, the results obtained might suggest immediate interventions to elements of the concrete social and environmental context that impact how collaborations develop. Beyond this, investigations of the cultural historical context, including the institution, neighborhood, and geographic location, could be useful in revealing the meanings of various shared activities.

In summary, this approach signifies a change to the way research within developmental psychology functions. Nonetheless, countless findings within the fields of social development and education are useful in informing the methods and measures necessary for the study of collaborative competence. Therefore, a large portion of this book is devoted to reviewing previous relevant literature. The purpose of these reviews is to enable a synthesis of what works for interactions at various ages and within different contexts.

The Content of This Book

This book includes four parts. Part I, which includes this chapter, lays out the two major arguments against the status quo in research on children's social development. The first, articulated by this chapter, concerns the problems of validity with current research methods, particularly regarding how the social development of children born into poverty is defined and studied. Chapter 2 reviews the issue of cultural validity in foundational conceptions of child development, especially social development. That chapter argues that the concept of collaborative competence rather than individual social competence reflects majority world cultural conceptions of child development and child-rearing values.

Part II of the book includes four chapters that examine the preexisting literature that informs the concept of collaborative competence. Psychological theories define subjectivity as an individual's perceptions and experiences of the world in varied ways according to different assumptions and areas of focus. Intersubjectivity is defined as a comingling of subjectivities between people that involves an exchange of thoughts, emotions, and intentions and is a major component of collaborative competence. Chapter 3 reviews theories of subjectivity and intersubjectivity from across various disciplines and within developmental psychology. Chapter 4 details how children of different ages and in varied contexts engage in peer interactions that demonstrate intersubjectivity. That chapter shows how, according to the theory being used, interactive behaviors may or may not be included as evidence of intersubjectivity. The purpose is to argue for a theory and method for documenting intersubjectivity among children that supports the construct of collaborative competence. Chapter 5 reviews the literature on interactions in different social contexts such as home and school. The focus of that chapter is on forms and qualities of interactive behavior that promote development across multiple contexts. The goal is to ensure that measures of collaborative competence reflect what is already known to comprise ideal interactions. Chapter 6 delves into the collaboration literature in depth, drawing parallels between the findings of studies of collaboration at multiple ages and in varied contexts. That chapter then introduces complexity as a component of construct of collaborative competence.

Part III builds upon the arguments and findings presented earlier to offer a detailed theory and method of collaborative competence. Chapter 7 outlines the full model of collaborative competence presented in this book. Examples of how the construct has been demonstrated with two related research paradigms – qualitative analysis of preschool peer interactions and elementary-aged guided learning activities – are provided. Chapter 8 describes the detailed principles informing the methodology for assessing collaborative competence. It then describes how these methods will be applied to preschool peer interactions. The application to both qualitative and quantitative approaches and the relationships between them are elaborated. Chapter 9 reports on the results of a quantitative study of collaborative competence during naturalistic preschooler peer play across five Head Start centers. This research addresses various questions about the processes by which children collaborate and the influences on the quality of their collaboration, including the impacts of various proximal and distal contextual factors. Chapter 10 details the results of a small-scale study of early elementary teacher-guided collaborations using some of the previously discussed measures and adding measures of dialogic communication. This method combines a quantitative and qualitative approach to illustrating how collaborative competence emerges at different points in an interaction and in relation to different components.

Part IV focuses on implications for both research and practice. Chapter 11 discusses concrete changes to education that would support the development of collaborative competence among children in school. Chapter 12 addresses the need for a theoretical paradigm that embraces the assumptions underlying the concept of collaborative competence. The goal is to align with an overarching theory that would allow the new methods required to study collaborative competence to emerge, as well as other ways of studying development using interaction as the unit of analysis.

In summary, this book sketches out a new concept and an accompanying new methodology for the study of social development, especially among the so-called at-risk population of children that has long been the focus of research in child development. Therefore, this book offers both an extensive critical review of the field and a road map for a more valid, inclusive, and meaningful way forward.

CHAPTER 2

Can the Self Be Relational?
Culture at the Root of Psychology

Psychology as Culturally Situated

Critical psychology, encompassing fields of sociocultural psychology and related subdisciplines along with the Indigenous Psychology movement within non-Western cultures, has brought to light the extent to which all mainstream psychology reflects the values of the globally dominant societies of North America and the postcolonial powers of Western Europe (Teo, 2015; Tomicic & Berardi, 2018). Within the Western world the values of the European Enlightenment period have defined psychology since its founding (e.g., Burman, 2017). These ideals, which support studying the human condition using the same assumptions and methods used in the natural sciences, continue to guide research and practice in psychology today. Yet related disciplines such as philosophy and social theory have long challenged the notion that logical positivism offers an adequate foundation for understanding the human condition (e.g., Morss, 1996). Indigenous psychological theories and methods provide alternative ways of defining personhood, the self, social relations, and psychological interventions that reflect cultural values across the majority world. Indigenous psychologies from Africa, Asia, and Latin and Indigenous North America share more commonalities with one another than they do with that of mainstream psychology derived from Europe and North America. The individualistic, objectivist framework of Western psychology represents a set of cultural values that are unique and distinct from the notions of self and society throughout the majority world (Henrich et al., 2010). Indeed, research shows that among European Americans, Western Europeans, and Asian respondents the group showing the most individualistic orientation is European Americans (Oyserman et al., 2002). This finding is relevant to understanding why individual deficits and skills have been the focus on research with "at-risk populations", as described in the previous chapter. This highly individualistic framing of socially determined challenges and strengths is counter to the ways resilience has been documented among majority world participants (Chua et al., 2019; Diaz-Loving, 2005; Ebersöhn, 2019). This research has shown that resilience is conceptualized and enacted as a collective response to adversity, such as poverty, violence, and marginalization. The construal of both adversity and protective factors as collective and tied to communal supports and identities has also been found among African American (Butler et al., 2018) and Latinx American samples (Morgan, 2004; Rogoff et al., 2018). This research raises additional challenges to the validity of the at-risk literature given that measures of both risk and resilience generally reflect the hyperindividualistic orientation of European American society.

Self, Subjectivity, and Intersubjectivity

Notions of self predate psychology in both Western and non-Western history as components of philosophy and religion. Subjectivity, on the other hand, is a conceptual foundation of Western philosophical thought. Discussed extensively by philosophers of the European Enlightenment period, subjectivity refers to the mind of a given individual – their perceptions and perspectives. The idea is that what is subjective is tied to the experience of an individual and their unique ways of perceiving the world. More recent formulations include phenomenology -the study of reality as experienced subjectively) and constructionism- (the idea that society constructs what is known to be reality rather than reality being something that can be perceived regardless of social context).

Intersubjectivity has been discussed extensively by the phenomenological philosopher Edmund Husserl, who is credited with its original definition. The most general understanding of the term is that intersubjectivity is a comingling of subjectivities – the sharing of internal states, including mental and emotional domains, between people (usually dyads). Along with much deliberation about the nature of intersubjectivity within Western philosophy, theoretical psychologists and psychoanalysts as well as a few developmental psychologists have devoted attention to the concept. Beyond the cerebral or affective components, the bodily dimensions of intersubjectivity have also been theorized. Other social science disciplines such as anthropology, sociology, and linguistics have occasionally made use of the concept. Across multiple disciplines and dimensions, intersubjectivity has primarily been conceptualized as occurring during dyadic interactions. Expanding beyond the subjectivist underpinning of theories of intersubjectivity, cultural historical activity theories (CHATs) contend that intersubjectivity may include: broader sociocultural contexts, culturally construed activity systems as well as discrepancies and disagreements. This broadens the concept beyond ideally attuned dyads.

Indigenous Psychologies

Psychologies derived from Chinese, Korean, South African, West African, and American Indigenous cultural worldviews and lifeways define the self in relation to the social. Among Confucian-heritage societies hierarchical relationism has been described as the normative view of the relational self (Liu, 2015). Reciprocal filial piety characterizes the contemporary East Asian ideal of social relations, wherein children and parents maintain hierarchically defined roles and interdependent obligations, yet affection and support are exchanged reciprocally within the boundaries of those roles (Hwang, 2012). South and West African psychologists have theorized a multidimensional self that is constructed and functions in relation to communal obligations and appraisals (Nwoye, 2006, 2022; Ratele, 2017). North American Indigenous psychologists similarly consider kinship ties, reciprocity, and responsibility to the community as implicit in definitions of self (Fish, 2022; Gone, 2019). These ways of conceptualizing the self as constituted by social relations imbue the psyche with a moral/ethical dimension (Hwang, 2023). For example, among South Koreans self-regulation is lauded as a means of maintaining emotional support from one's family and community (Kim & Park, 1999). Kim and Park (1999) studied conceptions of success and failure among South Korean adolescents and adults. Both groups attributed responsibility for their academic and occupational achievement to support from family and community members. Individual achievement and failure are perceived as being tied to emotion-laden relationships with as well as obligations to one's community members. This view of success and failure, as well as a focus on collective appraisals of one's worth, is repeated with slight variations throughout the majority world (Nwoye, 2022; Oyserman, 2011). According to Indigenous Psychology, individual actions are automatically rife with ethical and moral implications via family and community ties. The fulfillment of roles, obligations, and responsibilities relative to one's position in the family and community defines the boundaries within which the self is experienced and construed.

Beyond the relational versus individualistic notions of self, the conception of the psyche differs in fundamental ways between the Western and majority world. In African, South Asian and Indigenous North American views, the psyche is construed as multidimensional, wherein one's observable behavior and speech represent only one of many dimensions. Other dimensions include extrasensory phenomena perceived via spiritual connections to the natural environment, the realm of the ancestors, and components of situations and other people that can be sensed only when in close proximity to them (Chua et al., 2019; Fish, 2022; Nwoye, 2022). Consistent with this idea, the personal connection to the past through ancestors and to the future through one's impacts on the community adds a multitemporal dimension for both African and Indigenous North Americans. The mind as a portal to the ancestral or spiritual realms is another theme that occurs in both cosmologies and affects how subjectivity is construed and experienced. Although the cosmologies and guiding philosophical and spiritual principles differ widely, the blurred boundaries between internal and external, embodied sensing and observable reality are shared across Indigenous psychologies, impacting the basic ontology that would guide a culturally valid psychology throughout the majority world.

Subjectivity and Intersubjectivity
This view of the self, subjectivity, and intersubjectivity as including imperceptible elements that are not fully understood or explainable is most similar to the Western psychodynamic account of subjectivity. However, psychoanalysis is focused on cultivating insights and intervening at an individual, not communal level.

Alternative psychological interventions have been developed that build on the cultural value of communal support. For example, "relationship-resourced resilience" describes a collective form of resilience in South Africa in which a sharing of resources during a crisis leads to "flocking" as an effective communal trauma response (as opposed to the individual trauma responses of fight/flight/freeze;) (Ebersöhn, 2019).

Stemming from this Indigenous ontology, a "methodological relationism" has been advocated as a contrast with the "methodological individualism" that underpins Western-derived mainstream psychology (Ho et al., 2001). Isolating the observable behavior of individuals from the multiple dimensions – including social relations – that constitute the self is not a valid method of research with the majority world. An alternative "ground-up" methodology from which psychological constructs are developed according to local perceptions has been advocated (e.g., Diaz-Loving, 2005; Hwang, 2023; Nyota & Manpara, 2008; Ratele, 2017). A similar epistemological process entails developing a "scientific micro-world" derived from the "life-world" that represents the Indigenous knowledge systems (IKSs) of a given cultural group (Hwang, 2011). Research in Asia, Africa, Latin America, and Indigenous N. America using such methods have found that Western individual psychological constructs such as self-regulation, emotion, and achievement are construed as developed for supporting positive social relations. Rather than reflecting an individual physiological response, emotion is defined as an affective bond with others (e.g., Kim & Park, 1999). In many Indigenous psychologies, what are considered individual personality traits in mainstream psychology are understood in terms of the extent to which they maintain positive social standing and encourage social and emotional support from others in the family and community.

Other psychological constructs have their origins in common legends that reflect the spiritual or philosophical histories of a culture. For example, the concept of "thought-wish" is derived from North American Indigenous cosmology wherein strongly held thoughts can affect reality (Gone, 2019). Indigenous psychologists – themselves native to the community – are privy to the "folk psychology" that is necessary for testing the validity of psychological constructs. These psychologists are aware of specific IKSs and how they inform the psychological strengths and boundaries of their community. IKS have been referenced in studies of Zimbabwean children's games (Nyota & Mapara, 2008), postcolonial Indians' integration of Sanskrit texts and philosophy with Western psychology (Kumar, 2006), including Piagetian concepts (Mishra, 2014; Paranjpe, 2010), and North American Indigenous cosmology that guides the education of children by apprenticeship (D'Ambrosio, 2006; Prieto et al., 2015).

Despite the growing field of Indigenous Psychology, cross-cultural research has continued to use "methodological individualism" to study psychological constructs among non-Western populations. Using standardized measures for collectivistic versus individualist orientations, these studies have found class based differences among the same national groups (Hamamura et al., 2013). In addition, research has shown a distinction between collectivist cultural values and independent/interdependent self-construals. Research with Latin American samples has highlighted a highly independent self-construal along multiple dimensions together with a highly collectivist set of cultural values (Krys et al., 2022). This research suggests that the link between self and cultural value conceptions of individualism/collectivism found in Asian and Western societies may not apply in all societies. The authors draw a parallel between multiple factors of cultural historical context and societal functioning as the basis for these differences. The lack of detail regarding what exactly is meant by "collectivist" within cross-cultural psychology and how it applies to a wide range of differing nations and societies has been noted by other scholars (Hwang, 2023). Although self-construals of adolescents and adults are likely more complex than any given binary, interdependence among cultures with predominantly collectivistic values affects child-rearing norms and conceptions of ideal development.

A psychology that is inclusive of the relational, socially interdependent self acknowledges that intersubjectivity should be at the center of understanding human development. Intersubjectivity provides a unit of analysis that incorporates the relational ontology of the majority world. Nonetheless, the nature of intersubjectivity, like the nature of relational dynamics, is not fixed or universal in any given culture. Therefore, a culturally valid theory of intersubjectivity as a lens through which to view development must consider specific developmental processes that occur within the lives of children and families.

Theories of intersubjectivity span various disciplines and research traditions. Many accounts assume that perspective-taking is the primary mechanism for establishing intersubjectivity (see Stovanovich & Koski, 2018 for a review). On these accounts, individuals use skills such as theory of mind understanding, perspective-taking ability, and communication skills to perceive others' intentions, emotions, and knowledge. They apply these skills during interactions. When both interacting partners apply accurate perceptions of the other's mental states, intersubjectivity is achieved. This process is described as a negotiation of perspectives, in which each partner must share power and consider the perspective of the other (Rommetveit, 1979; Tomasello et al., 2005; Trevarthen & Aitken, 2001). This view of intersubjectivity is premised on the assumption that subjectivity exists within the individual mind. Interactions are described as primarily language-based exchanges of internal information between two or more individuals. Extending this account to developmental psychology adds a progressive dimension whereby children become increasingly able to engage intersubjectively as their associated sociocognitive skills develop. Accordingly, the intersubjective capacity corresponds to the development of more sophisticated language and more accurate understandings of the intentions and perspectives of others.

This conception of intersubjectivity is based on a view of the self and subjectivity that is culturally constructed within Western value systems. An alternative view of subjectivity as socially and culturally constituted means that intersubjectivity may characterize interactions more fundamentally in the majority world than is recognized by Western theories. Rather than focusing on individual skills, such an account shifts to a focus on the broader cultural historical contexts in which people interact, the activities that they share, and the culturally specific ways by which they embody and enact their subjectivity and intersubjectivity (Correa-Chavez & Roberts, 2012; Talamo & Pozzi, 2011).

Cultural historical activity theorists have called for a theory of intersubjectivity that considers the cultural and historical contexts of interactions as well as the central activity guiding interactions (Correa-Chavez & Roberts, 2012; Gillespie & Cornish, 2010; Stone et al., 2012; Talamo & Pozzi, 2011). The CHAT perspective includes the assumption that individual activity is mediated by the socially constructed meanings of tools and artifacts (Chaiklin, 2019; Edwards et al., 2019). Accordingly, collective activity is structured by the cultural historical context of a given society and culture. Therefore, the process of establishing and maintaining intersubjectivity will reflect particular cultural norms of interaction as well as the social organization of a given society (Fleer, 2006). In addition to acknowledging the cultural historical contexts that give meaning to everyday activities, the dynamics of interpersonal relations are heavily influenced by culturally specific norms of interactive styles and behavior (Correa-Chavez & Roberts, 2012; Rogoff, 2003).

Child-Rearing Practices and Ontogeny
Two forms of collaborative interaction that are highly developed among children from Indigenous, South and Central American and Mexican heritage backgrounds are not observed among European-heritage children or those exposed to extensive Western influence via schooling (Coppens et al., 2014; Mejía-Arauz et al., 2007; Roberts & Rogoff, 2012; Silva et al., 2010). These include learning by observing and pitching in (LOPI) as well as collaborating as a fluid ensemble (Alcalá et al., 2018). The latter collaborative type describes a culturally specific form of interaction in which children seamlessly adapt their actions to one another, share power, and distribute decision-making with very limited negotiation or conflict

(Dayton et al., 2022). Mexican-heritage, Indigenous South and Central American children and families have been found to use this style of collaboration, termed "fluidity" by researchers, twice as frequently as European-heritage families and children during the same task (Rogoff et al., 2018). One study showed that Mexican American dyads used "fluid synchrony," a collaboration style in which each partner anticipated and adapted their own responses to the other's contributions nonverbally three times more than European American dyads during a computer programming task (Mejía et al., 2007). This same pattern of fluid synchrony was found in a study of Guatemalan Mayan mother–toddler triads but was rarely observed among European American triads engaged in similar tasks (Dayton et al., 2022). In addition to the nonverbal mutual coordination, the Central American collaborators in both studies were mutually engaged, and the triads consistently engaged all three members at much higher rates than the European-heritage collaborators.

This body of literature is consistent with a relational ontology wherein intersubjectivity is a common state in which people live. The ability to sense the affect of others through proximity, a valued nonverbal dimension of the psyche in Indigenous psychology, is likely implicated in this interactive style as well. Incorporating forms of relating that are common among majority world cultures is necessary for culturally valid psychological constructs. Indeed, relational as opposed to individual-autonomous goals and practices of child-rearing have been found among American and European populations descended from other continents, especially among first-generation immigrants (Domenech-Rodriguez et al., 2009; Li & Yamamoto, 2020; Schweder et al., 2006).

Conceptions of Optimal Development

Consistent with the overarching framework of Western psychology, an emphasis on individuation is embedded within all major theories of developmental psychology (Burman, 2017; Morss, 2024; Valsiner, 2017). Although Western theorists such as Erikson and Piaget describe the role of society and interactions when framing identity and cognition, respectively, they each foreground the individual in describing developmental achievements. It is the individual who must master each stage before moving on to the next. In general, Western developmental psychology is devoted to explaining the growth of the individual surrounded by the sensory information of the external world.

Accordingly, social development is defined by mainstream psychology as comprising a set of skills that allow individuals to have positive relations with others. As with intellectual and linguistic domains, this theoretical orientation posits that as children age their social skills increase in abstraction and sophistication. The ability to infer others' internal states with increasing accuracy represents a social developmental advancement that has been extensively studied through research on theory of mind and related sociocognitive skills. Major cross-cultural differences in which cognitive skills were considered advanced reasoning were found between Western and majority world cultures (Cole et al., 1971; Heiphetz & Oishi, 2022; Sternberg, 2014). For example, abstract reasoning is considered less sophisticated than context- or task-specific problem-solving in many majority world cultures (Sternberg, 2014). Making claims based on general principles divorced from particular circumstances is considered immature and foolish (Schweder et al., 2006). Cultural differences in the development of other cognitive traits according to how they are applied to socially useful tasks have been found (Dasen, 1984; Maynard & Greenfield, 2003; Mishra, 2014). These findings reflect the tendency described earlier to consider individual traits in terms of their support for social relations and communal outcomes.

Research on emotional socialization, attachment, and autonomy has shown that most majority world cultures emphasize traits such as interdependence, parental control, and a relational orientation as positive features of social/emotional development (Desmond et al., 2009; Domenech-Rodriguez et al., 2009; Li & Yamamoto, 2020; McCord & Raval, 2016). Culture-specific concepts that reflect the interdependent norms and values of child-rearing such as *amae* A Japanese construct depicting over dependence and presumed indulgence as an indicator of closeness – shame with a positive connotation in parenting, shame – and a parenting style that combines authoritarian control with warmth and nurturing have been found among Asian/Asian American, African/African American, and Latin American cultures (Li & Yamamoto, 2020; Lieber et al., 2006; Nsamenang, 2013; Umemura & Traphegan, 2015).

Autonomy in the majority world is conceptualized in terms of autonomy-relatedness, whereby the child develops volitional autonomy while maintaining an interdependent form of the self that is psychologically connected to the family throughout the lifespan (Kagitcibasi, 2012). Indeed, a person who is psychologically detached from their parents in many majority world cultures would be generally perceived as pathological. Alternatively, interdependence, reciprocal filial piety, and shared decision-making with parents define ideal psychological development for adolescents and young adults (e.g., Leiber et al., 2006; Marbell-Pierre et al., 2019). Within and between national or ethnic groups, differences in emphasis by region, economy, industrialization, and religion exist, such as a focus on harmony in the family, resource-sharing among the wider community, or bringing pride to the ethnic or national group. However, among African, Asian, Latin American, and Indigenous cultures, both internationally and within Europe and North America, a shared goal of children's development and rearing is to foster a connection between the child and the family and community.

Within this broad orientation, three common overarching themes regarding the ideal methods and outcomes for child development include: (1) a holistic rather than domain-based view of development; (2) intelligence as indivisible from social responsibility; and (3) children's developing primarily via apprenticeship.

Each of these themes is reflected in detailed accounts of child-rearing, social orientations, and cultural practices. Viewing intelligence as a social contribution can be contrasted with defining intelligence as an individual capacity unrelated to the social sphere as reflected in Western systems of education. Children learning through apprenticeship is contrasted with the idea that children require special educational environments and materials separate from the life of the community and adult responsibilities. In the following subsections, each of these themes are elaborated as they have been documented throughout the majority world.

Holistic View of Development
Within African, Asian, Indigenous, and Latin American cultures, the approach to understanding psychological development from infancy to adolescence is inclusive of motor skills and social relatedness. Rather than separating cognitive, social, emotional, and motor domains, these areas of development are viewed as interconnected. Guidance and nurturing from parents and community members are designed to positively impact each of these domains simultaneously. For example, advances in motor development are celebrated as a sign of intelligence among African parents (Carra et al., 2014; Nsamenang, 2004). Indeed, African mothers "teach" infants to develop physical skills in a way that is analogous to how Western mothers focus on early learning by stimulating infants with books and toys (Carra et al., 2014). Despite the Western assumption that physical development is a universal occurrence resulting primarily from physiological maturation (Gessel, 1933; Heiphetz & Oishi, 2022), African babies who experience their own mothers' intervention show a three- to six-month advancement

in motor skill development compared to European-heritage infants (Rademeyer & Jacklin, 2013). By late toddlerhood, African children are expected to use their motor intelligence in the service of socially useful tasks (Ogunnaike & House, 2002). In this way, the physical, intellectual, and sociomoral domains interweave in service of the ultimate goal of child development in the majority world: achieving optimal social relationships. Children who help their families by running errands such as filling water jugs, supervising younger siblings, and helping in specific ways matched to their ages are described as both intelligent and responsible or emotionally mature by parents and teachers (Ogunnaike & House, 2002). Assessing and nurturing the physical, cognitive, and social/emotional domains separately is therefore impossible within the context of African views of child development (Nsamenang, 2008).

Indigenous and Mayan-heritage parents promote development in a way that considers each domain simultaneously and in relation to the other. Education, beginning in early childhood, is structured around tasks that are connected to the economic needs of the society (Greenfield et al., 2003). In many cases these include tasks requiring extensive manual dexterity along with cognitive skills, such as pottery-making and weaving (Rogoff, 2003). Research suggests a strong correlation between fine motor skills and cognitive development (Luo et al., 2007). General correlations between movement and cognition have been found in diverse American samples (Willoughby et al., 2021), while greater fine motor skills at early ages have been found among Asian and Asian American preschoolers than European Americans (Luo et al., 2007). These in turn were correlated with greater math concept development. The correlation between fine motor skills and cognitive development has not been researched widely. Nonetheless, among majority world cultures, including American immigrant populations, young children's increasing abilities to participate in the cultural life of their community are taken as evidence of their appropriate development – a combination of motor skills, attention to detail, and social reciprocity (Coppens et al., 2014; Rogoff, 2003).

Confucian-heritage societies have conceptualizations of psychology that reflect a holistic rather than a domain-specific view. For example, Japanese students conceive of psychology as pertaining primarily to the heart (Ashitaka & Shimada, 2014). This definition is reflected in the written character representing the word "psychology," which exists in the Chinese script as well. Accordingly, the ideal self is defined as knowing the unspoken emotions of others. In addition, both Japanese and Chinese parents value children developing early fine motor skills that allow them to be independent with self-care (Li & Yamamoto, 2020; Lieber et al., 2006). Similar to other majority world parenting values, early development of motor skills is one way in which independence is encouraged among young children. However, this conception of independence is defined as the ability to be helpful to the family and community (Umemura & Traphagan, 2015). This form of independence is different from the psychological independence reflected in the emphasis on individuation within Western culture.

Intelligence as Social Responsibility
Consistent with the holistic view of development, definitions of intelligence throughout the majority world differ from those of Western societies. For example, intelligence is not necessarily measured by academic achievement. Although Western models of schooling predominate throughout the majority world due to colonization, community elders, parents, and other adults do not necessarily consider academic achievement as the most relevant measure of a child's intelligence. Instead, intelligence is often conceived of as connected to social responsibility. This ideology is reflected in both child-rearing methods and beliefs about the nature of intelligence among parents and community leaders throughout the majority world (Gielen & Roopnarine, 2016; Harkness & Super, 1996; Nsamenang, 1992).

Throughout West Africa adults assess children's forms and degrees of intelligence according to how they complete different "errands," beginning from a very early age. Adults select children for errands that are helpful to the family or larger community based on the forms of intelligence that the errand requires and what they have observed about each child's proclivities (Nsamenang & Tchombé, 2012). Indeed, the word for "intelligence" in the Bamileke language has two components: one meaning "cleverness" and the other meaning "social responsibility." A child demonstrating cleverness without a strong sense of social responsibility is considered immature and, if the division persists, deviant and dangerous (Nsamenang, 1992; Ogunnaike & Houser, 2002; Serpell et al., 2011). A movement to tie learning in school with socially useful projects has been ongoing across Africa (Nsamenang & Tchombé, 2012; Serpell et al., 2011). Teachers and scholars within this movement have argued that combining conceptual learning and knowledge with socially useful projects will build on culturally valid conceptions of intelligence and improve home–school connections throughout the continent.

Another line of research on LOPI demonstrates how many Mayan-heritage community members support children's intellectual, physical, and social development. A number of studies beginning in the 1990s have documented a method of child socialization whereby adults gradually bring children increasingly into the center of culturally valued practices that serve the interests of the entire community (e.g., Coppens et al., 2014; Lave & Wenger, 1991; Roberts & Rogoff, 2012). Support for children's intellectual development begins with extensive observation of elders engaged in community tasks. The goal of such observation is for the child to develop "sharp attention" to both material and social details (Rogoff et al., 2003; Silva et al., 2010). Children are also encouraged to develop "broad attention" – an awareness of the overall social situation as well as of tasks requiring a variety of skills. Although European and European-heritage children may also engage in apprentice-style learning, it is not the central form of education, and tasks are typically divided based on age-based skill levels. Rather than deferring to educational professionals, in much of the majority world children's cognitive capacities are assessed by the extent to which they maintain focus for extended periods and contribute to their community by developing specific skills necessary for specific tasks. After practicing by pitching in, children's contributions gradually increase until they have developed mastery and can complete tasks independently with accuracy and skill.

These descriptions each depict a form of learning reminiscent of Vygotsky's (1987) zone of proximal development. However, among these cultures, the learning process is not designed to lead to eventual internalization allowing for independent use of knowledge or skills apart from the communal needs of daily life. There is no emphasis on the division between individual psychological functioning and functioning with and for the community. Indeed, throughout the majority world, a child or adult who acts only in their own interest is considered deviant and/or in need of training.

The idea of intelligence being relegated to academic learning as assessed by teachers separately from family and community is a unique feature of Western culture that does not occur in other cultures. In Confucian-heritage societies, a child's achievements (including intellectual ones) are traditionally viewed within the context of filial piety (Lieber et al., 2006). From this perspective, academic achievement is not considered an indicator of intelligence per se but rather is conceived separately from psychological traits. Academic achievement is considered the result of effort rather than innate abilities. Putting forth great effort to achieve is a way of honoring one's parents and contributing to one's family. Intelligence, on the other hand, is defined by the affective understanding of others (Ashitaka & Shimada, 2014; Li & Yamamoto, 2020). The realm of psychology on this view is characterized by one's connection with others, involving the intellectual, emotional, social, and moral domains.

This relational orientation is found in studies of causal attribution – how people explain the behavior of others – and in numerous studies showing that Asian children perceive analogies between similar objects and situations at higher rates and earlier ages than Westerners (Christie et al., 2020). For example, in laboratory studies when Asian children and adults are asked to explain why a figure fell, they are more likely to refer to elements of the environment as the cause, whereas European Americans are more likely to refer to personal traits, such as clumsiness or distractibility (Masuda & Nisbett, 2001) Known as fundamental attribution error – thought to be widespread based on research with Westerners – has been found to be very uncommon among Asian populations (Krull et al., 1999; Ma-Kellams, 2020). Perceiving similarities between distinct objects and situations is another sign that Asian populations are more attuned to relationality, whereas European American and Western European samples are more attuned to individuality. These abstract differences in focus are seen in everyday behavior through the concept of field dependence. Research has shown that East and South Asian populations reason in their daily lives about objects, situations, and people through a relational lens, to the extent that both their abstract and everyday problem-solving has been classified as field dependent (Masuda & Nisbitt, 2001; Schwalb et al., 1989). This is compared to the predominant style of reasoning among Westerners, who most often focus on elements independently from each other when problem-solving.

The field-dependent or relational learning style has also been found to be more common among students from Asia as compared to European-heritage students (Heiphetz & Oishi, 2022; Masuda & Nisbett, 2001). African American and Hispanic American students have also shown learning styles and preferences that share commonalities with field dependence (Oyserman, 2011; Tomes, 2008). Although the specific heuristic of field dependence/independence has mostly been applied in international samples of Asian versus European/North American contexts, research with American students descended from majority world populations suggests that holistic and relational styles of thought and learning are more culturally relevant for them (Hale, 2016). In addition, one study demonstrated that a field-dependent learning style characterized the learning of South African children significantly more than it did American children

(Engelbrecht & Natzel, 1997). This way of reasoning by considering contextual elements and relational factors means that fundamental forms of reasoning favor the relational over the atomistic in the majority world. Therefore, the disconnection between intelligence and social relatedness may reflect a culturally distinct form of thought that differs between Westerners and the rest of the world.

Children as Apprentices
Consistent with the holistic view of psychological development and the relational view of intelligence, the methods through which children's development is promoted differ between Western societies and those of the majority world. Constructivist, information processing, and psychodynamic views of development all describe increasing individuation, objective reasoning, and self-regulation capacities as the telos of psychological maturation. Social constructionism of cognitive development within the broader CHAT framework theorizes apprenticeship as the catalyst for early developmental processes (Bruner, 1978; Vygotsky, 1979a). However, within the zone of proximal development, the goal is mastery toward independence – consistent with Western cultural values. The apprenticeship models of child development in the majority world have a telos of increased participation in and responsibility toward the larger community (Rogoff et al., 2003). While increased skills indicate increasing independence at carrying out tasks and contributing knowledge, these skills are not intended to become generalized into thinking that is disconnected from cultural and community values. The emphasis on learning via apprenticeship is reflected in young children's ways of engaging with elders for the purpose of learning throughout the majority world. Children in Central and South America as well as recent immigrants from these cultures have been shown to observe teachers, parents, and elder siblings at higher rates, for longer periods, and with greater attentiveness than European-heritage children (Correa-Chavez & Rogoff, 2009; Mejía-Arauz et al., 2007; Roberts & Rogoff, 2012; Rogoff et al., 2003; Silva et al., 2010). Children in these societies are less likely to ask questions when observing a model "lesson," and if they do they are directed to observe more intently as an elder repeatedly demonstrates the skill (Alcala et al., 2018; Correa-Chavez & Rogoff, 2009). Within African nations adults assess whether children take initiative based on observing important tasks. Children are expected to provide aid to adults or older peers as soon as they detect a need that requires skills matched to their own capacities (Nsamenang & Tchombé, 2012). Three examples of children

learning via apprenticeship within the majority world are discussed in the following subsections.

Child-to-Child Program in Africa Throughout African societies, a common task that older children are responsible for is the care of younger siblings. Children aged six and above typically serve as primary caregivers for younger children. This practice is so widespread across the continent that it has been adapted into part of a government initiative for increasing child health and well-being (see Serpell et al., 2011 for details). The Child-to-Child (C2C) program trains older siblings in keeping track of infants' and toddlers' weight. Older siblings are tasked with monitoring toddlers' growth over time to ensure that they are receiving adequate nutrition. Throughout various African countries, younger siblings learn from older ones via games, apprenticeships of household tasks, stories, and songs (Nsamenang & Tchombé, 2012; Nyota & Mapara, 2008). The older children simultaneously receive apprentice-style instruction from parents or other adult relatives. This instruction is mainly in cultural values and necessary tasks as well as in stories, songs, and riddles that impart specific knowledge and understanding of importance to society. The apprenticeship model of teaching and learning is so interwoven in all aspects of life that during school peers often complete assignments in small groups, with younger children learning from older ones. Children naturally engage in reciprocal forms of teaching and learning according to the varied skill levels of the group members (see chapters by Serpell et al. and Mweru in Nsamenang & Tchombé, 2012). Indeed, African and African American children have been shown to easily coordinate group work among three and four peers of different ages, whereas European-heritage children consistently choose to work in dyads and are less able to coordinate with larger groups or those of mixed age (Mejía-Arauz et al., 2007).

Indigenous Math Practices Among Indigenous populations of the Americas, various mathematics traditions have been found. Much of what these Indigenous math practices and applications have in common is the connection to learning via apprenticeship. Other depictions of ethnomathematics describe a hybrid form of math learning wherein culturally meaningful practices are paired with academic Western mathematics teaching. In these cases, systems of measurement, geometry, and other math concepts are applied to practical cultural experiences, such as plotting a voyage across varied terrain or constructing a container for use in farming, rain gathering, or another social necessity (D'Ambrosio, 2006).

Mathematical systems that are tied to both the practical needs of the community and abstract contemporary formulas have been found in an ancient Ethiopian system. This system showed that the calculations used for the construction of historical buildings, the patterns of designs on everyday items, and the system's calendar were all consistent with modern mathematical formulas (Waldeana, 2016). As children and adolescents throughout the majority world take on increasingly challenging social problems, increasingly complex solutions are required. Hence, applying algebraic concepts to patterning or using geometric formulas to chart a path or to construct a three-dimensional object become integrated into older children's repertoires of necessary conceptual skills. Although these concepts require abstract reasoning, they are nonetheless tied to a particular social use. As children and adolescents participate in apprenticeship-style relationships that inculcate cultural norms and values, they simultaneously learn the more complex problem-solving skills necessary for more sophisticated tasks. For example, rather than an abstracted system of symbols and numerical relationships, the math of the Navajo is indivisibly linked with the language, cultural values, and cosmology of the culture Mathematical sciences research institute, 2019. Through the apprenticeship method, an understanding of this system, which is connected to broader customs and values, is transmitted across generations.

In summary, child-rearing practices and conceptions of child development in the majority world reflect the ideal of nurturing an interdependent, socially contingent self. From this cultural framework, intersubjectivity involving multiple others can be viewed as representing an ideal of psychological functioning. Such a state allows for shared activities that benefit the collective goals of a given society.

The expectation of most majority world cultures is that children will be raised via apprenticeship, which requires intersubjective forms of social engagement that are based in sensitive coordination with and observation of the actions of the other. Such a enactment of intersubjectivity is based in people collectively using materials while engaged in shared meaningful activities. This conceptualization of the role of intersubjectivity in children's development emphasizes the thriving of the community, borne out through everyday tasks and activities. Working together with objects makes this form of intersubjectivity inherently embodied.

Intersubjective interactions thus serve as a key driver of development within societies that view the function of intelligence and the ultimate purpose of child-rearing as social responsibility. Therefore, a theory of intersubjectivity that is culturally valid beyond Western populations must recognize that an intersubjective state of being is considered fundamental to healthy development in the majority world. Collaborative activities between peers and, more commonly, elders and novices give rise to shared meanings. Participation in such collaborations reflects an intersubjective stance that signifies culturally normative child development.

The research presented in this chapter suggests that a culturally expansive theory of intersubjectivity must reflect the relational ontology and child-rearing processes of the majority world. Rather than originating from individual sociocognitive skills, this perspective suggests that intersubjectivity develops through the interactive dynamics that occur in moment-by-moment exchanges between people. On this account, intersubjective skills cannot exist prior to interaction but develop at the group level over the course of interaction. Variations in the form and degree of intersubjectivity are contingent on the dynamics of any given interaction. In addition, intersubjectivity is embodied, both in terms of enacting shared activity and via the process of physical coordination with the actions of others.

To further understand how intersubjectivity can be extended upon to support collaborative competence in classrooms, it is necessary to consider how children from diverse cultural backgrounds enact intersubjectivity routinely with peers. In addition, contextual factors that lend themselves to intersubjective interactions must be explored. This will enable a culturally valid account of intersubjectivity to be discovered and supported among all populations of children. Indeed, an embodied, activity-dependent version of intersubjectivity is likely to be found among all children. The account argued for in this book does not contend that all interactions are intersubjective, or intersubjective to the same degree. Interactions among majority world populations are more likely to be highly intersubjective than interactions among Westerners. This is an area of cultural strength that must be researched and understood to support collaborative competence among all children. The next chapter will outline in detail the theory of intersubjectivity introduced in this book and how to delineate those ideal forms of collaborative competence from interactions that are less likely to promote development. Finally, as described earlier, Mayan-descended, Indigenous, and African children demonstrate the apprenticeship model of learning through their earlier and more wide-ranging participation in household tasks than European-heritage children (Dayton et al., 2022). Apprenticeship learning is woven into all aspects of daily life from infancy to adulthood; therefore, children are ready and eager to demonstrate their skills and to participate in socially valued tasks and problem-solving as soon as they are capable.

PART II

Elements of Collaborative Competence
Expanding on Prior Research

CHAPTER 3

Redefining Subjectivity and Intersubjectivity for a New Method

Subjectivity and Intersubjectivity

Competing theorizations of intersubjectivity reflect each scholar's philosophical commitments to the nature of subjectivity. As described in Chapter 2, the conception of the self is tied to cultural orientations that have existed over centuries. The idea of subjectivity – the individual perception of and experience in the world – has long been a focus of Western thought (e.g., Henrich, 2020). Dating to the period of the Enlightenment, European philosophers – both secular and theological – have sought to describe the nature of self and its boundaries and permeabilities with others. An entire subdiscipline within modern philosophy termed "philosophy of mind" has arisen to develop formulations of the individual mind. Within this cultural historical context, philosophical arguments that describe the individual as an artifact of language (Wittgenstein), of sensory perception (Merleau-Ponty), or of mind–body dualism that views the intellectual realm as separate from the embodied, emotional, and social (Descartes) have existed alongside theories that view individuality as a social construct (Harre, as discussed in Morss, 2024).

This Western tradition depicts a culture striving to make sense of subjectivity. Many of the questions at the center of philosophical inquiry are embedded in psychological theory as well. These include: (1) How and under what circumstances do we know other minds? (2) What are the boundaries between the self and others? (3) In what ways does language either create or obscure shared meanings, and how do we communicate our own and infer others' intentions? (4) What is the role of empathy in establishing and maintaining shared meanings, and can these meanings be understood psychodynamically? (5) At what age does the ability to coordinate behavior with others develop, and which other psychological/developmental capacities are necessary for this to occur? These questions demonstrate that investigating the nature of the self automatically involves the social realm.

As described in the previous chapter, many majority world conceptions of the human condition take as a given that the self must be understood in the context of relationships with others. Relational structures serve as the focal point for Indigenous psychologies and social theorizing in Asia, Africa, and Latin and Indigenous America. Rather than cultivating an ideal individual, within these societies children are raised with the goal of contributing to the good of the community and to harmonious interactions and relationships.

Theorizing intersubjectivity follows the ways that philosophers and psychologists define and investigate subjectivity. An expansion of the Vygotskian-derived cultural historical activity theory (CHAT), termed a "transformative activist stance" (TAS), reconciles the role of human agency with a focus on the cultural historical contexts of human activity (Stetsenko, 2005, 2016). By situating subjectivity within collaborative efforts at engaging with and transforming society, contributions to the shaping of one's own culture are described as inherently intersubjective. According to TAS, history and society are analogous to a zone of proximal development, wherein people working together, as apprentices, coconspirators, and collaborators, collectively construct their shared social reality in accordance with their own commitments, values, understandings, social positions, and goals. In this way, shared human endeavors transform their own cultural context continuously, expanding it even while that cultural context frames the meanings of those transformative activities. From this perspective, human development is always a product of socioculturally situated subjectivity, which is simultaneously intersubjective. Stetsenko's (2016) irreducibly dynamic view of development as always being transformative and activist echoes the view of play as a time when children create reality together with their peers to become the coauthors of their emergent selves (Perinat & Sadurni, 1999).

Theorizing Intersubjectivity

This chapter introduces a theory and method of intersubjectivity that draws from preexisting conceptualizations. The new concept acknowledges the dynamism inherent in social interaction and considers the continuous feedback loop between collective activity that generates meanings and the sociocultural contexts in which it occurs.

In everyday life, people share meanings according to the dynamics of their relationships as well as the context in which their interaction takes place – for example, friends discussing politics on the street as opposed to at a dinner party, coworkers in a project meeting as opposed to in a board meeting, or strangers watching a car accident as opposed to a sporting event. Each of these situational and interpersonal contexts elicits and requires different forms of intersubjectivity to allow for shared meanings to emerge during interaction.

Wide variations in the definition of intersubjectivity exist across disciplines. A key distinction among the major theories is whether to conceptualize intersubjectivity as a sharing or negotiating of individual subjectivities (usually dyads) or as an emergent product of interaction that cannot be reduced to individuals. The methods of inquiry used to support each theory are tied to which side of this question the theory falls on. The "subjectivist" theories study evidence of negotiating and coordinating subjectivities in the form of language use – looking for shared/mutually anticipated meanings where interacting partners accurately guess one another's perspectives. Accordingly, research in this tradition assesses the developmental capacities necessary for considering others' intentions and the social positioning of individual interactants relative to one another.

The "emergent" theories consider moments of intersubjectivity and what elements comprise those moments. These intersubjective interactions vary in duration and form and may include a wide range of mutual behaviors: physiological synchronization, coordinated enactment of activity, emotional attunement, and mutually constituted meanings. Research from this perspective highlights the ways in which intersubjectivity emerges from the space of interaction and the diverse forms it takes. Rather than measuring aspects of individual skills to explain how interactants engage in intersubjective relations, methods derived from this approach analyze moments of interaction and the contexts surrounding them that either support or detract from sustained intersubjectivity.

In this way, although both traditions investigate language, affect, joint attention, and shared activity, the methods of the "subjectivist" approach attend to how individuals, defined by developmental and psychological traits, use these domains to engage in intersubjective relating. The "emergent" view analyzes how the properties of the intersubjectivity establish and maintain an emergent interactive form beyond that of individual traits. Although each of the psychological domains is viewed as relevant to some extent by all theories of intersubjectivity, each conceptualization embeds intersubjectivity primarily within one or the other domain. The language-based views analyze discourse (or prelinguistic communication), the activity-based accounts analyze the activity at the center of the interaction, the attunement- and empathy-based views assess shared affect, and embodied views study the enactment of everyday physical and physiological coordination. Figure 3.1 depicts each construct of intersubjectivity according to the psychological domain in which it is theorized to occur, the theoretical construct used to define intersubjectivity, and the operationalization of that construct according to the scholars who developed it.

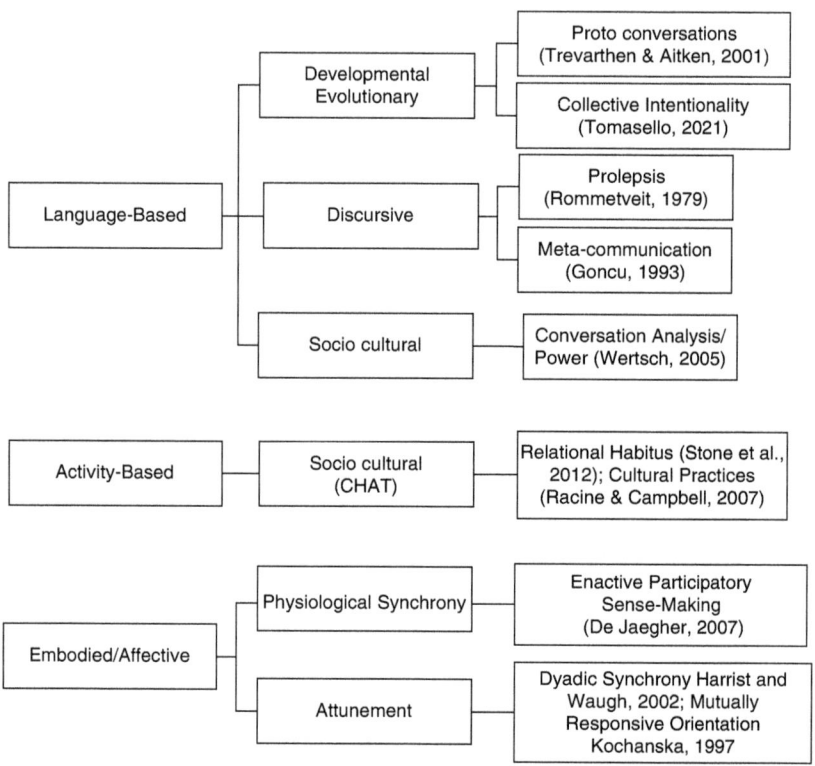

Figure 3.1 Constructs of intersubjectivity according to the domain, theory, and operationalization that are the focuses of each.

Language-Based Accounts of Intersubjectivity
Intersubjectivity as a developmental precursor for language development (Trevarthen, 2009; Trevarthen & Aitken, 2001) and as an evolutionary basis for human survival that simultaneously requires language (Tomasello, 2014) are included in the category of language-based accounts. These theories explain how intersubjectivity enables language during ontogeny. During infant–parent interactions, intersubjectivity is described as involving "proto-conversations." The argument in support of this view portrays language as embedded within a uniquely human intersubjectivity (Stevanovich & Koski, 2018; Tomasello & Carpenter, 2007). These accounts, led by Tomasello (Tomasello & Carpenter, 2007; Tomasello & Vaish, 2013) and Trevarthen and Aitken (2001) and their colleagues, define the social awareness of infants as primary intersubjectivity (PI). Intersubjectivity is demonstrated by following the mother's gaze and other early microcoordination of attention and affect. At around nine months of age, children begin to match their attention to objects, events, or other people with that of their primary caregivers. This shared referencing is thought to lay the groundwork for language acquisition. The implication is that the purpose of human language is to be able to share meanings with others. This collective meaning sharing is another way of describing intersubjectivity. Therefore, intersubjectivity is necessary for language and language supports intersubjectivity. Further support for this view contends that the evolutionary goal of both individual infants and the human species is to enable survival through highly attuned collaborations – first with the primary caregiver and later with the members of one's community (Tomasello, 2019). Tomasello details comparative psychology research that shows the distinctions between humans and great apes in sharing intentions and prioritizing social over individual benefits. He uses evidence from early hunter-gatherer societies to explain how collaborative interactions enabled survival among the first humans. He argues that joint attention and shared intentions are the foundations of the survival of the human species. On this view, evolution has primed infants to establish and maintain intersubjectivity with their caregiver for survival, which later extends into verbal language.

This functionalist paradigm of development casts intersubjectivity as the foundation of an innately social human development. By early childhood, the joint orientation to objects – termed "secondary intersubjectivity" – develops with the new awareness that another perceives the self just as the self perceives the other (Zahavi & Rochat, 2015). The child's use of language thus changes to reflect this new degree of intersubjective sophistication, serving as the tool that both supports and is enabled by growing intersubjective capacities. At the level of human society, the self–other awareness is represented by our cultural artifacts and history – a public accounting of socially shared meanings that depict culturally agreed-upon values (Tomasello, 2019).

The view of intersubjectivity as meta-communication builds upon the evolutionary foundation, highlighting the infant's affective drive to intersubjectively communicate with their primary caregiver. This instinct toward sharing meaning with others is extended to peers who engage with preschoolers during free play. Goncu (1993a, 1993b) argues that social pretend play is a ubiquitous and uniquely human activity. During early childhood, sociodramatic play serves as a bridge between preverbal forms of intersubjectivity and later social uses of language that structure sophisticated interpersonal relations.

Goncu et al. (2002) trace observations of attempts at intersubjective relating during peer play back to two years of age, wherein bids for joint attention are based in nonverbal interactions. Expanding on Trevarthen and Aitken's work, Goncu et al. argue that just as parents and infants are each inherently affectively motivated to interact with one another, peers are affectively motivated to engage in shared meaning-making, which then allows for pretend play.

Goncu's (1993b) measure of intersubjectivity highlights conversational turns that extend pretend play through joint agreement about the meaning of a play object, act, or situation. He refers to these linguistic exchanges as "meta-communication" because they represent talking about what something means – deciding with peers upon a new shared meaning. In this way, language is not being used solely to communicate but rather to decide collectively on the meaning of things and how to refer to them. The meaning agreed to by the pretend players is particular to that specific pretense scenario and therefore exists only in the context of the mutually constructed play activity.

Shared affect regarding the content of the play is required before meta-communicative exchanges can occur. Goncu's research shows that four-year-old children use more symbolic pretense forms of meta-communication (saying, "Let's pretend this is a phone," for example) than three-year-old or six-year-old children. This finding suggests that the preschool period is developmentally unique both in terms of children's new capacities for language, cognitive, and social development and in terms of their limitations relative to older children. Indeed, by six years of age children's play has moved from the players determining the structure of the play as it develops in the moment to games with rules that are predetermined (Elkonin, 2005; Piaget, 1971).

Social Constructivist Language-Based Theories   The discursive language-based account of intersubjectivity does not address questions of evolution and innate development. This account focuses on how intersubjectivity functions in language exchanges as a reflection of sociocultural norms and positions of individuals within a given society. Although, like meta-communication, intersubjectivity is embedded in language use, here it reveals differences in knowledge and status between interlocutors that reflect sociocultural historical factors.

Wertsch and Kazak (2005) and Mortimer and Wertsch (2003) have shown how this occurs in classrooms within disciplinary discourse. Rommetviet (1979) takes a more foundational view with his theory of prolepsis underlying all communication and often creating a barrier to intersubjectivity. Defined as the expectation of the speaker for how the listener will respond, prolepsis includes the presuppositions of shared knowledge required for effective communication. When these expectations are accurate, intersubjectivity develops and functions in an ideal state. However, in many cases a lack of intersubjectivity is both the cause and result of inaccurate prolepsis. The social positioning of two interactants impacts how they construe information and what they know or assume and may vary due to a vast array of potential factors such as social status, roles, developmental stages, and cultures, among others. Such differences in positionality, regardless of how subtle they are, will likely make intersubjectivity during conversation impossible, which in turn makes communication ineffective.

The language-based accounts each define intersubjectivity as a specific way of using language, which is reflected in their empirical research. Proto-conversations, meta-communication, and prolepsis each create limiting criteria for what counts as intersubjectivity, and yet the theories behind them claim that intersubjective interactions are required for ubiquitous forms of interaction, namely parent–infant attunement, preschooler pretend play, and effective communication within institutions. In this way, the language-based accounts can be seen as premised on a contradiction, arguing that intersubjectivity is both universally necessary for development and yet restricted to specific forms of communication that vary in frequency among different interactions and populations.

Activity-Based Accounts of Intersubjectivity
The activity-based approach to intersubjectivity does not apply evolutionary or developmental perspectives to account for intersubjective relations between people. Rather than language, intersubjectivity is described as embedded within shared practices. Joint activity gives rise to intersubjectivity as people collaborate and enact meanings while engaged in everyday collective actions. This view is consistent with that of activity theory (Leontiev, 1978). Accordingly, mundane tasks taken up by individuals are transformed when multiple people participate, imbuing them with social and cultural meaning. These socially meaningful activities become shared practices that either reflect or, as highlighted in the TAS framework, transform the values and understandings of a given culture or society. Here, intersubjectivity does not require agreement (Matusov, 1996) but rather collective engagement and commitment to an activity that is meaningful to all participants. A sprawling field of social meanings constitutes what has been termed "the relational habitus" (Stone et al., 2012). Within this field, intersubjectivity occurs at the intersection of culturally shared meanings and the specific practices of a given sociocultural frame.

Embodied-Affective Accounts of Intersubjectivity
Finally, the last category of theorized intersubjectivity focuses on embodiment. From cognitive science, participatory sense-making (De Jaegher et al., 2016; Fuchs & De Jaegher, 2009) describes intersubjectivity as an enacted third space with its own autonomy rather than a simple merging or negotiating between distinct minds. On this account, the many ways that we coordinate with others include a host of nonverbal forms, such as the physiological and affective. Unlike language- and activity-based accounts, this approach analyzes everyday microinteractions such as passing a plate at dinner or helping someone into their coat. A recognition that each of these social exchanges requires some extent of joint understanding makes every social interaction an intersubjective moment. To discover the process of how people cocreate meaningful actions, De Jaegher et al. (2016) argue that both social organizational structures and individuals coordinating their behavior with each other must be analyzed. In addition, as has been argued within CHAT, the individual is never subsumed within the interaction lest it ceases to be a social interaction (Stetsenko, 2005). Rather, individual autonomy is described as being in perpetual tension with the autonomy of the interaction.

The psychodynamic definition of intersubjectivity is like the "participatory sense-making" view in that both accounts decenter the role of language in intersubjectivity and do not require a collaboration centered on a specific shared activity. The mutually responsive orientation (MRO) construct (Feldman & Masalha, 2010; Kochanska, 2017; Kochanska, 1997) overlaps conceptually with a view of intersubjectivity as primarily affective, being tied to reciprocal attunement and mutual empathy. As with primary and secondary intersubjectivity, early in development the parent's sensitive responsiveness guides attunement, but in later stages the child mirrors this responsiveness with both parents and others. This responsivity can be viewed as a more structured form of empathy that includes attention to and accurate perception of the subjectivity of the other. Unlike proto-conversations, MRO does not lead to more sophisticated uses of language but rather allows for affective attunement, empathy, and moral behavior in relationships (Kochanska, 1997).

Empirical Support for Theories of Intersubjectivity

Research into Language-Based Accounts

Trevarthen and Aitken's (2001) research on PI and proto-conversations centers on face-to-face interactions between infants and mothers. Within these dyads both partners have been shown to anticipate and match their emotions and attention with one another, beginning early in infancy. Sadurní and Pérez (2016) extend this research, detailing primary, secondary, and tertiary intersubjectivity by accounting for six distinct developmental substages through which children and their mothers pass when the child is between the ages of nine months and three years. This research supports the proto-conversation depiction of PI during early infancy but describes a PI-attunement stage beginning at nine months of age. At this stage, PI includes "joint action routines," wherein both infant and parent repeatedly coordinate their attention, affect, and behavior to engage in repetitive, mutually enjoyable action sequences. Examples include peek-aboo, tickling, or other playful games. This formula depicts intersubjectivity as being embedded in relational exchanges that enable language while suggesting that, rather than proto-conversations, which prepare the infant for later language use, the emotional attunement and joint use of materials are developmentally the way in which infants create shared meanings with their parent. This subtle difference does not discount the role of proto-conversations but adds that between one and three years of age children are already actively engaged in joint meaning-making regardless of language use with their primary caregivers.

Extending into preschool, the ability to negotiate the meanings of objects connects to the symbolic representation of ideas and the language capacity necessary to communicate those ideas. This in turn enables joint pretend play (Goncu & Gaskins, 2007). This description of intersubjectivity appears to naturally lead to pretend play, wherein children negotiate meanings through a process of coordination with social partners that requires intersubjectivity. The approach taken by Goncu (1993a, 1993b) shares many core assumptions with the proto-conversation definition of intersubjectivity, including that intersubjectivity is a natural developmental outgrowth of the innate desire to share meaning with others. Goncu operationalizes intersubjectivity by utterances that signal shared meanings apart from the ongoing flow of activity of a pretend play scenario.

Research on the discursive approach to intersubjectivity departs from a developmental analysis and instead investigates the sociocultural elements necessary for and disruptive of intersubjectivity. These methods use adult and child–adult discursive moves to investigate how power differentials frame and/or hinder intersubjectivity. The analysis explains what happens under different conditions of communication when speaker and listener are asymmetrically positioned. The assumptions made about a partner's understanding or knowledge and the meanings attributed to various terms by differentially positioned individuals are tied to larger sociocultural factors. Consistent with methods for investigating the role of prolepsis in enabling intersubjectivity, conversation analysis focuses on how intersubjective relations among adults allow for and are formed by language-in-use (Peräkylä, 2004; see Stevanovich & Koski, 2018 for a review).

The goal of this research is to identify how participants understand the meanings of words, phrases, and concepts and where differences in those understandings occur. It is then possible to analyze how and why intersubjectivity fails and to make recommendations for enabling shared meanings in specific sociocultural contexts. As with meta-communication, focusing exclusively on language as the site of intersubjectivity means that each utterance is tied to the individual speaker. Although the degree of contingency between utterances may be analyzed in such research, the analysis never considers the interaction as a third space irreducible to individual subjectivities. Research in this vein uses the conceptual tool of intersubjectivity to analyze what works and fails in educational contexts (Beraldo et al., 2018). Inaccurate prolepsis during student–teacher interactions leads to disjunctions in intersubjectivity and a lack of common understanding. Without intersubjectivity, learning – as structured and guided by the teacher for the student – cannot occur. However, opportunities for intersubjectivity to flourish in the service of pedagogy or where partial intersubjectivity can be strengthened have been identified in these studies as well (Mortimer & Wertsch, 2003; Wertsch & Kazack, 2005).

Research on Activity-Based Accounts
The activity-based approaches take a major departure from individualistic, developmental accounts of intersubjectivity as located within discrete minds. From this perspective, Racine and Carpendale (2007) argue that during infancy joint attention emerges not from innate developmental capacities but rather from participation in shared practices. Research from this perspective focuses on the enculturation that enables infants to engage in joint meaning-making within specific activity settings. Bids for joint attention among young infant peers bear out the idea that intersubjectivity occurs in varying forms tied to the nature of a given shared activity (Selby & Bradly, 2003). Research showing that the form and meaning of intersubjectivity is emergent in a given interaction, within a particular sociocultural context, and tied to a shared meaningful activity includes evidence from parent–child scaffolding interactions during culturally valued activities among non-Western populations (Rogoff, 2003), infant peer triads (Selby & Bradley, 2003), elementary-aged peers working on a play (Matusov, 1996), and adults collaborating during work contexts (Keyton & Beck, 2009). In each of these situations, the analysis rests on the requirements of the shared activity as well as its relation to larger cultural historical norms, values, and meanings. In these examples, the shared meanings that emerge as intersubjectivity during interaction reflect a variety of relational dynamics.

Research on Embodied Accounts
Conceptually related to MRO and parental reciprocity, dyadic synchrony (Harrist & Waugh, 2002) describes a relational style in which two individuals are highly synchronized and coordinated in their behavior and affect, such that their interaction reflects its own subjectivity (Tunçgenç & Cohen, 2018). Rather than characterizing the nature of discrete interactions, dyadic synchrony describes how relationships function over time. Operationalizations of this concept have included both verbal and nonverbal behaviors. Research also suggests that, unlike MRO, high degrees of dyadic synchrony can reflect both positive and negative affect and can be harmful in dyads where the synchrony reflects a negative

psychological state (Healey et al., 2010). In these conceptualizations of intersubjectivity as affective reciprocity, there is often a nonverbal component. Indeed, research with clinical samples of mothers showed that neither affective or verbal coordination with their infants was possible due to the volatile and unpredictable psychological states of the mothers (Bateman & Fonagy, 2004). Rather than the proto-conversational behaviors of gaze following or emotion matching, infants coordinated their respiration and other physiological states to those of their mothers.

Theoretical and Empirical Assumptions Defining Intersubjectivity

Each theory of what constitutes intersubjectivity is tested using methods, situations, and populations that reflect the key assumptions about the forms of interaction expected to give rise to intersubjectivity. By investigating parent–infant dyads who enact Western norms of relating, primary and secondary intersubjectivities that indicate proto-conversations are discovered. Had this research been conducted within one of the many cultures in which face-to-face and object-related interactions between infants and parents are rare (e.g., Rogoff, 2003; Super & Harkness, 2002), this form of early intersubjectivity might not have been detected. Middle-class preschoolers engaging in pretend play within a laboratory setting using researcher-provided materials and social groups conveyed the meanings of their pretend play via verbal communication, using meta-communication as theorized. The same coding scheme for meta-communication during preschooler free play was applied to the verbal exchanges of low-income preschoolers in a naturalistic setting. Only 30 percent of utterances met the criteria for meta-communicative-based intersubjectivity (Whitington & Floyd, 2009). This finding led the researchers to wonder whether their population of preschoolers was less capable of intersubjectivity than the preschoolers for whom the measure of meta-communication was developed (Whitington & Floyd, 2009). Discourse between older children and adolescents and their teachers about scientific phenomena was analyzed within a setting with significant differences in knowledge, culture, and power between students and teachers (Wertsch & Kazack, 2005). In other examples, more subtle power differentials among assumedly symmetrically positioned individuals were also found in analyses of intersubjectivity from the sociolinguistic tradition (Stevanovic & Peräkylä, 2012).

Regardless of the sociocultural context, by looking for intersubjectivity in the ways in which individuals use language, evidence of shared meanings that exist outside of discourse are precluded. Indeed, Vygotsky's (1987) example of intersubjectivity is that it renders verbal communication unnecessary. From this perspective, sociolinguistic methods can be seen as discovering moments when intersubjectivity lapses or is impossible given the constraints of experiencing shared meaning through language alone. On the other hand, activity-based approaches allow for wide variations in what counts as shared meaning and for whom. Delineating intersubjectivity from other forms of mutuality such as joint attention or collective participation in an activity is a challenge. Empirical research in this tradition often focuses on the broader system from which interactions arise rather than identifying precise moments of intersubjectivity. For example, Matusov (1996) used examples of elementary children's play crafting episodes to argue for an activity-based conceptualization of intersubjectivity that includes disagreements. This method did not identify specific actions or utterances but rather considered the overall shared meaning and collective engagement in the activity as signifiers of intersubjective behavior. In activity-based accounts, the meaning of the shared activity is considered intersubjectively enacted once it is constructed collectively by all participants. This macro view of how shared meanings constitute intersubjective relations at various levels of mutual participation is reflected in Rogoff and colleagues' cross-cultural research, as described in the previous chapter. Their studies show how shared meanings continuously pass between parent and child through interactions that communicate common cultural values and norms. These communications simultaneously define the overall context of everyday activities as based in collective cultural meanings. The activity based approach thus produces two related levels of intersubjectivity that function in relation to each other. The interpersonally enacted shared meanings of everyday activities and the broader collective meanings prescribed by the entire culture and shared by all participants belonging to that culture. Taking a CHAT perspective allows for an analysis of intersubjectivity that includes everyday activities and interpersonal interactions along with culturally and historically based common meanings as well as the relations between them.

Embodied views of intersubjectivity use different methods of analysis from any of those described above. Research on dyadic synchrony examines asymmetrical (usually parent–child) dyads. The analysis includes dynamics of interactions over multiple time points with the same partners. In this way, an overall style that characterizes an interaction creates an intersubjective profile. Therefore, intersubjectivity is tied to a relationship rather than an activity, conversational exchange, or developmental capacity. The foundation for intersubjective relating according to synchrony is other relational traits, such as empathy and attachment. Here, the focus is less on joint meanings per se and more on affective and social attunement.

The participatory sense-making methods are unique, as is the account's definition of intersubjectivity (De Jaegher & Di Paolo, 2007; De Jaegher et al., 2016). De Jaegher and colleagues' concept of intersubjectivity is focused on how commonplace interactions that permeate daily life are experienced intersubjectively.

To investigate the nature and meanings of such interactions, a method is needed that attends to multiple modes of sensing, feeling, and perceiving the experience of mundane interactions, such as handing an object to another or holding a door open for someone. The methodology used to explore these experiences is designed to "investigate the experience of interacting" by recording the perceptions of self, other, and of a third-person observer (De Jaegher et al., 2017). The purpose of investigation is to draw out the multitude of meanings that arise from varied forms of perception during embodied interaction. Unlike any of the other approaches, rather than defining and measuring moments of intersubjectivity, this method defines social interactions as inherently intersubjective and then delineates the forms and meanings that the intersubjectivity takes. The unit of analysis in this approach is the phenomenological experience of the participants, with a particular focus on embodied dimensions. As a result, any social interaction – no matter how brief and how apparently meaningless – is rife for analysis of the ways in which meanings are cocreated through social interactions. Like the previously discussed methods, this approach creates a methodological frame that brings into awareness the area that the theory has chosen to highlight – in this case, embodied microinteractions of negotiated and coordinated meanings. Such a frame could be applied within any social context but is ideal for analyzing short moments rather than the extensive interactive sequence of a collaborative task as occurs in activity-based accounts.

A Theory of Intersubjectivity for New Insights

Each of these approaches offers insights into the nature and functioning of intersubjectivity. Given that the methods used to support the assumptions and focus of each theory are designed for specific domains and processes as articulated by the theory, it is not possible to use one set of evidence to invalidate a different theory. Rather, approaches to intersubjectivity capture unique aspects of the psychological phenomenon – the ways in which intersubjectivity develops and occurs at different points and at different levels of social life. The question is therefore which account of intersubjectivity has the greatest potential for providing useful insights. The account of intersubjectivity argued for in this book is concerned with illuminating developmental processes among children from a wide variety of cultural contexts and engaged in a wide variety of interactions and activities. Therefore, a theory that privileges some culturally based forms of interaction over others in its definition of intersubjectivity, such as verbal communication, or certain types of activities that may be provided more frequently to some children than others is not inclusive enough. At the same time, an overly broad theory of intersubjectivity that assesses general forms of interaction without delineating behavioral indicators that can be contrasted with nonintersubjective interactions is not useful for understanding which factors either support or hinder the development of intersubjectivity. Finally, given the premise that intersubjective interactions are widely beneficial and even necessary for many aspects of development, this book aims to provide an approach to investigating intersubjectivity that will offer practical implications for how to support its development among the most varied contexts and across wide variations among participants.

The account that will be elaborated in later chapters is characterized as activity-based given that it considers joint meaningful activity to be the anchor for intersubjectivity. In addition, consistent with embodied and sociocultural accounts, this theory views intersubjectivity as emergent in interaction and irreducible to individuals. In line with psychodynamic and developmental accounts of intersubjectivity, coordination of attention and affect comprise the primary dimensions. However, bodily orientation and physiological coordination are also potential indicators depending on the nature of the shared activity. This account allows for intersubjectivity to occur among both entirely aligned interacting partners or during interactions that include disagreements. In either case, shared meanings and joint participation in shared activity are required to enable intersubjectivity. Finally, embodied components are inherent in this account of intersubjectivity given that it emerges from shared activity and requires some degree of synchrony. On this account, synchrony is defined as a reciprocal coordination and attunement of affect, actions, and attention.

The theory introduced here that reflects each of these elements is termed the "sociocultural activity-embodied" (SAE) account of intersubjectivity. The SAE view makes use of the concept of interactional synchrony, defined by nonverbal affective and attention coordination. In this way, shared perspective-taking occurs via mutual observation and synchronization during interaction rather than as an individual sociocognitive skill. Synchrony has been referenced in the "fluid synchrony" of majority world collaborations (described in the prior chapter). In addition, the literature on "dyadic synchrony" has demonstrated this style of relating within close interpersonal relationships, such as between parent and–child (Harrist & Waugh, 2002), among Western populations.

The activity-based component of the SAE view highlights how shared meanings of collective activity are key to establishing intersubjectivity. The activity at the center of the interaction refers to the CHAT meaning of activity, in that cultural historical norms and symbols are enacted through engagement in the everyday activities that form the basis of a given society. On the SAE account, shared, meaningful activity determines both the extent to which an interaction is intersubjective and the form of intersubjectivity that it takes. At the same time, the activities carry into the interaction the cultural historical norms and values that are embedded within them. For example, playing hopscotch to a rhyme bounds an interaction within a particular set of shared meanings as well as imputing various cultural norms, values, and meanings. In summary, the theory of intersubjectivity elaborated in this book considers various levels of sociocultural historical context in elaborating both the meanings and goals of the shared activity that grounds the interaction and the nature of the interactive behavior itself.

Consistent with developmental and activity-based accounts, analysis of intersubjectivity attends to both the participants' developmental traits and to the socially meaningful contexts in which interactions occur. For example, an empirical application of this theory involved preschoolers, and therefore play – the leading activity of the preschool period (Elkonin, 2005) – was the focus for identifying intersubjectivity. In examples with primary school children, pedagogical elements were added because of the nature of the activity context and the developmental traits of the children. Consistent with a developmental perspective, the nature of the intersubjectivity observed is partially determined by developmental constraints and preferences. Consistent with a CHAT perspective, the nature of the joint activity and its shared meaning for the participants is in part determined by the cultural historical context in which it occurs, including cultural tools as well as culturally specific modes of relating among the participants. In this way, new implications for how to support intersubjectivity in that specific context arise from each interaction. Finally, unlike any of the previous accounts, the methodology used to apply the present theory is designed to allow for measuring intersubjectivity among groups of peers consisting of up to six participants. Grounding intersubjectivity in shared activity provides a wider "surface area" for mutual participation and joint coordination than would be possible if the measure assessed only a single domain, such as linguistic or affective dimensions.

The next chapter will provide further details of the theory and will then analyze samples of interactive episodes among children taken from other accounts to demonstrate how such a theory could be applied to a wide range of interactions, as well as which contextual details are necessary for measuring intersubjectivity in a way that is consistent with the proposed theory. This methodology will then be applied to a qualitative analysis of naturally occurring preschool play episodes.

CHAPTER 4

Framing Intersubjectivity during Children's Interactions
A Critical Examination of Theories and Methods

Prevailing Views of Intersubjectivity

As detailed in the previous chapter, the major distinctions between current theories of intersubjectivity are related to where the construct is thought to originate. Developmental accounts contend that intersubjectivity originates with the changing subjectivity of individuals at particular developmental stages. For infants this means parent–infant preverbal attunement, whereas for preschoolers intersubjectivity occurs during moments when two or more children engage in joint meaning-making apart from their individual understandings of reality. The developmental view of intersubjectivity grounds the construct in sets of individual developmental capacities, demonstrated via language use (or protolanguage for infants). The meta-communicative expression of intersubjectivity is specific to the pretend play of preschoolers because pretend play is the only context in which humans routinely create a new, imagined reality through language with peers.

The sociolinguistic account embeds intersubjectivity within interactive language exchanges but without the developmental context. Focused on communication between older children and adults, on this view intersubjectivity is demonstrated via prolepsis, wherein a speaker acts in accord with an accurate expectation of how a listener will respond (Rommetveit, 1979). This nondevelopmental account of language-based intersubjectivity extends it through the lifespan to any given conversation. Here, intersubjectivity is defined as the accurate perception of the perspective of a conversation partner. However, prolepsis is not analyzed among the conversations of young children given that it requires advanced perspective-taking ability, metalinguistic awareness, and sophisticated theory of mind. In addition, prolepsis can only be observed for the speaker during conversation. To be intersubjective both parties must accurately judge the other's perspective, thereby inhabiting the roles of both speaker and listener. In the examples given later in this chapter, the sociolinguistic analysis focuses on uneven power dynamics between speaker and listener in the form of teacher and student. The power analysis of discourse shifts intersubjectivity from a developmental achievement to a sociological and sociolinguistic phenomenon. Indeed, research from the sociolinguistic perspective applied to elementary and high school students has demonstrated how rare intersubjectivity is within educational contexts given inherent power differentials between the interacting partners.

The sociocultural view of intersubjectivity considers the overarching context of joint meaningful activity that develops between people. Here, the analysis turns to the ways in which shared meanings emerge from joint participation in an activity. Although examples tend to focus on activities that involve verbal communication, language is less the focus than the nature of the shared activity. Emergent, collective meanings derive from a complex mix of dialectical relations between the sociocultural contexts of the participants and the situations that give rise to their joint activity.

Each of these prior theorizations provides an analytical framing of interactions that demonstrate intersubjectivity. The purpose of this chapter is to contrast how each theory applies to empirical examples of children interacting. The argument is that none of the current theories provide a comprehensive enough account to assess naturally occurring interactions and provide implications for how to support them. To address this gap, a new conceptualization of intersubjectivity is introduced and demonstrated using examples of preschooler free play and preexisting empirical examples.

Sociocultural Activity-Embodied Theory of Intersubjectivity

The multidimensional concept of intersubjectivity proposed in this book provides a sociocultural activity-embodied (SAE) account that makes use of concepts from cultural historical activity theory (CHAT) along with the developmental construct of interactional synchrony. Interactional synchrony has been defined in prior research as a relationship type characterized by sensitivity, reciprocity, mutual orientation, and joint attention among asymmetrical dyads (Harrist & Waugh, 2002). In line with the conceptualization of intersubjectivity described here, research has shown synchrony to reflect a dynamic achievement that develops over the course of interaction (Healey et al., 2010). In the present conceptualization, synchrony indicates a coordination of emotional and attentional states as well as coordinated actions among two or more interacting people. The SAE concept of intersubjectivity includes the developmental characteristics of the interacting individuals as one of many contextual factors influencing the intersubjectivity that emerges from the interaction. Accordingly, the developmental period of interacting participants contributes to the form of intersubjectivity that develops between them. However, individuals' developmental constraints, capacities, or achievements do not determine the nature of intersubjectivity. Emergent, shared meanings of collective activity along with embodied and nonverbal indicators of interactional synchrony together comprise intersubjectivity on the SAE view.

Consistent with the sociocultural view, the analytical frame of the SAE account of intersubjectivity includes the activity itself and its shared, emergent meanings to the participants. The nonverbal coordination and synchronization of infancy that has been used to signify intersubjectivity from a developmental approach (Trevarthen & Aitken, 2001) is adapted for the SAE account by applying the construct of interactional synchrony to preschoolers and older children. Unlike in either the developmental or sociolinguistic view, language (broadly defined) does not serve as the structure for enacting intersubjectivity. Instead, verbal and nonverbal mutual behaviors are assessed for the degree to which they indicate interactional synchrony and shared meanings among participants. Figure 4.1 shows the components in the SAE model of intersubjectivity.

The three components of synchrony, shared activity, and intersubjectivity develop in a multidirectional relationship during interaction. The relationship between the shared activity and intersubjectivity is supported and mediated by synchrony. The collective meaning of the activity emerges at the intersection of all three components. Fluctuations in the degrees of

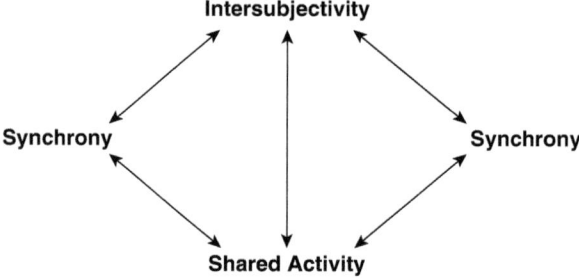

Figure 4.1 The theorized relationship between the elements of intersubjectivity.
Note: The dual arrows indicate a reciprocal relationship between synchrony, shared activity, and the shared meanings that comprise intersubjectivity. The level and form of each component develop in dialectical relationship with each other component.

each component trigger and are contingent upon those of the others. Therefore, intersubjectivity develops in dialectical relationship with shared activity and synchrony.

Framing Interactions According to Varied Accounts of Intersubjectivity

Different accounts of intersubjectivity each frame interactions with a different focus, zooming in when assessing how language is used during meta-communication or prolepsis and out when the focus is extended beyond language to capture the shared sociocultural meanings of the joint activity. The SAE theorization zooms in to examine interactional synchrony and out to observe the nature of the activity and the sociocultural and material context in which it occurs. The method for assessing intersubjectivity during interactions according to the SAE view uses continuous rather than categorical measurement. Therefore, interactions are characterized by degrees and dimensions of intersubjectivity rather than being defined as either intersubjective or not. This aspect of the SAE concept of intersubjectivity allows for measurement of nuances and fluctuations consistent with most major developmental concepts.

Indicators of Intersubjectivity
The previous chapter showed how differences in operationalizations of intersubjectivity determined what aspects of interactions are observed and evaluated for evidence of intersubjectivity. The major behaviors indicating intersubjectivity according to each operationalization are described below.

Developmental; meta-communication (Goncu, 1993a, 1993b): Behaviors include referring to an object, space, or situation as separate from its ordinary meaning. At least two children agree to this alternative meaning, demonstrating this agreement verbally, by showing an understanding of what the interacting partner means or by using the object during play with a shared understanding of its meaning. A typology of three major types of meta-communication with eight subtypes is provided in Goncu (1993b) and will be used in the subsequent analysis.

Sociolinguistic; prolepsis (Rommetveit, 1979; Wertsch & Kazack, 2005): The speaker demonstrates an accurate expectation of how the listener will respond. The speaker accurately takes the perspective of the listener into account, and the conversation partners then exchange roles. This operationalization is demonstrated via discourse and analyzed for shared understanding during linguistic exchanges.

Sociocultural view including conflict (Matusov, 1996): Behaviors include adding onto the ideas of others toward a common goal, engaging with others in the context of shared assumptions, goals, and values, and disagreeing on details while continuing to work within collective structures and meanings.

Sociocultural activity-embodied: Behaviors include joint participation in an activity defined by mutual understanding of its meaning. Mutual coordination and reciprocity are shown via nonverbal indicators such as eye contact, shared emotion, joint attention toward the materials, and coordinated use of materials to collectively construct the meaning of the shared activity.

Methods and Contexts

The remainder of this chapter is devoted to demonstrating where intersubjectivity exists within different types of interactions according to different theorizations. The purpose of this is to connect the theories and methods for defining intersubjectivity to goals for developmental psychology and education. A major goal of this book is to use intersubjectivity as it occurs among children in school to support a broader theory of collaborative competence. This endeavor requires being able to identify interactive competencies that rise to the level of intersubjectivity among populations of children who have typically been described as deficient within social development research. Therefore, the purpose of applying different theoretical and behavioral indicators of intersubjectivity to examples of children's interactions is to discover which account provides the broadest and most consistent frame for recognizing and analyzing intersubjective interactions.

The first example is taken from research into the SAE view introduced earlier. The segments will be analyzed according to each of the prevailing operationalizations. From Garte (2016):

Sarah walks over to the block area and asks "Can I play here?"

MARY: *"Okay, come in, we're making a bridge."*

Sarah takes a car, and she and Josh weave their cars through the columns, occasionally knocking them over.

According to the meta-communication scheme for identifying intersubjectivity, the mutual actions depicting agreement that the block structure is a vehicular bridge indicate intersubjectivity. These utterances would be coded as both verbal and nonverbal indicators of "agreement-acceptance," "expansion-extension," and "building-on" according to Goncu's (1993b) typology.

The sociolinguistic and sociocultural accounts would identify intersubjectivity based on the shared meaning of the activity and the apparently accurate perception of the other's perspective, wherein Mary demonstrates prolepsis in her statement to Sarah, who responds as expected.

Only the SAE operationalization would determine that this brief exchange does not clearly demonstrate whether a shared meaningful activity has emerged collectively. In addition, there is no evidence of social/emotional synchrony, only joint attention, indicating brief attentional intersubjectivity. Therefore, the SAE account would score this exchange with a low level of joint attention-based intersubjectivity.

Mary watches this and then removes the columns on the second tier. Josh and Sarah then drive the car over the horizontal block.

JOSH: *"This is a firefighter."*
SARAH: *"Do you want me to be a police?"*

According to the sociocultural account, this example of children adding to each other's ideas during a collectively constructed activity signifies intersubjectivity. Meta-communication is also indicated via "extension" and "building-on" in the exchange of mutually agreed-upon meanings of the cars as rescue workers as is prolepsis between Josh and Sarah.

Malcolm enters the block area and Sarah hands him a car. Mary also gets a car and joins in driving the cars around the floor.

According to the SAE view, the interaction has not yet reached a state of sustained intersubjectivity in that a clearly defined shared meaning of the collective activity has not emerged from the interaction. The children appear to be acting at the periphery of shared activity, with some moments of coordinated action and mutual observation that are not sustained enough to indicate synchrony. Again, as the only concept that allows for a continuous assessment of degree and a multidimensional assessment of the type of intersubjectivity, this interaction would be evaluated as showing brief attention-based intersubjectivity due to the joint use of materials on the SAE view.

This comparison highlights how differences in the methodology of each account determine what counts as social meaning. Meta-communication treats any agreement on symbolic meaning as indicative of intersubjectivity regardless of context, whereas the sociocultural view considers actions that occur within a mutually meaningful context as intersubjective. The SAE view considers moments of agreed-upon meaning that do not connect to an overarching shared meaning of an ongoing activity as representing a low level of intersubjectivity. The sociocultural definition of intersubjectivity as categorical rather than continuous does not allow for a distinction between fleeting exchanges that may constitute brief moments of shared meaning and longer interactions in which joint meaningful activity collectively emerges over time.

> *Sarah and Mary begin chasing each other around the classroom and laughing.*

This diversion from the shared focus on the blocks resulted most likely from the lack of sustained meaningful activity among the group. Only the SAE analysis would predict this lapse based on the low levels of intersubjectivity preceding it.

> *Josh comes over and all four children begin recreating the structure by adding multiple layers of horizontal blocks held up by two large column blocks on each end. The children place blocks in a highly coordinated fashion wherein each addition corresponds to the previous one.*

This nonverbal coordinated set of actions between four children indicates a high degree of interactional synchrony within the context of joint participation in a highly meaningful activity. However, due to the lack of dialogue, this segment would not be considered intersubjective by either the developmental or sociolinguistic account.

> *Each time a layer is completed, they drive their blocks over the horizontal surface in tandem. During this process, the children alternate their placement of blocks with one another and navigate around each other's movements to avoid collision.*

Although there is no explicit reference to a shared representational meaning, the children's use of materials shows that they are acting with a shared understanding of the meaning of the activity, including a symbolic representation. However, this interaction does not include signs of either meta-communication or prolepsis. The interaction would likely count as intersubjectivity according to the sociocultural view, but this would require the researcher's inference that the nature of the activity was commonly understood. Here, the multidimensionality and continuous measurement of the SAE view are helpful in that they would allow for specifying this exchange as highly synchronous along the dimensions of joint attention and mutual focus during joint coordinated action that involves a shared meaning among the participants. Characterizing the intersubjectivity in this way allows for an assessment of both the degree and form of intersubjectivity.

> *After a few moments, Sarah bangs into the structure's base with her knee and the whole building topples. She stares, saying, "Oops!"*
> *Malcolm immediately picks up the blocks to rebuild and Sarah begins a chant: "We can do it, we can build it!" which all four children join.*

Despite signifying clearly defined shared meanings as well as collective affect, this chant does not meet the criteria for meta-communicative intersubjectivity, as the children are not referring to an object or situation apart from its common meaning. Similarly, without a back-and-forth exchange, it cannot demonstrate prolepsis.

> *The four children work together chanting and quickly rebuild the structure following the same process as before.*
> *Sarah suggests, "Let's line up all the cars."*
> *Sarah collects the cars from the shelf and she, Mary, and Josh line them up on the top tier while Malcolm adds smaller shapes to the top, fitting them into each other carefully.*
> *The children take turns adding small triangles, arches, and other "decorative" shapes to the top tier. Once there is no more space, all four children drive the cars through the crevices between the top blocks, moving in perfect coordination with one another.*

With a high degree of synchrony, the foursome acts as a collective subject (Leontiev, 1978). The collective subject refers to participants acting together for a common purpose within a given socioculturally defined activity system. The goal of creating a "bridge for cars" is collectively defined as a very tall, stable structure. Overall, this episode demonstrates a highly meaningful joint activity. The sociocultural view would characterize the episode as intersubjective. However, it would not be able to delineate how that intersubjectivity changes and builds over discrete segments of interaction. Meta-communication is evidenced through the brief conversational exchanges at the beginning of the episode. The first exchange between Mary and Sarah and the second between Josh and Sarah signify both meta-communication and prolepsis regardless of the extent to which they were constructing a meaningful activity or demonstrating synchrony. However, the latter sections would not qualify as intersubjective on these accounts due to the lack of language exchange. In this way, the developmental and sociolinguistic accounts serve to detach moments that demonstrate intersubjectivity from the ongoing flow of an interaction. The sociocultural view perceives intersubjectivity as a global characterization of the entire activity but cannot delineate fluctuations over the course of interaction. Only the SAE view is able to provide a moment-by-moment analysis of peaks and dips in intersubjectivity, taking into consideration both the overall shared meaning of the activity and the microinteractions that signify synchrony, as well as the relations between both levels of interaction.

The following example of intersubjectivity as meta-communication from Goncu (1993b, pp. 105–106) contrasts with the highly synchronous, coordinated, nonverbal shared activity of the previous "bridge for cars" episode.

> *One of the boys introduces a play idea by announcing to his partner "Hey let's play workers."*
>
> *A boy picks up a pan and says: "I'll just use this" and his partner in an extension responds "that's that's the water pan."*
>
> *(Verbal): A girl says, "They can play having cooking," referring to imaginary children expected to come to an imaginary party. Her partner first responds by saying "Yeah, they can play." Then she builds on the idea in her turn by saying, "Not the grown-up ones. Right?"*
>
> *(Non-Verbal): A girl says, "We're gonna put this orange juice in here" while she opens the refrigerator door to put the juice can in it. However, she changes her mind after she opens the refrigerator door, and in an act of BUILDING-ON, she gets a milk bottle out of the refrigerator and pours the play dough that was in the juice can into the milk bottle.*
>
> *(V): A girl says to her partner, "Hold this bow, get your ponytail out" while she tries to tie a bow on her partner's braid. The partner says "It's a braid." The girl responds in a compromise, "I know but let's just call it a ponytail."*
>
> *(NV): A girl pulls the bottle that her partner was joyously shaking. For a short while neither releases the bottle. Then, in an act of CONCILIATION, the partner lets the girl have it by giving the bottle to her with an ostensibly inquiring eye contact as a plea to maintain the play interaction.*

Goncu (1993b) created a typology of eight distinct subtypes of meta-communication to allow for the coding of utterances as seen in this extract. These exchanges exemplify the operationalization of intersubjectivity as meta-communicative turns. As such, it is not possible to determine the dynamics of when intersubjectivity peaks and falls over the course of an entire activity. Here, nonverbal behaviors are represented by agreements on symbolic meanings for the purpose of maintaining the pretend play. Theoretically, intersubjectivity resides in the mutually created pretend world and the extent to which players contribute to maintaining and elaborating on that world.

Only certain exchanges count as a contribution. In addition, there is no measure of affective or embodied interpersonal connection. This limits intersubjectivity to the activity of pretend play. In addition, verbal and nonverbal communication is construed as not being for the purpose of furthering the interpersonal connection between the interactants but rather between individual players and the pretend play activity. Unlike the SAE view, it is not necessary to determine the extent to which an emergent activity is collectively meaningful because, developmentally, pretend play is by its nature collectively meaningful to preschoolers. Nonetheless, interpersonal coordination is the foundation for the developmental account of infant intersubjectivity that Goncu (1993a) theorizes meta-communication to be an extension of. By removing the component of affective and attentional mutual coordination from preschooler intersubjectivity, the theory applies solely to pretend play, excluding other kinds of interactions or activities in which preschoolers might engage with peers.

Neither the sociolinguistic, sociocultural, or SAE view could determine intersubjectivity from these anecdotes because they are isolated from the ongoing interaction, with limited conversational exchanges. An analysis of an entire activity, on the other hand, provides insight into multiple interactive dimensions, as seen in the following (Garte, 2016, pp. 265–267):

> *The boys simultaneously take hold of opposite ends of the string stretching it out between them and taking turns alternatively cutting and holding the string. One boy pulls the string taut to the edge of the "cutter" while the other boy strikes the cutter down on the string. After each successful chop, the string falls and the boys immediately break into uproarious laughter. The two boys experiment with different versions of the "cutting" activity, responding to the string dropping after each chop with mirth.*

This activity has taken on a specific form and meaning. The exploration of the material has turned into a game. Both boys construe the moment of the string being chopped and falling as hilarious. Their common perception of an ambiguous phenomenon with high emotional synchrony and shared meaning indicates intersubjectivity on the SAE and sociocultural views, but again, due to the lack of discourse, this exchange does not demonstrate either meta-communication or prolepsis.

The examples of the "string game" and the "bridge for cars" show high levels of synchrony, joint attention, affective attunement, and embodied mutual coordination and synchronization. During peaks in these indicators of intersubjectivity, there is no discourse among the participants. Similarly, these moments of heightened intersubjectivity cannot be fully understood without the larger context of the shared activity and its vicissitudes over the entire play episode. The antecedents of intersubjectivity demonstrate how, depending on the nature of the activity, the relative importance of interpersonal, material, and sociocultural factors varies in terms of the influence of these factors on the form of intersubjectivity that develops at different points throughout a given interaction.

The following example from a naturalistic study seeking to replicate intersubjectivity as meta-communication shows how the language-based operationalization constrains the researcher's focus even when more context is provided (Whitington & Floyd, 2009, pp. 148–149).

> *To this point, Brenda and Bruce had been playing doctors. Brenda was on the phone when Bruce left the room. He re-entered carrying a large white stuffed rabbit calling for the nurse (Wendy) to put the bunny into bed. However, the girls had changed to veterinary play. Brenda began to leave "doctors" to join veterinary play.*
>
> *Onlooker Wendy looked at Bruce (observation) as he called "Nurse" (building-on) but she quickly pulled off her cap and joined Grace on the lounge chair (rejection).*
>
> *Grace said "I can be Mum. I can be Mum dog" (introduction).*
>
> *Wendy replied "Yes, 'n this is the vet. We went to the vet" (extension). Both girls curled together on the chair – like puppies.*
>
> *Meanwhile Brenda had taken the phone to Wendy and Grace.*
>
> *Wendy said to Brenda "We're in the vet's now" (extension).*
>
> *Grace and Brenda made yappy noises acceptance) as Brenda climbed into the chair and huddled (extension; rejection of Bruce and previous play theme) with Wendy and Grace.*

The inclusion of the entire episode in this naturalistic transcript allows one to note moments of coordination and mutual engagement along with shifts and transitions that lead to changes in partners as well as in the nature of the agreed-upon activity. However, by segmenting the episodes into linguistic categories, the children's limitations of verbal communication rather than their capacities for interpersonal coordination of actions are highlighted. In the examples provided by Goncu's (1993b) laboratory study referenced previously, each coded category of shared meaning is provided in discrete one- or two-turn interactions. How these interactions relate to ongoing dynamics of shared activity is unknown. In the naturalistic study, key details that could have evidenced shared meaning creation, joint attention, or affective synchrony are left out by the authors providing summaries such as "They had been playing doctors," and, "The girls had changed to veterinary play," without describing how these shared play themes emerged and then collectively shifted. By focusing only on discrete verbally expressed joint meanings according to a priori criteria, the emergence of intersubjectivity during play and the extent to which the overall play episode reflects intersubjective joint meaning-making are not visible to the researcher.

Next, the transcripts of interacting groups of older children engaged in classroom activities are compared. The analysis of intersubjectivity during such interactions reflects the sociolinguistic approach in the first example and the sociocultural perspective in the second example. These transcripts highlight elements that influence where and how intersubjectivity is detected during interaction. The structures of both the interpersonal and material contexts differ greatly, despite both interactions occurring among school-age peers within an educational setting. Although similar on the surface, the roles of the children in relation to each other and to the shared task vary. In addition, what counts as evidence of intersubjectivity and therefore the focus of the description differs between the accounts.

The first example takes place during a science lesson (Mortimer & Wertsch, 2003, p. 238). The anecdote demonstrates how inaccurate prolepsis on the part of the teacher regarding the students makes both intersubjectivity and effective pedagogy impossible.

> EDW: *A supposition ... it has to be a vacuum ... supposing, it is only an example, one way is to put the gas there, inside ...*
>
> ALE: *(to the teacher, who comes over to the group) Teacher, all gases can be transformed into a liquid state?*
>
> T.: *Yes, all can be transformed, but some have to be in perfect condition; otherwise they can blow up.*
>
> ALE: *Sort of ...?*
>
> T.: *Like methane, natural gas. What do they do with natural gas? (The teacher explains why natural gas must be transported through pipelines and cannot be stored in containers like butane and propane.)*
>
> EDW: *See, now it changes completely ... to put (the gas) in a pipeline or inside a butane bottle ...*
>
> T.: *Hey, pay attention: What should you do in this question, now? You have proposed a model for each one of the previous situations. This model now, the final model, isn't it the same model for all the situations? Then, what is this? It is to generalize. Which is that model? What model is it?*
>
> ALE: *It is a compact model, isn't it?*
>
> T.: *No, it is not this. Forget the butane bottle! It is constituted by ...*

> Car: *Particles!*
> T.: *By particles, it this. All the gases, then . . .*
> Ale: *Particles!*
> T.: *Particles. And what are the characteristics of the particles? Then, what you should discuss is this. Particles and what else? . . . How the particles . . . what happens to them . . . how do they behave? (The teacher leaves, going to another group.)*
> Ale: *If they undergo modification . . . I'm not understanding . . .*
> Car: *Nether do I (All laugh.) . . .*
> Ale: *The thing is: It has to be made a characteristic of a gas. Of gases . . .*
> Edw: *We were talking about that, totally wrong! Here it doesn't say anything about a container . . .*
> Car: *But here it is asking to describe the model.*
> Edw: *Then, the model . . . (Inaudible.)*
> Edw: *Maybe he said it this way: Draw a ridiculous square there and put the model inside the square.*
> Car: *Yes, then it is this. (They begin to draw.)*
> Car: *The particles of a gas are the same as the particles of the air?*

The analysis discusses how there is not only a chasm between the knowledge of the students and teacher but also that the discourse of the teacher assumes an abstract perception of scientific phenomena, but this way of thinking is misaligned with the students' cultural norms. In a later paper by Wertsch and Kazack (2005), scientific discourse between teachers and elementary-aged children reveals a similar issue. The discourse used by the teacher presupposes knowledge as well as a conceptual way of perceiving scientific phenomena that is foreign to the children. Nonetheless, because of the nature of the sociocultural context – a classroom – and the prescribed roles for students and teachers within such a context, the students make repeated attempts to appropriate the teacher's perspective through adjusting their discourse.

From Wertsch and Kazack, (2005: pp. 6–7):

> *There, Leona points out, "So, somehow we need to show 225 numbers on the paper," and in response Jessica, Erica, and Tanner start to calculate how many squares are on the graph paper, apparently in order to determine whether there were enough for their data. They continue to talk in terms of simply writing down numbers in the squares on the paper, whereas Leona is talking in terms of the range of values and how these values might usefully be divided into segments and displayed in the form of a histogram. When she realizes that they are calculating the number of squares on the graph paper, Leona finally asks them what they are doing and responds by noting, "Well, we don't want to know how many squares there is altogether, right?"*

This example expands the analysis to include a focus on the cultural tool "graph paper." Indeed, the authors agree that, despite the frequent mismatch between the teachers' expectations of student knowledge and their responses to students' speech (lack of prolepsis), the common cultural tool served as a bridge to enable limited intersubjectivity and made it possible for the teacher to eventually (after understanding the students' perspective) scaffold student learning toward greater alignment.

The following example from the sociocultural approach reveals intersubjectivity as it emerges from shared meaningful activity among child peers. This paper by Matusov (1996: pp. 36–37) aimed to demonstrate how disagreements within the context of shared meaningful activity can ultimately strengthen intersubjectivity if they contribute to the shared space in which collective meaning-making occurs.

STACY: *It's supposed to be Snow White not Black Night.*
ROBIN: *Yeah, but remember? We were gonna change it!*
STACY: *Yeah. but [sic] it's supposed to be called Snow White!*
LESLEE: *Except it could be called Black Night. (Robin mumbles something) Let's ask Cathy [the teacher]. Cathy, can you change the name? Can you change the name like to Black Night instead of Snow White?*
TEACHER: *Sure. That can be your thing. Just do whatever you want.*
CAROL: *(interrupts) But we don't like it!*
ROBIN: *Well, some ... most people do!*
TEACHER: *When people don't agree, how do you solve a problem?*
LESLEE: *We had, we had the last play. Heather liked it, everybody liked it and then ...*
TEACHER: *Now who's not happy? (Stacy and Carol raise their hands) Can you think of how would you like it?*
STACY: *I'd like to change the form. Like make it exactly opposite.*
LESLEE: *But it's not opposite.*
TEACHER: *We need to hear out Stacy and Carol. I think it is real important that you put your ideas in front of them.*
ROBIN: *Like we can get everybody, we can mix all the ideas so everybody will have their own idea and then we can mix them up together.*

These examples are early episodes of an extensive play-crafting activity that took place over many days. Three more transcripts are presented in the paper in which the children come to increasing degrees of agreement, with occasional disagreement, and a final shared product is created that reflects the equal participation of all the children. During these later episodes the teacher is either absent or silent.

Had any of the conversational turns been analyzed outside of the context of the overall activity and its shared meanings to the participants, this narrative would have been viewed as demonstrating limited intersubjectivity.

However, an inclusive definition of intersubjectivity as joint engagement in shared meaningful activity considers the dialogue within the context of the entire activity, its development over time, and how the cognitive and affective contributions of the participants together result in a process that is highly coordinated and whose meaning is, in the end, a collective product that emerged entirely from the interaction.

Contrasting these elementary-aged children's small-group interactions within educational settings highlights factors that influence the development of intersubjectivity that are not included in meta-communication. These include: the extent of shared knowledge and equal power exchange among participants; the sociocultural context framing the interaction; the role of cultural artifacts and their use and meanings to the participants; the goals of the activity for the participants and the pedagogue(s)/teacher(s); the sources of the participants' commitment to the activity; and how the teacher navigates their power relative to the students.

Each of the science classroom examples consists of a group of students provided with limited materials (pencil and paper in the first and graph paper in the second) while the teacher circulates from group to group attempting to scaffold understanding through discussion. However, we do not have information about additional details of the space or materials provided, nor of the sociocultural dynamics of the school. For example: Is the teacher from a different racial or socioeconomic background from the students? Is this a remedial or advanced class? How was the lesson introduced initially? Did the children select their group members or were they chosen by the teacher? These details, among possible others, constitute the "relational habitus" (Stone et al., 2012) surrounding the dialogue that is presented. Providing the full sociocultural, historical activity context of an interaction offers multiple entry points for analysis. Within this larger context might be additional opportunities for collective meaning-making among the participants. These opportunities might be situated within dimensions other than dialogue or signaled by nonverbal means. Instead, the analysis is limited to analyzing how the discourse between teacher and students demonstrated a lack of prolepsis and therefore intersubjectivity. As with meta-communication, the narrow definition of intersubjectivity as prolepsis makes the theorization applicable only to particular types of exchanges and bases analysis entirely on verbal turns.

On the other hand, the play-crafting exchanges are provided with extensive contextual details. Episodes of meaningful shared activity that occur over consecutive days are reported for the purpose of tracking the emergence of intersubjectivity and the dynamics that support and detract from it over time. Beyond this, the respective roles of the teacher and of shared cultural artifacts are the opposite of those in the science lessons. In the play-crafting episodes, the child participants collectively choose every aspect of the activity. The teacher serves as a facilitator to maintain dialogue, offering neutral support and then backing away once they are no longer needed. The cultural artifacts are stories and movies that the participants have a common relationship to and that are personally relevant and meaningful to them. Indeed, every aspect of the play-crafting activity is selected by the children themselves rather than by the teacher. They construct the activity and the intersubjectivity. Therefore, the sociocultural context surrounding them is collectively meaningful. Their interactive styles and cultural references are also shared due to a common developmental period (middle childhood) and cultural background (as evidenced by common cultural references). In addition, the participants are symmetrically positioned regarding power. The teacher maintains this equilibrium by taking the role of an unobtrusive facilitator at the beginning and then recedes into the role of a silent observer.

Had the first science lesson begun from the students' common knowledge base, asked them to investigate their household uses of gas (the concrete representation of gas in a stove, which interfered with their ability to shift to abstract reasoning), and made use of shared cultural artifacts and their common sociocultural context, the teacher could then have adapted their pedagogical perspective and discourse to that of the students, established intersubjectivity, and then gradually connected their knowledge to more abstract ways of thinking. As described by Rommetviet (1979), power must be shared to enable intersubjectivity. When interlocutors are as asymmetrically positioned as students and teachers, it is the more powerful interactant who must take the perspective of the least, thereby reversing the power differential to enable dialogue on an equal basis.

These transcripts of elementary-aged children's attempts to engage in a shared activity and collective problem-solving reveal how power differentials impede dialogue. Only with the use of a concrete referent – graph paper – were the students and teachers able to perceive the others' perspective. Given the differences in power and knowledge, it was impossible to guess the knowledge or understanding of the other through language alone. Once the discordant perspectives were revealed, both teachers and students were able to make some progress toward considering the others' perspectives, but only by using the shared cultural tool of graph paper – already imbued with a common meaning – to represent their thinking. On the other hand, the play-crafting children were able to resolve differing interests and opinions solely through dialogue given the shared sociocultural context, knowledge base, and equal power exchange, as well as a common commitment to the shared goals of the activity. In this case, disagreement did not signal a lapse of intersubjectivity because there was no disjunction in the collective meaning or in the agreed-upon overall purpose of the activity. The criteria for intersubjectivity as meta-communication are too narrowly defined to apply to forms of interaction beyond pretend play. Although the play-crafting activity depicts conversation that could be viewed through the lens of meta-communication (collectively agreeing on symbolic meanings that exist only within the context of the play), it would be difficult to apply the coding of turns in the long narrative according to the meta-communication coding scheme.

Unlike the language-based operationalizations requiring either meta-communication or prolepsis, the SAE and sociocultural conceptualizations can be used to determine the intersubjectivity of a given interaction among any age group in varied contexts. The sociocultural view provides a global, categorical assessment of intersubjectivity as joint participation in any collectively meaningful activity. However, by specifying synchrony and identifying discrete mutual behaviors, the SAE approach allows for an assessment of the extent to which intersubjectivity occurs on a continuum that ranges from brief to sustained or constant.

Analysis according to the SAE view includes the influence of space and materials on intersubjectivity. Returning to preschooler's free play, another episode highlights the impact of the immediate environment. Similar to how the graph paper corresponded to the particular developmental context of elementary-aged children, preschoolers – whose capacity for linguistic expression is still developing – are reliant on concrete referents for much of their communication (Cazden, 2001). In the following episode, the shared meaning of the play activity and the synchrony among the participants are highly influenced by the nature of the materials and space (Garte, 2016, pp. 267–270).

> *Juan who's pretending to be a baby lies on the floor crying like an infant in a highly realistic manner.*
> *Jorge who's pretending to be the caregiver pats the baby, bends towards him, and repeats loudly in Spanish a refrain of: "Calm down," "Go to sleep," "Calm yourself."*
> *Alessandro comes and kneels beside the "baby."*
> *Maxine and Jennifer who have been playing in the kitchen area come and stand over the baby.*
> *Jorge announces repeatedly in Spanish "The baby is cold!"*

Framing Intersubjectivity during Children's Interactions 81

The children appear drawn to this shared activity based on a common script (Nelson, 1998) that relates to a shared cultural context of the importance and ubiquity of caring for babies. This shared cultural context automatically makes the scenario meaningful to the children. This is analogous to how common cultural references imbued the play-crafting episode with shared meanings.

> *Alessandro quickly brings a blanket from the kitchen area and covers the baby. Jorge announces "The baby is hungry!" in English. Alessandro, Maxine, and Jennifer go back and forth from the adjacent kitchen area bringing plastic food and other props for the baby.*

This episode includes many verbal and nonverbal signs of meta-communication according to Goncu's (1993a, 1993b) formulation and typology. However, such an analysis does not include the role of shared cultural scripts and reference points. The sociocultural view does consider how this element facilitates intersubjectivity in the construction of the shared activity. However, only the SAE account can both acknowledge the role of culture in creating a shared meaning of an activity while also assessing the extent to which interpersonal synchrony is present at different points in the interaction.

> *The girls drag chairs from other parts of the room to the rug area then begin "shopping" in the kitchen. Maxine says "We have to get some stuff for the baby," and Jennifer agrees.*

This side activity is tangentially related to the larger group's play theme and is not inclusive of the others. This break in the shared activity leads to a total dissolution of the interaction. Such a break in intersubjectivity would be predicted by the SAE view given the lack of interactional synchrony preceding it. On the other hand, meta-communication would be coded for this exchange regardless of its disconnection from the rest of the group and the ongoing activity.

> *Jorge circles around the baby talking loudly to no one in particular. A brief argument ensues over the chairs between Jorge and the girls which the teacher resolves from a distance. Alessandro continues busily collecting materials from all over the classroom and piling them up beside the baby. After a moment, Jorge approaches the other children to distribute the contents of a doctor's kit to each of them, saying "The baby is sick, the baby is sick" "Give him medicine" "He needs a shot" alternating between Spanish and English.*

Jorge reestablishes intersubjectivity by engaging the group with objects and actions whose meanings are collectively defined in relation to the shared activity. This segment demonstrates intersubjectivity according to all four theories. His use of both English and Spanish to include all of the group members serves to reestablish interactional synchrony.

> *All four children simultaneously use the doctor's tools on the baby who begins crying loudly and squirming around. Jorge repeats his earlier refrain to quiet down. The children begin offering the baby the different foods that have been collected.*

Here, collective activity in relation to the shared meaning of the scenario corresponds to highly synchronous actions with materials and interpersonal coordination. Again, this segment counts as intersubjectivity according to all four theories; however, the operationalizations that focus on specific forms of discourse would be difficult to apply empirically.

Explicit reference to the sociocultural and environmental context is missing from the language-based operationalizations and is not defined in the sociocultural view. However, both contextual elements influenced the nature and extent of intersubjectivity to varying degrees within each example.

The baby and the play-crafting episodes involved multiple participants, whereas the meta-communication examples tended to focus on dyads. Theories that include indicators of intersubjectivity beyond dialogue provide a greater "surface area" of a given interaction. Therefore, the theory can accommodate larger group activities than conversations that hinge solely on contingent utterances between interacting individuals. In the activity-based examples (the preschoolers' free play and play-crafting episodes), behaviors that indicated shared meanings were counted as evidence of intersubjectivity even if they were nonverbal or included disagreements.

The elementary science episodes and each of the naturalistic free play episodes highlighted the roles of both space and materials in sustaining and constraining intersubjectivity during peer interactions. During the free play activities, joint attention, moments of collective meaning-making, and agreed-upon goals and themes for the episodes were inextricably tied to the materials used. The physical space created boundaries around the episodes that brought the children back to one another's imagined worlds. When those boundaries were ignored, this flung them out of each other's realm of influence, thus severing the shared play narrative and the intersubjectivity. In this way, an analysis of intersubjectivity during preschooler play that ignores physical actions on objects and within spatial configurations cannot capture or predict how intersubjectivity develops during interaction. Similarly, older children huddling over a piece of graph paper with their teachers showed how materials are a crucial element in prolepsis-based intersubjectivity, given that intersubjectivity could not have occurred through discourse alone.

Contrasting Approaches to Intersubjectivity

In summary, a definition of intersubjectivity as limited to linguistic exchanges or specific forms of pretend play provides decontextualized examples of each type of interaction divorced from the whole. When these limited definitions of intersubjectivity are applied to naturalistic settings, the evidence suggests that differences between participants regarding power, knowledge, cultural norms, interests, goals, or assumptions make intersubjectivity impossible. Therefore, the examples supporting the sociolinguistic and developmental theories of intersubjectivity suggest that, although they are necessary and ubiquitous for human development, intersubjective interactions are nonetheless rare and effortful phenomena.

The sociocultural view encompasses a wide range of interactive dimensions that support collective meaning-making. This holistic account of interactions over time captures peaks and lapses in intersubjectivity. However, categorizing intersubjectivity as joint participation in any socially meaningful activity does not provide an analytical tool for determining patterns within and between interactions. Therefore, this theory cannot predict when intersubjectivity is most or least likely to occur. Without such an analysis, it is impossible to draw conclusions about which contextual features are most supportive of intersubjectivity and how practitioners can best support it among their students.

Considering the episodes from both the SAE and sociocultural views allow us to consider how children develop common meanings over the course of ordinary interactions. However, only the SAE analysis provides insight into those contextual features that both support and detract from intersubjectivity. Acknowledging that meanings may be constructed via the shared use of materials, affective attunement, synchronized physical behavior, and various other modes of collective intentionality rather than solely within linguistic exchanges means that intersubjectivity can occur among speakers of different languages, with different cultural references or norms, and with different assumptions about how to talk or think about things. Intersubjectivity can occur in a moment when two children who speak different languages fly cars over their heads making noises in synchrony, or when a teacher draws a pictograph to demonstrate a concept that suddenly makes sense to a student because it does not require the language of abstraction. Or intersubjectivity can emerge slowly over time when multiple participants contribute, debate, and engage with differing degrees of agreement regarding a shared third space that represents a collectively meaningful shared activity.

This inclusive conceptualization reveals how specific details of the spatial, material, social, and cultural context enable and sustain intersubjectivity. Within educational settings, observing the ways in which children interact with each other provides insights into the types of activities that, by corresponding to what is developmentally and culturally shared, emerge as sites of collective meaning. The SAE view identifies details of dynamic relationships between multiple factors that support and detract from intersubjectivity over the course of an entire interaction. In doing so, opportunities for empirical research regarding a wide variety of interactive situations are made possible.

In conclusion, this chapter sought to illustrate how theoretical assumptions about the origins of intersubjectivity determine the behavioral focus of empirical research. The methodology thus reflects this focus, highlighting some elements of how intersubjectivity develops between children while ignoring others. Each theory is supported by methods that exclude behaviors that go beyond its definition or framing of intersubjectivity. Applying methodologies to empirical examples selected to reflect a different theoretical concept of intersubjectivity revealed how the analytic frame that is applied to an interaction could distort how intersubjectivity is perceived. An inclusive approach to both theory and method would capture varied modes of shared meaning-making across diverse forms of activity and sociocultural context. The SAE view acknowledges the ubiquity of intersubjectivity in interaction while detailing elements of process during interaction, allowing for an analysis of how and under what circumstances intersubjectivity develops. This approach furthers the goal of making intersubjectivity an empirically supported and generalizable concept. The next step is to define what constitutes ideal intersubjective moments and their corollaries. To accomplish this, the findings from studies of interactions will be helpful.

CHAPTER 5

What Makes for "High-Quality" Interactions at Home and School?

To measure interactions, it is necessary to evaluate the sociocultural contexts in which they occur. Collaborative cognition, based in a Vygotskian approach, defines thought as initially external, embodied within social interaction that becomes internalized later in development (Forman et al., 1993). Vygotsky's (1979a) zone of proximal development describes learning as inherently social, wherein learning can only occur in the context of social support. According to Vygotsky, to fully assess a child's intellectual level, one must consider what they can do or understand with the help of a more expert interactant. The concept of scaffolding was developed to provide a model of how teaching or assistance within the zone of proximal development ideally occurs (Bruner, 1978; Fernandez et al., 2002). According to the scaffolding paradigm (Bruner, 1978), a teacher matches their guidance to the present level of the student while providing whatever support is needed to promote higher levels of mastery and independence. The teacher must continuously adjust the support provided to match increases in student learning. For an effective scaffolding interaction, the teacher must be highly sensitive and responsive to the students' development over time (Fernández et al., 2002; Litowitz, 1993).

Developmental studies have shown that young children are capable of effectively "tutoring" one another (Shenderovich et al., 2016; Verba, 1998). A meta-analysis found that collaborations between dyads – the most frequently studied format for assessing collaborative cognition among ages four to seven – does indeed benefit specific types of learning (Sills et al., 2016). In addition, some studies have shown that peers take turns at the expert and novice positions at different points in their interactions (Pino-Pasternack, 2018).

Interactions in Classrooms

The past two decades of research on classrooms have shown that the dimensions of teacher–child interaction are uniquely significant in predicting student outcomes (NICHD Early Child Care Research Network, 2005; Pianta, 2016). As a result, widely used measures of classroom quality focus on methods for assessing the quality of teacher–child and classroom peer interactions. The first of two major approaches includes a global assessment named the Classroom Assessment Scoring System (CLASS) by Pianta and colleagues (Hamre et al., 2014; Pianta et al., 2008). This observational scoring system measures how teachers support children along the dimensions of emotional support, instructional support, and learning formats. Each dimension includes two to three domains with more precise behavioral indicators such as positive and negative classroom climate, quality of feedback, and behavioral management.

The other approach considers "high-leverage practices" that assess domain-specific teaching competence (Ball & Forzani, 2009; Cabello & Topping, 2018). These measures include a mixture of general teaching practices, such as facilitating discussions, along with subject-specific competencies, such as effective use of modeling in math instruction. Within this category are measures such as the Elementary Instruction Observation Scale (Stipek & Chiatovich, 2017). These assessments consider teachers' content knowledge within a specific subject area as well as pedagogical content knowledge (PCK) – the ability to help students make sense of concepts within the subject area by planning for common misconceptions, tying new information to previous information, and elaborating on students' ideas to enhance their conceptual understanding. The CLASS and PCK measures have each shown correlations with student outcomes in prior studies (Burchinal et al., 2010; Fauth et al., 2019; Vandenbroucke et al., 2018; Watts et al., 2021). However, correlations and the validity of each measure have varied with student academic level (Watts et al., 2021), grade level (Sandilos et al., 2019), and culture (Longobardi et al., 2020).

These assessment measures define classroom interactions by teacher behaviors, providing snapshots of teachers in classrooms, but they do not consider teacher behaviors within a broad sociocultural context. The importance of such a context is illustrated by findings showing the emotional support dimensions of the CLASS as unstable over time, with increases in several domains observed within the same classroom between the fall and spring (Buell et al., 2017). The Measure of Effective Teaching showed a lack of stability of ratings across lessons and raters (Mantzicopoulos et al., 2018). Further highlighting the crucial influence of the broader relational context, studies have found that the classroom composition (student makeup) may have a greater impact on classroom quality than teacher characteristics (Fauth et al., 2021; Stuhlman & Pianta,

2009; Sutton et al., 2021). One study showed that students with the most risk factors (i.e., poverty, having special needs, and being academically at risk) are clustered in classrooms with lower quality scores (Fauth et al., 2021). Another study looked within high-poverty schools and found that students with the highest risk profiles in terms of academic, emotional, and behavioral challenges were in classrooms where teacher quality indicators were lower than those with lower-risk profiles (Sutton et al., 2021).

A study that assessed both dyadic and classroom-level teacher–student relational climates showed their impact on students' concurrent psychological adjustment but with limited longitudinal effects. In addition, the effects of teacher–child relational quality did not extend to students' academic achievement (Buyse et al., 2009). Together, these studies show that by isolating pieces of teacher behavior from the broader sociocultural and relational context a full understanding of how teacher–student interactions shape child development is eclipsed.

In response to the need for a contextualized approach to assessing classroom quality, a measure entitled the Classroom Assessment of Sociocultural Interactions (CASI) has been developed (Jensen et al., 2020, 2021; Reese et al., 2014). The CASI indicators reflect the specific ways in which teachers respond to their students in a given classroom. More specifically, the CASI has been designed to reflect the cultural norms of children from the majority world, as described in detail in Chapter 2. Classrooms are rated on a continuum that assesses the extent to which teaching practices and social organization reflect these norms. For example, the measure of social organization of the classroom has indicators ranging from competitive to communal, with more communal classroom structures being scored as more culturally responsive.

Classrooms where children are explicitly engaged through their personal experiences, home languages, and elements of their families' cultural experiences and norms receive high scores on the CASI. In addition, by assessing to an equal extent teacher behaviors, student behaviors, and classroom climate, the measure comes closer to capturing the interactive, multidimensional effects of student and teacher behavior rather than treating teacher behavior as having unidirectional effects on students. Preliminary use of the CASI as a research tool suggests that it could help explain gaps in the understanding of how teacher responses to children from diverse cultural groups impact those children's classroom functioning (Jensen et al., 2020). This approach challenges the idea that there is a universal set of "high-quality" teacher–student interactions divorced from cultural norms.

Although each of these three approaches acknowledges the primacy of interactive quality in determining classroom quality, none attempts to measure moment-by-moment interactive classroom dynamics. Research on parent–child interactions, however, is based in this microanalytic methodology.

Parent–Child Interactions

The tradition of using observations of parent–child interactions to predict child outcomes has a long history in developmental psychology within the Western world. Attachment theory and research have reliably identified interactive behaviors from birth and up through the various stages of childhood and adolescence that consistently correlate with and predict a host of developmental outcomes (Cassidy et al., 2013). Although both the CLASS and CASI measures contain dimensions of sensitivity and autonomy support, they are scored by assessing teacher behavior without regard for how the children's contributions influence the interaction. Observational methods designed to measure parent–child interactions represent ways to capture the reciprocal and mutually influencing behaviors of both partners. For example, the concept of "mutually responsive orientation" (Kochanska, 2017) has shown that parent–child affective attunement is a unique factor that predicts aspects of children's moral development and empathy for peers. Parent–child synchrony as described in earlier chapters is in line with these approaches. By measuring both the type and contingency of parental responsiveness, researchers have found associations of highly synchronous parent–child relationships with positive child outcomes (Lindsey et al., 2009).

Parents' coregulation of their children's affective and cognitive states is also linked to children's self-regulation and school adjustment (Feldman et al., 2013). Mutual responsivity, synchrony, and coregulation are all aspects of contingent responsiveness between the parent and child that are powerful drivers of development. However, whether the effects are positive or negative depends on the affective and developmental context of the interaction, as well as the cultural context of the parent–child relationship (Birk et al., 2022). A study wherein affective content (negative, positive, and neutral) and flexibility were assessed separately from the degree of contingent responsiveness found that high affective contingency within the context of negative emotion and highly flexible affect had the greatest effect on child outcomes, which included lower self-regulation and affective lability (Lobo & Lunkenheimer, 2020).

Longitudinal research supports the idea that the way in which parental sensitivity impacts children is dynamic and varies within different relational and developmental contexts. Parenting that includes positive social and emotional support has an equally powerful impact on children's cognitive and language development as it does on social and emotional development (Roger Mills-Koonce et al., 2015). The research reviewed here suggests that highly responsive and attuned parent–child interactive dynamics may be either positive or negative depending the type of emotion and relationship.

Another consideration is the sensitivity of measurements. One study showed a discrepancy between global measures and microanalysis of parent–child coregulation (PCR; Bardack et al., 2017). Only the lower-inference microanalysis measure of PCR showed a relationship with children's problem behavior, and neither type of measure predicted social skills with peers and prosocial behavior. The authors discussed how different activity contexts, such as types of tasks requiring different forms of skills, might influence transfer between PCR and child behavior in school. In addition, teacher report of individual children's social skills with peers was not correlated with other measures – in this case, PCR.

Teacher–child and parent–child interactions both involve asymmetrical relationships, with the child in a vulnerable position relative to the adult. However, the literatures on these topics have not developed methods wherein the child's contributions to such interactions are counted as equal to those of the adult. The parent–child literature has shown that contingent responsiveness can be characterized by negative emotionality. This likely occurs during teacher–child interactions as well. However, the microanalytic methods used to measure parent–child interactive dynamics have never been applied to teacher–child interactions. Similarly, the impacts of the broader social context on classroom climate and teacher–child interactions are likely analogous in parent–child interactions. Yet these elements have not been included in studies of parent–child interaction. For example, household chaos – assessed via parent report – has been shown to have extremely robust impacts on child functioning (Marsh et al., 2020). Yet this measure has never been entered into models assessing parent–child interactive dynamics.

One factor that has been applied in both parent–child and classroom interactions is the degree of awareness of interaction and psychological processes. Parents who direct their children's attention to their internal states have children with greater recall of events, more developed theory of mind, and other foundational aspects of metacognition (Fernyhough et al., 2002; Lemche et al., 2007). The same has been found among teachers who reference internal states (Kienbaum et al., 2001; Lucariello et al., 2004). In addition, group metacognition and attention to collaborative processes have benefited peer-group collaborations in school among multiple age groups (Bertucci et al., 2012; Smith & Mancy, 2018)

The broader sociocultural contexts of socioeconomic status (SES) and culture have rarely been considered in parent–child interaction research. Most research on parent–child interactive dynamics has been done with middle-class samples. One study included both high- and low-SES samples and defined the lower-SES group as "at risk." None of the expected relationships between parents interaction styles and child compliance with adult authority were found among the low-SES sample (Lincoln et al., 2017). Instead, factors related to negative outcomes in middle-class samples, such as parents granting less autonomy to children, positively predicted compliance with authority for low-SES children. One important conclusion from this research is that parental responsiveness does not occur in a sociocultural vacuum. Without considering cultural differences (e.g., in the meanings of autonomy support) or whether parent–child relations are connected to a broader societal context, the link to child outcomes is unclear. Given known cultural differences in parent–child relationships, child-rearing values, and parent–child interaction styles (Bernstein et al., 2005; Clegg et al., 2021; Lieber et al., 2006; Mejía-Arauz et al., 2018; Mizuta et al., 1996; Rogoff et al., 2003; Siekiera & Białek, 2021), it is likely that there would be cultural variance in what constitutes optimal parent–child interactions.

Peer Interactions

Moving from asymmetrical partnerships to peer interactions, the role of the central tools and tasks of a shared activity is brought into focus by Yuill's (2021) CoEnact framework. Based on studies of technologically mediated collaborations among young children, the framework defines the crucial components for effective peer collaboration as collaborative engagement, attention, contingency, and control. Each of these elements reflects the importance of mutuality during collaboration. For example, "collaborative engagement" refers to mutual cognitive and emotional interest in a shared phenomenon between interactants. "Attention" is directed toward the actions and inferred intentions of the interacting group members. "Contingency" refers to the extent to which each group member's actions are related in real time to those of the others, leading to shared intentionality. Finally, "control" refers to the equitable sharing of control over objects, goals, and activities.

The CoEnact framework puts the shared activity at the center of peer interaction, with the expectation that the interactive dynamics are organized mainly by the affordances and demands of the materials and tools required for the activity. This is a different conception from dialogic or "negotiation"-type interactions that may be entirely based on verbal discussion (Mejía-Arauz et al., 2018). The traditional developmental conceptualization of how interactions based on negotiation occur considers them to be outgrowths of individual capacities such as theory of mind and perspective-taking ability (Siekiera & Białek, 2021). However, research on human–computer interaction, on which the CoEnact framework is based, shows that group competence in collaboration is based on the nature of the shared activity and the design of the tools that are central to it.

Peer Collaboration in the Majority World

This description of ideal peer collaborations is in line with accounts from the majority world that have shown children, especially Indigenous and Mayan-heritage children, to have sophisticated collaborative abilities (Rogoff et al., 2018). Rogoff and colleagues describe "learning by observing and pitching in" (LOPI) as the main way in which children learn from family and community members, as well as being how they transfer this method to learning from peers and teachers in classrooms (e.g., Coppens et al., 2014; Mejía-Arauz et al., 2018; Rogoff, 2016). In addition to the specific content and skills required to master the activity, LOPI requires sensitive adaptation by child novices to more expert participants, ensuring that their involvement neither disrupts nor takes over the work. In this case, learners are enculturated into learning socially valued skills via participation in authentic community activities.

This contrasts with the Western norm wherein adults provide activities specifically tailored to children for the sole purpose of instruction without serving any authentic social need of the community (Clegg et al., 2021). The skill of mutual adaptation, which is a prerequisite for learning by participating in ongoing cultural activities, requires the elements of the

CoEnact framework, whereby the learner or novice must pay attention and adjust themselves to both the demands of the activity and the actions, goals, and needs of the expert – whether adult or peer – with whom they are interacting. On this account, collaborative competence is not an individual set of skills but rather is embedded and emergent within the activity and the interaction as it develops.

As discussed in Chapter 2, culturally based ways of learning observed among some African and Asian children share similarities with those that have been widely documented among South, Central, and Latin American and Indigenous populations (Hurley et al., 2005; Li & Yamamoto, 2020). For example, Serpell et al. (2011) report on how collaborative group learning tied to a socially meaningful task such as measuring and maintaining the health of the infants and toddlers of the community led to increased academic engagement and improved egalitarianism in rural Zambia. Sternberg (2014) reviews research on adaptive intelligence in non-Western contexts, showing that children who did not attend formal schooling demonstrated skills in math, science, and geography when applied to problem-solving regarding a community issue, such as where to place a well, and were able to learn more sophisticated concepts when presented in the context of culturally meaningful activities. These authentic, apprentice-based learning processes are similar in structure to the pedagogy of "project-based learning." However, unlike Western samples, when children are given socially important problems to solve they do not rely on adult assistance to structure their collaborations in order to ensure equal work distribution and a productive interaction (Garcia-Carrion et al., 2020; Rogoff et al., 2018). Rather, children distribute tasks and leadership according to skill levels among the group members, which all agree upon. Because siblings play a key role in early childhood development in most African countries, there is little debate among the children over the control of different aspects of a shared problem-solving task (Nsamenang, 2008; Serpell et al., 2011). As described in Chapter 2, adults assess and recognize the different strengths, skills, and innate abilities in each child, and this becomes community knowledge. Rather than ranking children's intelligence, children are described in terms of the kinds of intelligence that they demonstrate for the purpose of being useful to meeting shared community needs (e.g., Ogunnaike & Houser, 2002). This distributed view of intelligence posits that individual traits are defined in relation to collective goals (i.e., everyone is useful in some way), so concepts of intellectual superiority or inferiority are not culturally salient.

Early Elementary Peer Collaboration

Most studies of collaborative learning involve children above third grade. Of the few studies of collaborative learning in first to third grade, the structure of the learning situations diverges extensively from the CoEnact framework (Yuill, 2021). Peer interactions are more associative than collaborative and tend to be highly structured and managed by teachers in advance of child engagement as well as during the interaction. Unlike research with older children (fifth or sixth grade and up) or preschoolers, early elementary-aged children are often significantly prompted and trained in specific ways of using language as a prerequisite for engaging in collaborative learning activities (Artut, 2009; Souvignier & Kronenberger, 2007). The expected outcomes from these scenarios are also predetermined to allow for comparison of the efficacy of collaborative formats with control groups that use individualistic learning (Young et al., 2019). Therefore, there is little room for emergent or enactive forms of collaboration. When such studies investigated whether there were differences in academic achievement due to children participating in either teacher- or child-directed formats, none were found (Souvignier & Kronenberger, 2007; Tarchi & Pinto, 2016).

Among preschoolers, older children, and adolescents, high degrees of language development and collaborative cognition were found when the outcome was open-ended or process-oriented and the teacher took a background, observer role (Gillies, 2014; Hamre et al., 2014; Howe & Abedin, 2013; Sills et al., 2016; Zillmer & Kuhn, 2018). Student-directed collaborative learning activities that were centered on discipline-specific content showed increased conceptual understanding and more consideration of multiple perspectives on the content (Garcia-Carrion et al., 2020; Kazak et al., 2015). It is likely that the lack of empirical findings regarding the impact of format (child- versus adult-directed) among early elementary-aged children is due to differences in the design and measurement of collaborative activities rather than a unique age-based difference in the importance of student-led collaborations for learning.

One area where early elementary-aged children learn through child-directed collaborations is the method of play-based pedagogy. Play-based pedagogy is generally a transition between preschoolers' free play and the highly structured learning experiences of elementary school. Therefore, research investigating the efficacy of play-based pedagogy for learning and development usually focuses on children in the age gap between early childhood education and later elementary schooling – most often using samples from kindergarten and first grade, occasionally including preschool.

Play-Based Learning and Pedagogy

Research on preschooler's play has not investigated how children learn specific academic concepts and skills through play-based activities and interactions with peers. Play-based pedagogy or playful learning has been considered a way to guide young children toward greater academic learning within a playful context. This literature spans from preschool up through third grade. The role of the teacher in guided play or play-based learning has been investigated, and this research supports child-directed play with teacher scaffolding and involvement (Paterson, 2020; Portier et al., 2019). In some instances, allowing a greater role for teacher guidance while children engaged in a teacher-structured playful activity was shown to be the most effective method for specific learning such as vocabulary development among certain populations of children (Weisberg et al., 2013). A continuum of play-based learning has been identified in the literature by Pyle and Bigelow (2015). This shows that kindergarten and first- and second-grade classrooms tend to endorse specific philosophies of the role of play in learning, which in turn lead to different ways of using play in the classroom. Hands-on activities that are nonetheless teacher-directed have been criticized as not meeting the definition of play as child-directed and child-chosen (Bodrova & Leong, 2015). However, attempting to teach academic concepts at school via child-directed and child-chosen free play would require teachers to embed content knowledge and skills within children's variegated interests while somehow connecting their ongoing play to learning outcomes. This is an unrealistic method of teaching for most early elementary school classrooms and teachers (Paterson, 2020). Between these two extremes is the goal of harnessing those elements of free play and scaffolded instruction that can be combined to produce highly engaging, collaborative, and personally meaningful experiences through which to support learning of new concepts and skills. However, to do this, the most development-supporting elements of both free and guided playful activities must be identified.

Missing from the play-based pedagogy literature is the in-depth analysis of interactions that characterizes the parent–child and dialogic education literatures. This analysis details specific forms of communication that are most conducive to peer collaboration. Without this information, it is difficult to gauge which formats of activities, teacher roles, materials, and/or content most impact how much can be learned from play-based activities or from teacher-guided or scaffolded play.

The diverse literatures summarized here each have implications for which kinds of interactions impact children's learning and development in varied contexts. From the CLASS, we know that interactions matter more than structural elements. However, global measures that fail to consider cultural differences are inadequate. The CASI provides a step toward assessing the extent to which classroom interactions and organization are culturally relevant and meaningful while considering both student and teacher roles. However, these global indicators do not account for the details of interactive processes. To determine how teacher–child interactions impact children's cognitive, social, and emotional development, research delineating how parent–child interactive qualities coregulate children and support positive development is instructive. Reciprocal, sensitive, attuned, and contingent parent–child dynamics have all been shown to directly influence child self-regulation and both their emotional and cognitive development. However, in classrooms, collaborative forms of learning often involve peer groups; therefore, the research on collaborative cognition and the forms of peer interaction that are most conducive to learning must be identified and then facilitated. To determine which are the most efficacious forms of peer interaction, the literatures describing dialogic education, computer-supported peer collaborations, and cultures where highly sophisticated collaborations among children are common are all instructive.

Taken together, the research presented here suggests that there is a crucial role played by peer collaboration in learning. Conceptual depth, problem-solving, and creativity have been shown to particularly benefit from collaborative forms of learning among school-aged children. The following principles can be extracted from the literature to suggest ways to structure learning activities in early elementary classrooms.

Collaborative learning activities should:
(Gillies, 2014; Legare et al., 2017; Mercier et al., 2017; Nieminen et al., 2022; Pino-Pasternack, 2018; Sills et al., 2016; Yuil, 2021).

- be related to the authentic interests, meanings, and goals of the children;
- accommodate multiple methods of engagement wherein children can participate in different ways and at different levels and time points during ongoing activities;
- focus on conceptual depth, application of ideas, problem-solving, and creative solutions or applications and should be open to multiple end points and formats (equifinality) of learning outcomes.

Teachers should:
(Bertucci et al., 2012; Buyse et al., 2009; Häkkinen et al., 2017; Howe & Abedin, 2013; Hurley et al., 2005; Jensen et al., 2021; Kazack et al., 2015; Kerawala et al., 2013; Li & Yamamoto, 2020; Reese et al., 2014; Smith & Mancy, 2018; Vanderbrooke et al., 2018; Wegerif, 2011; Yuil, 2021).

- facilitate the structure of conversation toward dialogism by restating ideas, modeling questioning, wondering aloud, and directing children to one another's contributions;
- establish sensitive and contingent ways of responding to children nonverbally as well as verbally;
- attempt to use children's own preferred language forms as well as culturally valued forms of relating (physical touch, observation, translanguaging);
- direct children to the internal states of peers, including affective and physiological states such as body orientation, engagement, and emotional states;
- scaffold collaboration and dialogue, becoming another participant or observer, jumping in only to clarify or make subtle adjustments in the case of discord once peer-to-peer engagement occurs fluidly;
- design materials to support peer coordination, shared control, and contingency of responses and actions among group members;
- encourage exploratory and dialogic forms of talk among children.

CHAPTER 6

Collaborative Competence
A New Model of Development

This chapter details the construct of collaborative competence to serve as both a theory and a method for understanding children's social development as a collective developmental achievement, analyzed at the group level. Prior research on collaboration is instructive for suggesting how to define ideal collaborations and the most appropriate methods for capturing them.

Distributed Cognition

The "cultural-cognitive ecosystem" was theorized by Hutchins (2014) to explain how human culture creates activity systems in which cognition is distributed between multiple individuals acting at various points of the system. The public meanings of the practices that maintain these systems and what they produce are determined at the cultural level. Hutchins argues that culture provides predictable systems that enable group-level cognition, but that the nature of specific activity systems determines the type of distributed cognition and collective knowledge required to maintain the system. To illustrate this abstract conceptualization, Hutchins uses the example of navigation at sea (1995). He refers to the collaborative processes required to guide a ship as an example of how ship navigation represents an activity system that requires highly distributed and collaborative forms of reasoning and problem-solving drawing on collective knowledge. To demonstrate the ways in which culture intersects with collaboration in each system, he compares methods of collective navigation between two distinct cultures of sailors. This analysis shows that cultures impose their own collective forms of distributed cognition that are neither reducible to individuals nor generalizable to universal forms of reasoning. On Hutchins' account, cultures create their own activity systems that give rise to unique forms of distributed cognition, and much of human functioning relies on this. His analysis bridges the fields of anthropology and cognitive science, providing computational models of cognition along with cultural analysis.

Technological Support for Collaborations

Hutchins' theory is relevant to understanding how problem-solving can be distributed and the ways in which diverse cultures structure activities among children of different ages. The details of the interactive dynamics and patterns of behavior that he observed as elements of distributed cognition during concrete activities have since been made more visible with technology. Computing technology allows both joint and contingent interindividual processes to be made apparent in real time as well as documented for later analysis. Technologically mediated shared surfaces such as multitouch tablets and augmented play equipment can provide an extra set of cues that aid participants during distributed tasks. This technology explicitly directs interacting children to one another's actions and intentions, incentivizes contingent actions, and supports equitable control of equipment by design (e.g., Mercier et al., 2017).

This type of support for distributed cognition and collaboration has been found to be especially useful with children on the autism spectrum who may not be innately attuned to subtle social cues, and it has even allowed parallel play types of interaction that are nonetheless collaborative among these populations (Yuill, 2021). Such technology also supports collaboration among larger groups of typically developing children, including young children. In one study, technology enabled a play interaction to develop into collaborative emergent literacy (Wohlwend, 2015). Other research reviewed by Yuill (2021) demonstrates how such technology supports collaborations that would otherwise be exceptionally challenging, such as in the case of a shared design task.

Augmented technology makes interacting partners' intentions more visible through highlighting the actions of participants to the other group members and creating a shared focus that might not emerge on its own. Talk Factory software both documents how dialogue functions in real time and provides a concrete referent to scaffold collaboration and productive dialogue by directing participants' attention to one another's contributions (Kerawalla, 2015; Kerawalla et al., 2013). By making conversational responses visible to all participants, Talk Factory software enables significantly enhanced degrees of exploratory talk (Kerawalla et al., 2013).

Studies of the technological mediation of collaboration among adults (e.g., multiplayer gaming or shared work on a network) show that, like traditional collaborations, each member's engagement in the collective activity is contingent on one another's (Avnet, 2016). In these types of collaboration, nonverbal actions are the only type of representation of individual contributions, and yet they are sufficient for robust collaboration and mutual adaptation.

Dialogic Support for Collaborations

The low-tech version of support for effective collaborations includes dialogic training. Dialogic-based collaborations are most productive and generative when children attend to a conversational structure. These structures often relate to specific concepts and/or problem-solving within a given subject area (Garcia-Carrion et al., 2020; Kazak et al., 2015). An ideal form of dialogue occurs when reciprocal questioning among interacting participants leads to more complex, creative, and higher-order thinking. The dialogic education approach advocates for designing learning situations that support this dialogic ideal. Wegerif (2011) adapts Bakhtin's (1981) notion of dialogue as multivocality, wherein a new space is created between speakers engaged in dialogue that cannot be reduced to any individual utterance. This dialogic space exists entirely in relation to the collective product of contingent utterances between speakers. By focusing on ways to make talk most likely to generate productive outcomes, dialogic education has developed specific types of communication that interactants should learn prior to engaging in a learning interaction (Howe & Abedin, 2013; Wegerif, 2011). These include "ground rules" for talk, which have been shown to lead to greater learning outcomes via dialogue (Wegerif, 2019). The goal of these rules is to allow for evidence-based collective reasoning, in which each interacting participant is expected to fully explain their thinking as well as to challenge and add on to the thinking of others. This form of talk, termed "exploratory," leads to collective awareness of new ideas and ways of thinking that are creative and critical (Kazak et al., 2015). Additionally, participants must demonstrate an "intersubjective orientation" (Wegerif, 2011). This orientation is defined as openness to the perspective of the other – the dialogic partner(s) – and a willingness to strive to comingle perspectives through dialogue. Exploratory talk during small-group activities has supported greater conceptual understanding in math and science as well as creative problem-solving, literacy development, and more sophisticated text analysis (Gillies, 2014; Kazak et al., 2015; Pino-Pasternak et al., 2018; Rojas-Drummond et al., 2014; Tarchi & Pinto, 2016).

Collaborative Meta-Cognition and Group Solidarity

Among older children and adolescents, directing the interacting group to analyze its own collaborative and shared cognitive processes has been shown to increase group-level conceptual understanding (Bertucci et al., 2012; Kumpulainen & Kaartinen, 2003; Smith & Mancy, 2018). Whether high- or low-tech, collaborative meta-cognition or group-level awareness of collaborative reasoning processes seems key to high-quality collaboration. One study found that groups who engaged in process analysis of collaborative activities had higher degrees of meta-analytic strategies tied to higher academic achievement than groups that did not analyze their processes in a follow-up activity (Bertucci et al., 2012).

The field of "team cognition" refers to adults working toward a shared goal. The structure of these collaborations reflects an infinitely complex set of contingency loops driven by reciprocal exchanges (Kozlowski & Bell, 2003). The importance of group members' awareness of and adaptation to one another's contributions as well as group-level awareness and evaluation of collaborative processes has been well documented in research on team cognition (e.g., Avnet, 2016; Chou et al., 2012; Gevers et al., 2020).

Collaborative cognition among children and adults has also highlighted the importance of relational messages and their construal during collaboration (Graesser et al., 2018; Löfstrand & Zakrisson, 2014; Schindler & Bakker, 2020; Stengelin et al., 2020). Solidarity among collaborating group members may be indicated through their expression of positive emotions (Löfstrand & Zakrisson, 2014), although this has been shown to vary cross-culturally (Stengelin et al., 2020). A higher frequency of reciprocal exchanges and positive relational messages and greater social proximity of team members have all predicted more effective adult collaboration (Chou et al., 2012; Keyton & Beck, 2009). Such social/emotional dynamics enhance group members' feelings of solidarity with one another (Keyton & Beck, 2009; Peräkylä, 2004; Schindler & Bakker, 2020), a key component of effective working groups (Chou et al., 2012). The importance of solidarity and emergent dynamics among the group is highlighted by findings showing that external group rewards for project completion lack impact as compared to the conditions of the interaction itself (Morgan, 2004; Pino-Pasternak, 2018; Stengelin et al., 2020), and that the outcome of group work cannot be predicted from individual team members' abilities alone (Chou et al., 2012). Consistent with these findings, across age groups collaborations that promote interdependence, wherein each participant is only able to reach the goal if all group members also reach it, are more effective than those of groups without positive interdependence (Johnson et al., 2014; Sills et al., 2016). Differences in collaborations between developmental periods reflect the support needed to enable reciprocal, contingent, and adaptive responses among group members.

Contexts for Collaboration throughout Development

Play in Early Childhood

Among young children, free play is an ideal context for analyzing collaborative processes. During children's free play, the goal, structure, and outcome are entirely co-constructed out of dynamic collaborative interactions. The only rule of peer play is that everyone must agree on the meanings at the center of the play (Goncu, 1993). Like the infinite feedback loops of team cognition, children's play episodes are collectively created in the moment and impossible to predict based on the characteristics of individual players. Young children's play can occur through a variety of media, as it can be primarily physical, affective, task-oriented, creative, and/or discursive. Much of the play of young children is entirely nonverbal. Most play makes use of materials as props, tools, or concrete referents. Play interactions can be long and complex or short and simple. Sustained play activities can involve dyads as well as much larger groups. They can be situated in a particular area or roam through an extensive space. The meanings of the play itself and its tools and goals are never predetermined. Activities with predetermined meanings cease to be play.

Rakoczy (2006) argues that young children's pretend play represents the earliest form of collective intentionality. Rather than describing pretense as based in several individual cognitive capacities, such as the ability to perceive others' intentions, Rakoczy analyzes research showing that by two years of age children engage in pretense with objects in response to others' pretense with objects. However, these actions are not solely imitative, as their experimental results show that the young child matches their intention to that of the adult pretender. Rakoczy acknowledges that this cannot be explained by a two-year-old's sophisticated cognitive understanding of others' minds but rather requires a view of collective intention as "primitive." In other words, collective intentionality – acting in accordance with the perspectives and goals of another person – is a primary human capacity that is present prior to the development of conceptual understandings of others' internal states.

Pretending provides an opportunity during early development to enact an understanding of the intentions of others behaviorally. Therefore, simply perceiving the intention behind another's behavior by observing them engaging in pretense is adequate to trigger young children's ability to enact joint intentionality. Tracing this capacity for cooperation back to two years of age demonstrates that pretend play provides a unique context not only for the basis of human cooperative behavior but also for the development of the collectively shared meanings – including status functions (see Searle, 2009) – that comprise human culture. More broadly, this analysis suggests that the ubiquity of pretense among young children is evidence of a primarily social, innately cooperative orientation that predates individualistic concepts of other minds in ontogeny.

The free play of preschoolers shows developmental continuity with children's capacity for collaboration and collective meaning-making at an age when sophisticated linguistic capacities first become available in development. At this stage, peer play develops apart from the adult world, as children collectively create and transform the meanings of a culture that is still largely foreign to them (Perinat & Sadurni, 1999).

Collaborative Learning in Middle Childhood
Among middle-childhood peer collaborators, open-ended negotiating and coordination of ideas are crucial for effective collaboration (Häkkinen et al., 2017; Hennesy et al., 2016; Ogden, 2000). Rote learning does not benefit from collaborative forms of cognition and may even be negatively impacted, whereas all other types of learning – ranging from brainstorming, creativity, problem-solving, and conceptual comprehension – do benefit (Bearison & Dorval, 2002; Brennan & Enns, 2015; Johnson & Johnson, 2002; Legare et al., 2017; Pai et al., 2015; Pino-Pasternak, 2018; Sills et al., 2016; Zillmer & Kuhn, 2018). Conceptual learning in science often requires rejecting individual "made-up theories" of scientific phenomena in favor of those that can be perceived by the group as being based on evidence (Kaartinen & Kumpulainen, 2002). Research into cooperative learning across domains such as math, science, and literacy learning (Gillies, 2014; Ucan & Webb, 2015) has shown that structured collaborative learning tailored to the subject is most effective (Hurley et al., 2005; Shenderovich et al., 2016). However, both structured and unstructured groups have greater transfer of conceptual understanding during group rather than individual learning (Pai et al., 2015). The same has been found among groups that are asymmetrical (in which child group members are at different levels) or symmetrical (in which the peer participants are cognitively equal at baseline; Zillmer & Kuhn, 2018). In addition, elements of the task such as multiple entry points, affordances, and an open-ended structure have been related to the most cohesive and productive collaborations (Fawcett & Garton, 2005; Forman et al., 1993; Gamberini & Spanolli, 2004; Legare et al., 2017; Nieminen et al., 2022).

Adolescent Collaborative Problem-Solving

Collaborative problem-solving (CPS) has been named a twenty-first-century skill by various international educational assessment bodies (Graesser et al., 2018; Scoular et al., 2017). Methods of evaluation and analysis that focus on determining ideal processes for supporting CPS have been considered via meta-analyses and theoretical summaries (Cukurova et al., 2018; Graesser et al., 2018; Scoular et al., 2017). Empirical analysis of CPS processes in classrooms has been conducted most prolifically within science, technology, engineering, and mathematics (STEM) content areas. For example, research on aspects of CPS within math education has focused on shared student agency (Nieminen et al., 2022), dynamic affective fields (Schindler & Bakker, 2020), collaborative meta-cognition (Smith & Mancy, 2018), and sociomathematical norms (Tatsis & Koleza, 2008). Each of these concepts was shown to impact collaborative mathematical problem-solving processes in classrooms over time. In addition, open-ended outcomes, collaborative processes that are not managed or directed by any one person, and positive interdependence have been identified as crucial for effective CPS and conceptual learning (Graesser et al., 2018; Johnson et al., 2014). More specifically, CPS interactions must be structured and assessed in a way that acknowledges and promotes the emergent nature of collective cognitive competencies rather than fixed outcomes (Ricca et al., 2020).

A critique of attempts to extrapolate generalizable guidelines for enabling ideal collaborations cited the lack of contextual information provided, especially relating to the ages of participants and the content of their problem-solving tasks (Cukurova et al., 2018). The lack of developmental considerations was noted in a critique of the CPS literature (Gauvain, 2018), specifically regarding individual developmental capacities for cognition and the sociocognitive skills thought to support collaboration. Gauvain's (2018) concern was tied to the use of assessments designed for group processes rather than individual functioning. The possibility that development could be adequately addressed through group-level analysis is a major goal of the present account of collaborative competence.

Adult Team Cognition

Agreement on the nature and priorities of the group task as well as a shared understanding of the time required to complete them have been shown to predict group effectiveness among adult collaborators (Gevers et al., 2020). Group-level meta-cognition and progress monitoring of the group increases with the age of group members. These capacities enable more cognitively sophisticated CPS among adolescents and adults.

When comparing the youngest play interactions of the preschool age to those of adult project teams, the following commonalities can be observed: (1) Contingency of responses is necessary and may occur in both verbal and nonverbal forms; (2) technological mediation can support interactions by facilitating shared attention among group members and promoting awareness of and mutual adaptations to member contributions; and (3) solidarity among the group is both crucial for effective functioning and results from positive affective messages, social/emotional construal, and interdependence.

The Developmental Considerations of Collaborative Competence

A developmentally valid approach to studying collaborations among young children would not involve a priori goals for the interaction – imposed by either teachers or researchers. Although prior research has demonstrated the importance of shared goals, agency, and perspective-taking as associated components or subskills of effective collaborations, the present formulation views intersubjectivity – defined along multiple dimensions – via nonverbal mutual behavior as the primary component of collaborative competence. Although sensitive to the developmental traits of the interacting group members, the operationalizations of intersubjectivity and collaborative complexity can be applied to any collaborative interaction.

Collaborative competence is therefore defined as a process by which two or more people engage in an interaction that is characterized by optimal degrees of mutual engagement, allowing for the interaction to spur positive development among the group. In this model, intersubjectivity is conceptualized as the semiconscious microbehaviors that reflect the degree of synchrony experienced among the interacting partners as well as the extent to which the meaning of the shared activity in which they are engaged is jointly understood.

Whereas an interaction can be fleeting and meaningless, a collaboration implies a structured, goal-oriented form of mutual engagement and participation. A high degree of intersubjectivity as defined by the SAE account enables an interaction to become a collaboration. In this way, high intersubjectivity is a prerequisite for a competent collaboration. The second component of the present theory of collaborative competence is collaborative complexity. To determine whether a given interaction reflects collaborative competence, there must be criteria for which mutual behaviors distinguish a mere interaction from a collaboration. The concept of collaborative complexity is operationalized as both categorical (reflecting the type social complexity) and continuous (reflecting the extent to which it is observed over the course of the episode). Highly complex collaborations occur when interacting partners are mutually engaged with one another in extensive contingent and reciprocal exchanges that include behaviors within both the cognitive and socioemotional domains. These contributions may be conversational, but they can also occur in the form of nonverbal coordinated actions on a shared material or within a joint task.

Complex collaborations are characterized by interacting partners iteratively elaborating on one another's contributions to a shared endeavor. This is why complex collaborations often produce jointly created outcomes. During such a collaboration, group members work within an emergent goal-directed framework in which actions are tied to group goals, which in turn shift and emerge collectively in response to shared contributions toward the goal. This is analogous to the activity theory notion of how individual everyday actions transform into socially meaningful activities when they reflect goals that are shared by members of a society. On this formulation, to meet the criteria for collaboration, the interaction must be grounded in shared meaningful activity, not simply related actions. This definition is consistent with long-standing accounts of young children's developmental progression. The progression describes two- to three-year-olds engaging in functional social behavior, during which they play beside each other using toys repetitively, or associative play, which involves children engaging in similar actions without a shared purpose. By the middle of early childhood, play shifts toward more socially and cognitively complex forms (Howes & Matheson, 1992; Rubin, 2001).

Thus, intersubjectivity and collaborative complexity combined enable increasingly coordinated, collectively meaningful and socially, emotionally, and cognitively complex group activities. As each of these components is heightened among the group, the shared engagement and collective meaning of the activity is also increased. Therefore, collaborative competence develops over time as degrees of intersubjectivity, collaborative complexity, and mutuality of engagement and common meaning peak and wane at different points during the interaction. Accordingly, each component is mutually constitutive, contingent, and emergent.

A few illustrative examples demonstrate how interactions function in line with this conceptualization throughout the lifespan. Among very young children, functional play (i.e., banging an object repeatedly) can become a game when a second or third child joins in with an object of their own. As they bang together, they laugh, exchange eye contact, and begin to synchronize and coordinate their banging to create a pattern, growing increasingly excited and engaged.

Among adults (or older adolescents) engaged in a project meeting, brainstorms often begin awkwardly, with averted gazes and statements by individuals that are not taken up by the group and that seem to dissolve as soon as they are spoken. The longer this "awkward" period persists, the more signs of individual withdrawal and distraction characterize the behaviors of group members (checking phones or emails, excusing themselves for brief periods). However, at some point, at least two people become excited about the same idea – eye contact and proximity increase, and reciprocal exchanges of ideas that build and extend upon one another in rapid succession occur. A third and fourth member joins in, and soon the group is enthralled in some collective meaning-making. This "rapid-fire" intersubjectivity ideally leads to goal-directed actions, and periods of heightened coordination continue to characterize the team. In between these two bookends of development lies childhood.

During the preschool period, an extension of the toddler's nonverbal banging game may include adding language, role-play, and even a mutual focus on an outcome, as in the case of group construction with blocks or other materials. Middle childhood adds a greater element of structure, as the team collectively creates group rules and roles for each member. Older childhood work groups might define collective goals with added precision and might pause to take stock of shared progress and reevaluate. Conflict becomes a necessary and potentially helpful element as factions or individuals argue for a particular direction. Adolescent work groups resemble adult project teams in that there is a greater developmental capacity for progress monitoring and group-level self-regulation. Although these developmental shifts affect the overall functioning of a collaboration, the underlying prerequisites change little between toddlerhood and adulthood. In other words, the level of social/emotional and cognitive attention intersubjectivity within the group – in relation to levels of synchrony and shared meaning – bounds the extent to which a group collaborates, regardless of the age of group members.

Intersubjectivity combined with collaborative complexity comprise the full construct of collaborative competence. Complexity is defined by the form that the collaboration most often takes over the entire course of the interaction. Intersubjectivity provides the underlying relational glue of an effective collaboration, whereas complexity defines the overall structure of the collaboration. Three degrees of social complexity – imitative, reciprocal, and cooperative – have been delineated as steps in a developmental sequence (Howes & Matheson, 1992). However, the present concept of collaborative competence builds on research that shows that all three of these components are present during most interactions (Robinson et al., 2003). Although imitation was originally defined as characterizing the collaborations of toddlers, this form of collaboration occurs at all developmental stages. Imitation is extremely common during all developmental periods and ages – for example, during early childhood free play, middle childhood group work on an assigned task at school, older childhood teams, or when an individual or pair of any age gets a group of others to participate in a common task by following their ideas. Groups in which one member dominates and the others simply agree or add on very slightly to that member's ideas are common during childhood, adolescent, and adult collaborations. Imitative collaborations include those in which two members lead and the others follow or in which members switch roles from leader to follower and back over the course of the collaboration. However, to meet the criteria for an imitative collaboration, the interaction cannot develop beyond the leader–follower form for any extensive period. Regardless of who plays what role when group members follow the lead of another rather than making unique contributions, the structure of the collaboration is considered imitative.

The next level of complexity beyond the imitative is the reciprocal. This form of collaboration is based on turn-taking. Members take turns exchanging contributions. The contributions relate to each other but do not build into something new. A conversation between two or more people may proceed in this fashion, wherein each conversant shares a related observation or opinion but no new ideas emerge from the talk. Some examples of this common collaborative form include: children taking turns adding to a structure or a mural, with each contribution accounting for that of the previous ones; a sports game in which team members take turns passing the ball but no new plays emerge; or a project meeting in which people take turns fleshing out the same idea with different applications or reciprocally add to computer code that elaborates on the same process but does not create a new algorithmic extension. These forms of collaboration require intersubjectivity – people have to be attuned to one another's contributions, share a common understanding of the meaning of the joint activity, and exhibit a certain degree of emotional and attentional synchrony with their group members.

The most complex form of collaboration – cooperation – requires the greatest amount of intersubjectivity to be sustained. In this type of collaboration, group members collectively contribute to a shared effort, producing a joint creation that goes beyond the input of any individual. During early childhood, cooperative forms of play are traditionally associated with sociodramatic play. In this case, multiple children play different roles that all contribute to a shared storyline. Each member plays a part that emerges in response to the roles of the other members. As the story unfolds, the nature of the common narrative emerges, shifts, and develops, becoming increasingly complex. This narrative form of play is based on the dynamics that develop between all of the members and could not exist without their collective contributions. Although the product of sociodramatic play might resemble an actual drama performed on a stage, the process is entirely emergent and an outcome of the mutual participation of all members. Most formal theater is not produced in this fashion, except for experimental improvisation. Many other forms of early childhood play beyond forms of play, sociodramatic role-play can also be characterized as cooperative. Group construction projects with varied materials are frequently characterized by cooperative processes, although a collaborative use of materials rather than verbal exchanges may predominate. Play that appears functional and task-based might also become cooperative if children collectively use materials and coordinate their behavior in such a way that a joint product emerges – for example, collaborative use of instruments, joint use of open-ended materials that develops into a game, and other collective behavior that yields new forms. This can occur among children and adults using both verbal and nonverbal modes of communication and mutual engagement. Cooperative forms of collaboration will be stymied by any imposed structure – for example, children playing a game with predetermined rules or college students collaboratively working on an assignment with predetermined content and format. Cooperative collaborations require that something new emerges from all members' unique contributions, therefore, predetermined outcomes limit the extent to which a collaboration can be cooperative. However, during pre-determined group efforts there may be space for a truly cooperative collaboration to develop. For example, college students trying to answer an essay question might collectively develop a new insight or method, preschoolers completing a puzzle might develop a new strategy together, or children engaged in a science experiment might together develop a new finding that diverges from the expected outcome. Additionally, there may be moments of cooperation that occur over the course of a collaboration that is primarily reciprocal. For example, while taking turns replicating a diagram, the group might diverge from the assigned task and create a structure that leads them to change the original diagram, or a group might become so collectively enthralled in a cooperative activity that they decide to ignore the original task and instead argue for the superiority of the new one. It can be argued that these are the collaborations that lead to the greatest innovations among adults and the greatest developmental achievements among children.

In summary, the collaborative competence introduced here reflects a typology of complexity ranging from imitative to reciprocal to cooperative. The relevance and accuracy of this assessment of collaborations are supported by a range of research into the processes, outcomes, and influences that have been found among a wide range of collaboration types and participants. Taken together, the collaborative complexity construct synthesizes what has been shown to support the most productive collaborations while allowing for a wide range of interactive situations and forms to be included in the criteria for collaborative competence.

PART III

A New Theory and Method for Assessing Development via Collaborative Competence

CHAPTER 7

Capturing the Complexity of Collaborations in Varied Settings

The rationale for both a new theory and corresponding method for studying collaborative competence has been laid out in Parts I and II of this book. Pooling findings from prior research, I argue that our current approach to assessing social development, especially among children from majority world cultures, is inherently flawed. Luckily, much research has already demonstrated the impact of interactions and collaborations on all areas of development. In addition, this research supports the idea of a collaborative form of competence that cannot be reduced to the individual. The components of the model of collaborative competence I have proposed must now be formalized to enable further research. It is also important to outline how a comprehensive account of collaborative competence could influence the research and practice of developmental psychology and education.

Collaborative Complexity and Intersubjectivity

On the current account, collaborative competence is composed of two major components: intersubjectivity and collaborative complexity. Competence develops when intersubjectivity and collaborative complexity each reach high levels and intersect during interaction. In this way, the model is both descriptive and prescriptive: It describes how this happens during interaction and what should be done to make it possible.

During interaction, intersubjectivity emerges from synchrony in conjunction with a mutual understanding of an activity. The form of synchrony and the type of shared meaning influence the type and extent of collaborative complexity. Collaborative competence develops when intersubjectivity enables a form of collaboration that supports the joint activity at the center of the interaction. Therefore, the form and degree of synchrony, the meaning of the activity, and the extent to which it is shared among the group relates to the form and degree of collaborative complexity. When this relationship functions in a mutually sustaining feedback loop, collaborations grow in complexity and become highly competent. When mismatches between the form or degree of synchrony and the type of collaboration occur or when the type of synchrony or form of collaboration does not support the meaning of the shared activity, lapses in intersubjectivity and/or collaboration occur. This negative side also occurs in a feedback loop whereby lapses in one component lead to constraints or breaks in the other. When this happens, the interaction either ends or ceases to be collaborative. Therefore, although intersubjectivity is considered a catalyst and support for collaborative complexity, there are bidirectional relationships between each element in the model.

Sociocultural Activity-Based Embodied Intersubjectivity

The mutual behaviors that indicate high intersubjectivity according to the sociocultural activity-based embodied (SAE) account have been found to promote ideal interactions, as discussed in the previous chapters across Part II of the book. These include signs of emotional attunement, reciprocal engagement, and proximity seeking, as well as shared attention in the form of joint attention to tasks and materials and a mutual focus on the shared activity. This multidimensional account of intersubjectivity captures the unconscious, synchrony-based, nonverbal dimensions that characterize high-quality parent–child and peer interactions. Synchronization among interacting groups may be primarily affective and social or attention-based and cognitive. Social-affective synchrony reflects emotional attunement and reciprocity, while attentional-cognitive synchrony supports mutual engagement in the activity via joint attention and focus on the central activity. Although these elements may be analyzed separately, during the flow of interaction they are mutually contingent and reciprocal. For example, increases in collective meaning and joint engagement with an activity can trigger greater synchrony, or a high degree of synchrony can lead to an increase in shared meaning and engagement. Shared meanings generally coincide with either social-affective synchrony in the form of eye contact, emotion mirroring, and increased reciprocal actions or attentional-cognitive synchrony in the form of joint attention to materials and tasks and a mutual focus. Often in highly engaging collective activities both forms of synchrony are heightened. This conceptualization of intersubjectivity defines collaborative competence as processual and in a state of flux.

As children engage in shared actions, these actions often develop into a shared meaningful activity. This may be a leading activity for their age or an activity that is tied to a larger collectively meaningful sociocultural context. For example, caring for a baby, playing weddings, and building trains reflect both common developmental and sociocultural meanings among preschoolers in an urban environment who live in multigenerational families. Young children enter any experience or interaction with their own desire for making meaning. Through shared actions, their "ideas" – not yet fully formed via internalized language – have the potential to become concretized through collaborative enactment with others. The more meaningful that the shared activity becomes to the participants, the more their interaction is expected to become intersubjective and vice versa.

As detailed in Chapter 4, SAE intersubjectivity is a product of synchrony and shared meaning. Each element varies in both degree and form. Synchrony may be high, medium, or low and primarily social-affective or attentional-cognitive. The extent to which an activity is agreed upon and meaningful to all participants also varies at different points in the interaction. The shared goals, structure, and form of a given collective activity may vary from one interaction to another and at different points in a single interaction. These elements combined produce intersubjectivity that reflects the nature and degree of synchrony along the dimensions of social-affective or attentional-cognitive (potentially also physically focused on physiological coordination, like in a team sport). Intersubjectivity enables collaboration and influences the complexity and form of collaboration that develops. The components of intersubjectivity – synchrony and shared meaning – support specific forms of collaboration, as defined in the previous chapter, by determining the moment-to-moment needs of a given interaction. For example, laying bricks and making a tall tower with blocks have shared goals and meanings – both require specific coordinated actions with materials. An imitative collaboration, wherein one worker or one child simply follows the lead of the other, making sure to match their placing of materials in a coordinated way that furthers the common goal, is supported by attentional synchrony. The shared meaning of accomplishing a useful task supports the type and amount of intersubjectivity necessary for this imitation-based collaboration. Therefore, the activity at the center of the interaction grounds both elements of collaborative competence. Within the context of the specific shared activity, the intersubjectivity gives rise to, influences, supports, and in the case of lapses detracts from the extent to which the interaction is collaborative and the type of collaboration it employs. At the micro-level, the degree and type of synchrony and the extent and nature of the shared meaning interact with the amount and type of collaborative complexity. Although many shared activities maintain a constant state of intersubjectivity and collaborative complexity, many others reflect the dynamic relationships between each of the elements and change in both form and degree over the course of a given interaction.

Components of Collaborative Competence

As described in previous chapters, a variety of approaches to measuring collaborative interactions have been conducted within different fields. Parent–infant dyads are perhaps the most assessed interactions and have been subjected to various methodologies. The most common approach for studying interactions is the statistical analysis of individual contributions. In this approach, the behavior of each member of an interaction is assessed separately and entered into a statistical model to determine the correlation between the individual contributions. The method most divorced from the moment-to-moment dynamics of interaction involves surveys completed by each interactant, whose responses are statistically analyzed for correlations. This method does not actually assess an interaction but rather how each participant relates to each other according to the items on the survey. The method next most proximal to the interaction is to code the behaviors of each participant separately from video or live in situ and then to use various analyses to assess the extent of contingency between the behaviors. The most sophisticated of such approaches considers microseconds and microbehaviors such as the direction and duration of a gaze. This type of methodology takes apart and then reassembles the interaction. It allows researchers to document moment-by-moment attunement between the utterances and nonverbal behaviors of interactants. This method is most commonly applied to dyads, especially parent–child interactions, within a laboratory.

One method that generally employs less technical methods falls under the umbrella of "conversation analysis." Conversation analysis combines sociology and psychology to analyze discourse as well as nonverbal communication. Although dyads represent the most common interactive structure assessed using conversation analysis, this method has also been used in larger groups. Some conversation analytic approaches extend to narrative, analyzing subtext, power relations, and other dialectic moves.

These approaches look at meaning as encapsulated within the text, either written or recorded.

Regardless of the method used, the question is: What are assessments of collaborations designed to measure? A handful of recent research has investigated elements shown to be critical for effective collaborations. These include response contingency, emergence, multidimensionality, and complexity. Each of these elements has been measured using innovative methods that inform the present approach to capturing collaborative competence and will be reviewed in the following subsections.

Response Contingency
Response contingency refers to the extent to which an individual member's responses are influenced by the prior responses and/or behaviors of other group members. This "contingency" can be conscious or unconscious, and methods have been developed that assess both. For example, conversation analytic methods have been used to assess contingency of both verbal and nonverbal components of interactions, such as the timing of responses to group members (Edwards-Groves & Davidson, 2020).

Other methods use technological mediation to enhance the likelihood that group members' responses will be contingent on one another's. One study involved secondary school student teams in which every members' actions on a circuit board affected the others' boards. The assessment tracked responses of individuals to the shared task at multiple levels: mouse clicks, communication logs, and changes made to the equipment (Andrews-Todd & Forsythe, 2020). Another use of technological mediation to both encourage and track contingent responses during interaction was used with younger children by Yuill et al. (2014). Their experiments measured the effects of an augmented play structure that alerts players to their peers' actions. Software coded the play behaviors of small groups using both the augmented and nonaugmented structures. The results showed that cooperative play was significantly more common when using the augmented version and solitary play was significantly more common during the nonaugmented version. Furthermore, the research identified "bids for attention" as being the key element that supported greater response contingency in the augmented version and led to more complex play. These results were borne out during both free play and when a structured task to create a narrative was added to the experiment. Triads of fifth graders engaged in an engineering design cycle collaborative problem-solving (CPS) task were shown to engage in talk turns in sequences that varied predictably during the different phases of the design process (Ricca et al., 2020). The response contingency of talk turns occurred at both the micro-level of talk sequences and at the macro-level of how the talk sequences varied according to which stage of the CPS task the group was engaged in. This finding suggests that the collectively generated dynamics of a collaboration at the group level are related to response contingencies between individual members.

Another study with secondary school students supported this individual–group response contingency finding. Using video-recorded data combined with group student reflections, aspects of different emotional states were coded along with examples of problem-posing from within a math problem, wherein the focus of the problem is restated, expanded, or given a different emphasis (Schindler & Bakker, 2020). The results showed that changes to one individual's affective field corresponded to group-level shifts in emotions. More positive group-level emotions corresponded to moments of problem-posing (i.e., reframing the original question). This led to more complex CPS. These last two studies coded collaborations for both individual sequences of response contingencies and macro-level collaborative dynamics. Each of the methods showed that greater response contingencies predicted more effective collaborations.

Emergence
The next characteristic of effective collaboration is emergence. The study of fifth grade triads made this the focus of the research (Ricca et al., 2020). The talk turns were coded with categories that measured the extent to which each turn contributed to group CPS. The group was also coded by episodes reflecting each phase of the engineering design process: problem-scoping, generating ideas, testing, and reporting. Although the task was provided to the groups, it was open-ended and provided little guidance. The results highlighted how the phases emerged organically out of specific talk turn sequences. In addition, an equation showed that entropy among the sequences peaked just after a shift to a new phase and then became predictable shortly after.

The study quantifying the affective field among math problem-solving groups also demonstrated how emergence was key to enabling shifts in group-level and individual attitudes toward math (Schindler & Bakker, 2020). More complex ways of thinking about the nature of a problem by refining it emerged in concert with social and emotional changes among the group. These changes emerged due to multiple factors that could not be predicted by a single antecedent. In addition, group dynamics were studied over multiple days, and some changes were gradual, whereas others were sudden.

Multidimensionality

Two studies highlighted the crucial role of multidimensionality, specifically the mutually reinforcing roles of social, emotional, and cognitive components within collaborations. The first, a study of five-year-olds engaged in predetermined age-appropriate collaborative tasks, coded indicators of self-regulation, coregulation, and social regulation, social dynamics regarding positive or negative social-emotionality, social role positioning (one of four potential roles taken in the service of completing the shared task), and three forms of dialogue (Pino-Pasternak et al., 2018). The groups were analyzed holistically and categorized over four different problem-solving conditions. Measures included micro- and macro-coding schemes as well as a narrative description of the flow of each element of interaction. In addition, scores of self-regulated learning (SRL) ability had been given to each individual child prior to engaging in the collaborative tasks. The findings indicated that positive social-emotional interchanges and role positioning were crucial to enabling a productive collaboration. Most important was that the positioning flowed away from the "owner role" (most often taken up by high-SRL children) and toward the participant role (egalitarian). The high-SRL children who took on scaffolder versus owner roles were most successful at supporting this.

A very different study created a theoretical ontology of CPS based on secondary student assessments that delineated social and cognitive components according to a highly detailed schema (Andrews-Todd & Forsythe, 2020). This schema included social and cognitive components, with subsets of specific strategies and behaviors organized hierarchically. To assess collaborations in real time, this approach – termed the "evidence-centered design framework" – used rubrics to score the data according to how they corresponded to the ideal model of CPS represented by the schema. The authors profiled groups according to CPS competence along the two dimensions of cognitive and social skills, wherein each group could be scored low or high on each dimension. Those scoring high on cognitive and social skills were the most effective groups, whereas those scoring low on both dimensions formed the least effective groups.

In addition, the affective field study demonstrated the significant influence of different affective states at both the individual and group level on students' initial engagement with problem-solving of open-ended math challenges and later in the ways in which they were able to restate problems to enable more complex and creative approaches and solutions (Schindler & Bakker, 2020). Taken together, these studies show the inherent multidimensionality of collaborations, wherein social and affective components play an equally significant role to cognitive elements and wherein all components are mutually reinforcing and constituting.

Complexity
The final characteristic that is key to effective measurement of collaborations is complexity. The previously described traits of response contingency, emergence, and multidimensionality all point to the idea that collaborations are by nature complex systems. Methodological elements focused on capturing rather than reducing complexity include the use of both qualitative and quantitative measures as complementary and necessary for measuring the full range of collaborations. In addition, the recognition that collaborations function at multiple levels (micro and macro; individual and collective) and that those levels occur in relation to each other rather than separately is key to implementing effective methods for measuring collaboration. The ontology of the CPS framework showed that individuals had negative and positive influences on group scores relative to their own skills and contributions. This method utilized multiple techniques for analyzing components of the collaborative process: semantic analysis, holistic rubrics, algorithms to construct predictive models, and even an artificial agent to track responses at both the individual and the group level as well as the relationships between these levels. This approach recognizes the complexity inherent in assessing collaborations and does not try to simplify or reduce it.

The study of augmented play structures used a methodology for assessing collaboration that uniquely captured complexity in a few ways (Yuill et al., 2014). First, the mean scores of the triad of interacting children in each play state measured in seconds were used. The "bid for attention" code was assessed by the behavior of all of the children within the triad – the one who sought the attention and the other two who responded or did not respond. For this code – shown to be crucial for collaboration to develop – the triad served as the unit of analysis. The narratives produced collectively by the children were coded in terms of the narrative quality of creativity. However, individual roles were also coded to determine the extent of equal distribution among the group. Therefore, most of the measures used the group as the unit of analysis either in the initial coding or in the use of the data. The micro-codes provided a real-time map of children's behavior during interaction along multiple dimensions. This demonstrated the processes of collaboration as well as depicting the varied elements that influence the quality of collaborations. A unique aspect of the methodology used in this study is the way in which the qualitative and quantitative data complemented each other. For example, photos of moments when children responded to each other's bids for attention and engaged in cooperative collaborations were used to demonstrate the reciprocal sequence of interaction that occurred in the augmented play state but that did not occur in the nonaugmented one. Similarly, full transcripts of the interactions were provided to exemplify how narrative roles occurred over the course of the entire play narrative. Finally, the relationship between individual child play type and the group-level outcome was illustrated by the micro-coding of each child within a given triad and the length of time they participated in each play state as this corresponded to the other group members' time spent in each play state.

The study analyzing CPS of an engineering design process among fifth grade elementary school students used a method that was designed to reflect the theoretical assumption that collaborative groups represent complex systems (Ricca et al., 2020). Data were coded at both the individual and the group level and made use of a combination of qualitative, categorical analysis for coding of the design phases and quantitative analysis for coding of the patterns of dialogue sequences and an equation that calculated entropy (by comparing the distance between predicted and random sequences of interaction) as it emerged at different points in the collaboration.

The study of influence of "affective fields" during collaborative problem-posing/CPS within math provides another example of coding and mapping both individual and group processes during specific episodes (Schindler & Bakker, 2020). The results showed multiple bidirectional influences of the type of affect and the type of reasoning among both individual and group processes. The relation between these levels was mapped using quantitative methods, whereas the categorizing of affective states made use of qualitative analysis.

Each of these methodologies demonstrates that complexity is key to measuring collaborations. To capture complexity, multimodal methodologies must be used. Rather than flattening the picture of what happens during collaboration, a complex system is analyzed using various perspectives, units of analysis, and mixed methods.

Collaborations as Complex Systems

Taken together, these methods share several commonalities. First, each study spends significant time theorizing and then operationalizing the constructs of interest that will be applied to the analysis of the collaboration. In this way, there is a direct line from theory to operationalization to observational indicator of individual and group behavior. Second, each methodology considers the relationship between individual and group-level analyses as distinct and dynamic but not causal or derivative. Third, they use a combination of qualitative and quantitative approaches, wherein the two approaches are mutually informing. By viewing an interaction in this way, it is possible to account for concepts such as emergence and flow. These elements are key to understanding collaboration and cannot be isolated or studied atomistically. The variable of time is crucial to understanding how collaborative interactions function over the course of an entire shared activity. The variable of entropy or randomness helps to explain that not every sequence of responses is directly connected to the previous one or to anything that can be predicted. Patterns of group-level behavior over time arise from a complex mix of factors that is heavily influenced by affect and social cohesion. In addition, the more open-ended or "ill-fitting" the problem or task, the more likely it is that the group will participate in effective CPS that engages all members.

Developmental Components of Collaboration

Finally, the developmental component is key to understanding collaborations. The study by Pino-Pasternack et al. (2018) described above with the youngest children who were given CPS tasks with predetermined goals and no adult support showed very low levels of productive collaboration, with only one group out of six achieving collaborations in multiple tasks. The second youngest children in the Yuill et al. (2014) study were given a free play and a guided play activity. The groups showed high collaboration and joint creativity only when the material provided support for interactivity in the form of directing children to peer contributions. The engineering design study with upper elementary-aged children showed that randomness of students' talk turns was concentrated during the times when the group had just begun a new phase in CPS (problem-scoping, generating ideas, testing, or reporting) (Ricca et al., 2020). In addition, the group spent most of the collaboration on generating ideas and the least amount of time on testing. This difference likely reflects the cognitive challenge of testing a hypothesis or method (as part of an engineering challenge) as opposed to generating ideas. Among the secondary school populations in the Schindler and Bakker (2020) study, problem-posing was the central driver of collaboration, wherein progress in completing open-ended challenges was made when positive changes in group and individual emotions coincided with reframing the problem. Both studies that involved secondary-aged students explicitly measured cognitive and social-emotional components separately (Andrews-Todd & Forsythe, 2020; Schindler & Bakker, 2020). This likely reflects the adolescents' capacity for emotion-masking and for sophisticated sociocognitive skills that are separate from reasoning, whereas younger students have less distinct capacities in these areas.

Therefore, although developmental considerations were not highlighted in these studies, each method for operationalizing and measuring collaborations as complex systems automatically took into consideration developmental characteristics. However, only the augmented play structure used the context most relevant and familiar to young children – play – and, perhaps most important for these results, this study created a context in which collaboration could be observed with explicit support for social awareness and concrete referents for verbal communication (Yuill et al., 2014). The qualitative study with five-year-old children used age-appropriate tasks but provided no support for methods of interacting or communicating (Pino-Pasternak et al., 2018). Given the constraints on young children's social perspective-taking and social use of language and on their ability to hold multiple ideas, foci, and goals in mind simultaneously, it is not surprising that the groups in this study showed an overall low level of collaboration. Without the scaffolds provided by an augmented play structure or a multitouch surface, the young children could not focus on completing a predetermined task while simultaneously considering peer contributions and adapting their contributions to those of their peers. Had this study involved a wholly open-ended use of props, it might have been possible to engage with peers through play that did not pose the challenge of fulfilling a predefined task.

Applying the Theory of Collaborative Competence

The theory and accompanying method argued for in this book build upon many aspects of the studies described in the previous sections. First, every factor investigated among children is operationalized in behavioral detail. These operationalizations are directly tied to theory: (1) the SAE view of intersubjectivity and its components; (2) the definition of collaboration in terms of complexity; and (3) the theorized relationship between those two components. Second, the methods designed to measure collaborative competence use both qualitative and quantitative approaches.

Two studies designed to measure collaborative competence will be reported on later in this chapter. Each of them reflects the components discussed earlier. The methods used will illustrate possibilities for studying collaborations as complex systems within naturally occurring educational contexts.

The first study used quantitative coding of mutual behaviors during free-play episodes of preschool children (Garte, 2019). The scale was designed to capture the frequency and duration of each microinteractive code. Each categorical behavioral indicator is scored for the extent to which it is observed over the course of the episode. Select episodes were transcribed from the videos for qualitative analysis as well. This analysis provided a holistic understanding of the interactions' ways of functioning over time. The coding scheme that defined the variables of intersubjectivity and collaborative complexity as observed during preschooler free play was developed and validated based on extensive in-situ observation of the same a similar population to whom participated in the study. Both quantitative and qualitative analyses show how intersubjectivity assessed via microinteractions corresponds to the measure of collaborative complexity. The quantitative analysis shows distinct relationships between interactive and environmental factors that were not automatically apparent in the qualitative data. The qualitative analysis shows the peaks and plunges of intersubjectivity and collaborative complexity as they occurred over the duration of an entire play episode.

The second, unpublished study (reported for the first time in this volume) provided a preliminary analysis of early elementary teacher-facilitated playful learning activities. The analysis combines qualitative and quantitative methods by mapping the codes for intersubjectivity and dialogue over the entire episode. This overlay depicts how different behaviors were concentrated and dissipated over time, as well as displaying correlations between distinct behaviors. The measure of intersubjectivity was scored without dialogue and included codes of joint engagement and collaboration in lieu of the collaborative complexity categories used for free play (imitative, reciprocal, and cooperative). As the activities in this elementary-aged study were teacher-facilitated, collaboration did not emerge as organically as in the preschool study. Otherwise, the coding scheme was the same as that used with the preschool children. However, for this elementary-aged study, dialogue was coded with a separate scheme that included indicators of exploratory talk. Teacher talk and student talk were coded separately. One code for internal state language was also applied. The codes used for the elementary-aged study are detailed in Table 7.1. These behavioral codes were overlain across the entire episode and time stamped so that correspondences and overlaps between different codes as well as what was prevalent at different points in the interaction were made visible. Although the conceptualization of collaborative competence did not change between the coding of preschoolers' free play and that of early elementary playful learning, the specific indicators changed slightly to reflect the difference in context as well as developmental changes.

Table 7.1 *Codebook for early elementary collaborative competence.*

Name	Description
Brainstorm	Children give original ideas about a topic that are not connected to personal experience or to anything they have learned
Brief eye contact	At least half the group makes eye contact for a short period
Challenge thinking	The teacher questions children's ideas or understanding using logic or counterexamples – not the same as clarifying questions or asking for elaboration
Children coordinate actions with one another	Children adapt their movements and/or position to those of the other group members
Content connection	Teacher explains contents or concepts by connecting them to students' prior knowledge
Content connection child	Children connect new content to something they learned or observed during the lesson/activity
Coordinate activity	Children, with or without teacher, coordinate their behavior in relation to group members. This might include actions with objects, movements, or other behavior – it is broader than simply adapting movements and encompasses shared engagement
Direct to peer	Teacher directs children to attend to their peer's dialogue or actions
Elicit ideas	Teacher asks open-ended questions to generate ideas about the topic/content
Internal state	Use of words by both children and teachers that refer to internal states, such as think, know, wonder, question, predict, expect, mean, or remember
Joint attention with the material	All group members – including teacher – pay attention (through gaze/handling) to the same material(s)
Mutual positive emotion	All group members – including teacher – show positive emotion, smiling or laughing at the same time

Table 7.1 (*cont.*)

Name	Description
Off topic	Children say something unrelated to the topic/content/concept of the learning activity
Participate equally in task/shared activity	Children and teacher collectively engage in the same activity with an agreed-upon goal
Personal connection	Children make a connection between their own personal experience and the content/topic that is the focus of the lesson/learning activity
Prompt for elaboration	Teacher responds to children's utterance by asking for more details or clarification
Question content	Children ask a question about the content/topic/concept at the center of the lesson/learning activity
Respond to peer	Children respond to their peer directly with dialogue
Shared meaning of activity	Children, with or without teacher, demonstrate a shared understanding of an activity in which they are engaged. They verbally show a common understanding of what they are doing, demonstrate common purposes and meanings, and engage collectively
Sustained eye contact	All of the group members maintain eye contact for an extended period of time

Measuring Collaborative Competence during Preschooler Free Play

The major difference between the free-play coding scheme and most other measures used in prior research for analyzing collaboration is that dialogue is not used to indicate the degree of collaboration. Language is coded only in terms of whether the language exchange is reciprocal and whether the interacting group members are attending simultaneously to the language uttered. This coding reflects the developmental norms of the preschool age, such as egocentric speech, in which children might speak without directing their speech toward another person or expecting a response. Therefore, the codes "reciprocal conversation" and "joint attention conversation" are used to capture the jointness and reciprocity of whatever utterances occur. The remaining indicators of social-affective and attentional-cognitive intersubjectivity were entirely nonverbal and coded according to the degree of mutuality/synchrony that they demonstrated. This points to another unique element, wherein all codes were applied only to joint or mutual behaviors among the group. Although qualitative transcription documented the behaviors and speech of each child, the analysis focused on the moments of intersubjectivity and joint meaning-making.

For example, the following extracts represent a 20-minute episode of interaction between two boys. Julio is 3.1 years old and monolingual in Spanish and Marco is 4.7 years old and bilingual in Spanish and English.

> *Activity setting: Water table*
> *Julio mixes water in a bowl using a strand of plastic, stringy material.*
> *Marco walks up to the water table and bends over, looking up into Julio's face closely. He then points at the bowl and makes a stirring gesture, saying "Alli, alli" (like this, like this).*
> *Julio smiles up at Marco and holds out the string in his direction.*
> *Julio reaches into the table and produces a much larger piece of the material which he shows to Marco.*
> *Marco smiles widely at Julio and the string; Julio matches his expression.*

This initial sequence demonstrates synchrony based on joint attention and matched emotion. Although a definitive meaning of the activity has not yet emerged, a collective subject is established as the boys begin a joint, reciprocal exploration of the material.

> *Marco inspects the string, holding it up as Julio begins "plucking" at it with a shovel.*
> *The two boys explore the material simultaneously, taking hold of large sections, pulling them apart, dividing the strings, dropping and scrunching them.*
> *While exploring, the two boys make eye contact, smile at each other, and nod whenever the other boy tries a new use of the material.*
> *Together they push the string into a bucket filled with water. Marco says in Spanish: "Drown it," then, "Now let's cut it."*
> *After some experimentation, they find it can be "cut" with the shovel while held taut.*

This transcript is focused on describing the details of nonverbal actions and especially on highlighting signs of synchrony and shared understandings. The transcript itself often moves from describing an individual child's action to describing joint actions. Verbal utterances must be attributed to an individual speaker; however, much of the nonverbal communication and coordinated actions happened simultaneously and are described as occurring jointly. In this way, the transcript defines the collective as the unit of analysis.

> *Both boys begin to "cut" their own pieces of string with the other water table materials.*

Here, the transcript could have detailed each boy's individual actions with the materials. This would have given the impression that their actions occurred separately in a temporal sequence, although they occurred simultaneously, with the parallel use of the materials occurring as a contingent response to one another's actions.

> *Marco holds up a long piece and says in Spanish: "This is big."*
> *The boys simultaneously take hold of opposite ends of the string, stretching it out between them and taking turns alternatively cutting and holding the string.*
> *One boy pulls the string taut to the edge of the "cutter" while the other boy strikes the cutter down on the string.*
> *After each successful chop, the string falls and the boys immediately break into uproarious laughter.*
> *The boys experiment with different versions of the "cutting" activity, responding to the string dropping after each chop with mirth.*

At this point, the activity has taken on a specific form and meaning. With the support of high social-affective and attentional-cognitive intersubjectivity, an open-ended exploration of materials has turned into a structured game with collectively determined goals and meanings.

> *Marco and Julio collect some of the smaller pieces and put them in buckets. Marco says in Spanish: "Let's cook."*
> *Marco stirs the water for a moment while Julio watches him without moving.*
> *They both return to more of the cutting game.*

Marco's sudden detour away from the jointly established meaningful activity creates a break in intersubjectivity. The lapse is prompted by Marco uttering a new idea, cooking, that is not agreed to by Julio. Instead, the other child simply watches him without participating. The transcript reflects the lapse as jointly enacted – one child plays a new game while the other does not engage with the game. Depicting both children's simultaneous behavior highlights the joint meaning of the lapse and foreshadows its continuity with renewed intersubjectivity.

> *The boys then stretch the string out further and further, cutting at different points and testing different materials as cutters.*
> *The boys coordinate with each other's positions while holding the string to maintain the tautness, leaning towards each other and nodding in affirmation at each other frequently.*
> *Marco calls to the teacher in English, "Josh, look we're cutting it!"*
> *The teacher offers the boys another large bunch of the material to which they open their arms simultaneously.*

Once received, they begin tossing it to each other and laughing.

Here, the construct of intersubjectivity as a combination of emotional and attentional synchrony plus meaningful shared activity is embedded in both the data provided and the analysis. From the same 20-minute video recording an entirely different transcription could have been presented. Had the focus been primarily on verbal utterances or had it described one boy's actions as separate from the other's, an analysis based on the SAE view of intersubjectivity would not have been possible.

The methodology used for the preschooler free play study included 277 episodes that were coded holistically for intersubjectivity and collaborative complexity. In addition, a small sample of episodes was transcribed and analyzed qualitatively as described earlier. In this way, although they were complementary and mutually informing, the qualitative and quantitative analyses were conducted separately.

The quantitative assessment of this episode shows that high social-affective and joint attention intersubjectivity with micro-codes such as eye contact, mutual positive emotion, and joint attention task were scored as sustained and joint attention materials and mutual focus were scored as constant. The type of collaboration that characterized most of the episode was cooperative, in which the boys collectively created something new (the string-chopping game). In addition, reciprocal collaboration occurred at certain points when the boys took turns with different aspects of the activity.

The materials in this episode were highly flexible. The quantitative analysis was able to show that the flexibility of materials systematically influenced the collaborative competence that developed across multiple episodes. Not captured in the quantitative analysis was the shared meaning of the activity, how it developed over the course of the episode, and the nature of its meaning to the interacting children. In addition, the momentary lapse in intersubjectivity, how one child responded to the lapse, and how – once repaired – the joint meaning of the activity peaked, leading to heightened degrees of both collaborative complexity and intersubjectivity, were depicted in the qualitative analysis. These sequential relationships between the different components of collaborative competence could not be used as measures within the quantitative analysis. Instead, the quantitative analysis showed the correlations between each component but not how they related in real time. Therefore, the full theorization of collaborative competence requires both quantitative and qualitative methods. The quantitative analysis demonstrated that these correlations were not unique to a single episode but were repeated across multiple episodes in different contexts and with different participants.

Another episode highlights the ways in which an inflexible material constrains the nature of a shared activity and, in turn, the extent to which a joint meaning can emerge from it. Nonetheless, intersubjectivity can still develop from other sources during an interaction.

> Zaria and Jessica share a puzzle, Zaria standing, Jessica sitting. Most of the pieces are out of the puzzle on the table beside it. Zaria turns a piece around in her hands. Jessica looks at the piece Zaria is holding and asks, "Is he upside down?" Zaria: "No, no, the legs, the legs have to be upside down." Zaria places the piece randomly in the puzzle frame and Jessica laughs heartily. Zaria doesn't respond but adjusts the placement of the piece.

There is a disjunction between the girls in terms of the meaning of the activity. Zaria perceives the goal as completing the puzzle, whereas Jessica seems more interested in the social possibilities of the interaction.

> The girls both begin randomly putting pieces in the puzzle, sometimes on top of each other.
> Zaria places two pieces together that fit and Jessica stops placing pieces to watch Zaria's placement.

This moment of joint attention introduces the possibility of synchrony between the girls.

> The girls resume simultaneously taking pieces in and out. Another piece is matched by Zaria.
> Jessica smiles at the match and says, "Yeah," nodding her head.
> The girls take turns placing the other pieces, this time slowly and watching the other's placement before placing their own.

Here, there is a negotiation of meaning that occurs through joint action. Once Zaria's goal for the activity is accepted by Jessica, the two proceed as a collective subject. Could this negotiation of perspectives have taken place linguistically? Most likely not among preschoolers. Perhaps older children would have argued: "Let's finish the puzzle." "No! Let's just play with the pieces, it's more fun." This dialogue would likely have led to a protracted debate. In the episode here, Jessica's desire for social cohesion led to her adapting her initial construal of the activity to match Zaria's without requiring any verbal negotiation. This interaction does not demonstrate a high degree of collaborative competence, as neither intersubjectivity nor collaborative complexity occurred at a high level. Therefore, the episode would receive low scores on interactive measures. However, the qualitative description shows that despite the girls' limited moments of synchrony, their desire for social engagement and mutual connection is enough to maintain the interaction. Consistent with the quantitative results, the transcription and qualitative analysis also shows how an inflexible material can make the development of a shared meaningful activity difficult, thereby limiting collaborative competence.

These episodes show how quantitative and qualitative analyses of preschooler free play show consistent results that overlap while also providing unique insights. Conducting separate analyses allowed for capturing patterns of relationships that occurred both across episodes containing a large sample and within episodes of a small sample. The finding that what was observed to occur systematically over multiple episodes was consistent with the details of microinteractions within individual episodes lends validity to the theorized model of collaborative competence. However, in the teacher-guided playful learning episodes of early elementary-aged children the quantitative and qualitative analyses were combined.

Collaborative Competence during Early Elementary Playful Learning Activities

Using *NVivo* software, videos of playful learning activities were segmented according to time stamp and speaker. Each new dialogic turn was coded in sequence by time. If multiple participants spoke at the same time, their speech was listed with the same time stamp. The time stamps served as segments for intersubjectivity codes that were added to the transcript without dialogue as the video played. For example:

> 0:00:20.720,0:01:42.220
> Intro: Teacher makes brief eye contact with
> all 4 children
>
> 0:01:42.220,0:02:32.500
> Children direct gaze toward teacher
> 3/4 children demonstrate sustained eye contact
>
> 0:02:32.500,0:03:18.360
> while responding to question
> Teacher responds to all child utterances with
>
> 0:03:18.360,0:04:08.629
> verbal and nonverbal acknowledgment
> children follow teacher's gaze to make eye
>
> 0:04:08.629,0:04:49.480
> contact with the child who is speaking
> Mutual positive emotion and eye contact are

0:04:49.480,0:05:15.230
sustained between teacher and 3–4 children
Teacher nods and gives nonverbal signs of

0:05:15.230,0:05:24.910
recognition whenever a child speaks regardless
of content

Coding for each video was conducted three times: once with the sound off to code for intersubjectivity, once with the sound on to code for dialogue, and a final time to code for "shared meaning of the activity" as indicated by both nonverbal and verbal interactive behavior. For this code, the content of children's utterances was used to determine shared meaning, such as using the same words and/or agreeing on what was happening. In addition, nonverbal communication and use of materials was also considered if it supported a mutual understanding of the concepts. The codes of the transcripts and the videos were then integrated to produce a visual depiction of how each code occurred over the course of the activity in terms of frequency, duration, and overlap with other codes. An example of just the dialogic codes as they occurred over the entire course of an episode is depicted in Figure 7.1. The bars indicate how long each type of dialogue lasted and when it occurred during the 15-minute episode. The intersubjectivity codes from the same episode are depicted in Figure 7.2.

The full set of codes overlain throughout the episode are depicted in Figure 7.3. In addition to the dialogue and intersubjectivity codes, Figure 7.3 also includes the collaboration codes of coordinate activity, participate equally in task/shared activity, and children coordinate actions with each other, as well as a code for internal state language and a code showing teacher talk.

In addition to each coded item, the "coding density" depicts the amount of coding at a particular point. More specifically, the black segments represent a high degree of intersubjectivity and/or exploratory talk, whereas the white segments indicate points at which minimal signs of exploratory talk or intersubjectivity occurred. Therefore, the darker segments represent the periods of the greatest collaborative competence over the course of the activity.

By overlaying codes in real time, insights into how behaviors emerge, recede, peak, and dissolve at different points are captured within a single analysis. The preschool interactions were often too short and did not follow a clear enough structure to code in this manner. On the other hand, due to the teacher facilitation of the elementary-aged activities, holistic coding would not have allowed for distinguishing between child

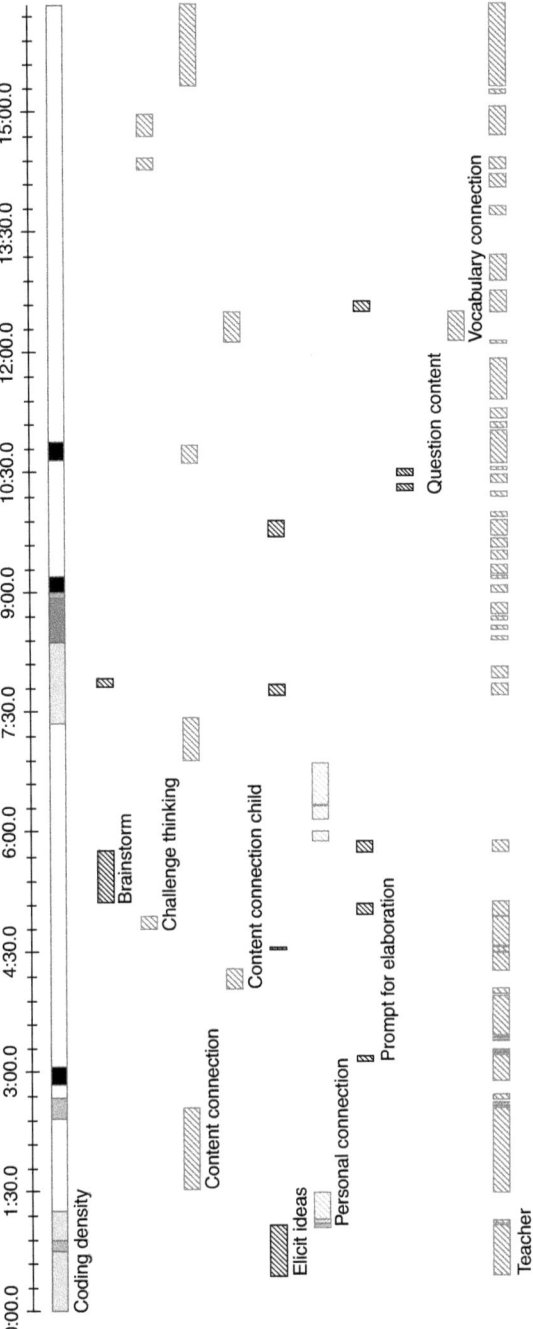

Figure 7.1 Dialogue codes as they occurred over the course of a playful learning episode. "Coding density" refers to all codes applied to this video, not solely the dialogue codes depicted here.

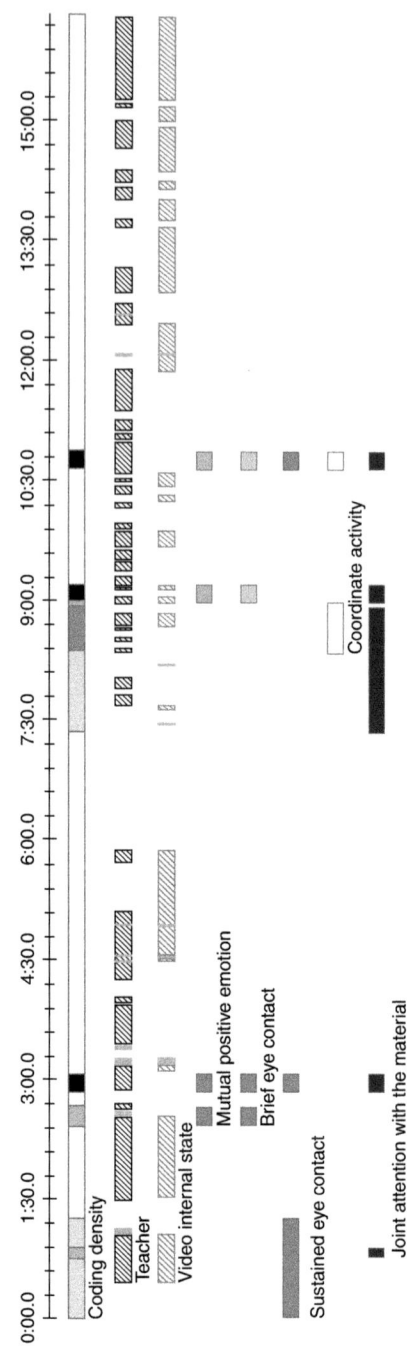

Figure 7.2 Intersubjectivity codes as they occurred over the course of a playful learning episode.

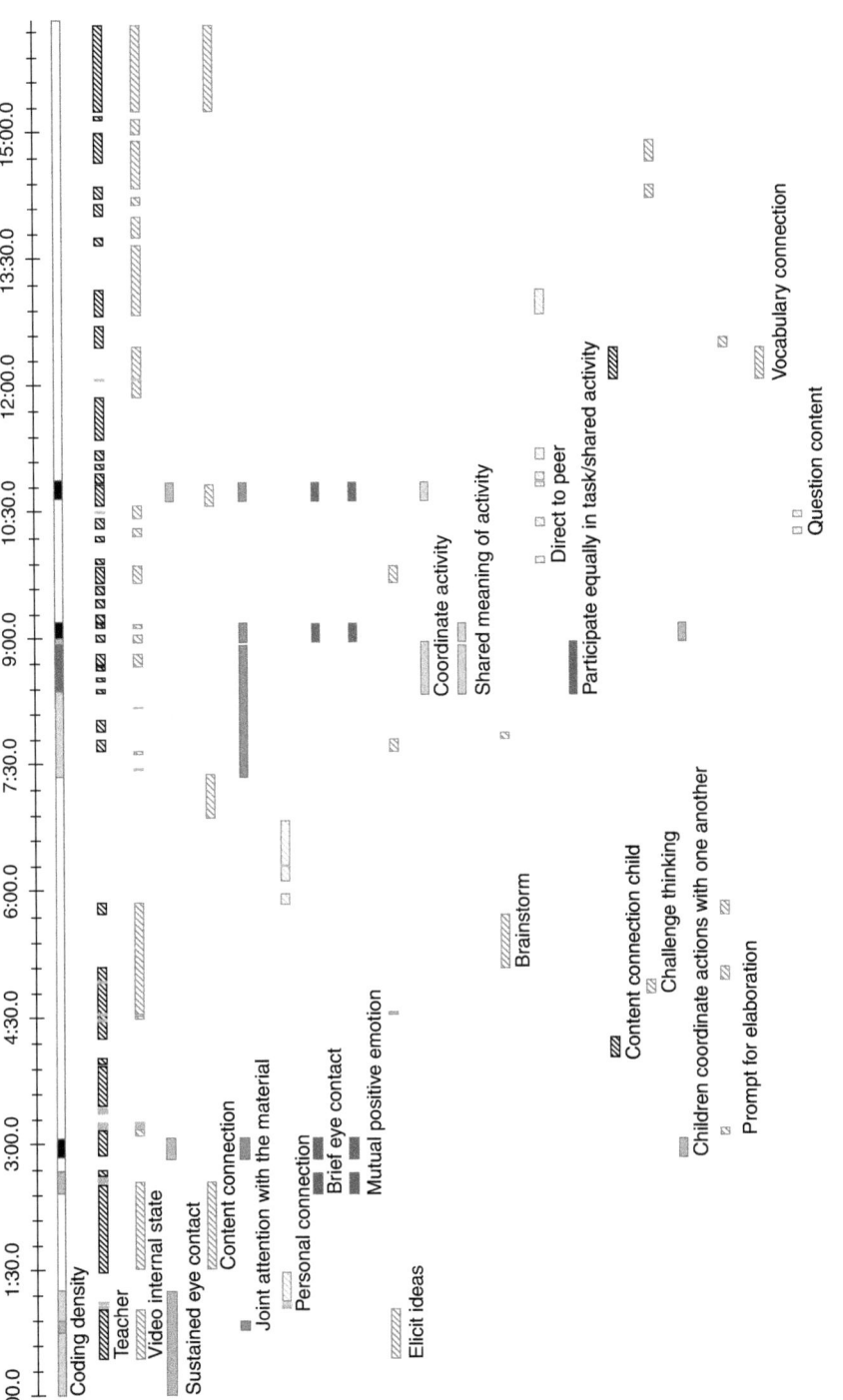

Figure 7.3 All interactive codes across an episode of playful learning collaboration, including exploratory talk, intersubjectivity, collaboration, internal state language, and teacher talk, as well as the coding density over the course of the playful learning episode.

and teacher dialogue/behavior and would have resulted in teacher discourse dominating the analysis.

Although the methodologies of these two studies differed, general principles based in the same conceptualization of collaborative competence were adhered to. This demonstrates how measurement can be designed to reflect the particularities of the interactions under study rather than choosing elements of interactions to be observed in order to suit a given method. In these cases, it was possible to adapt the methods to reflect what was meaningful for the age and structure of the observed activities without diverging from the general construct of collaborative competence. The methods used were designed to allow for consideration of the developmental norms of the participants, the structure and nature of their shared activities, and the most practical ways to capture the emergence and contextual influences of interactive behaviors. The methods for capturing collaborative competence in both studies maintained the unit of analysis as the interaction, even when dialogue was introduced. The codes defined utterances in terms of exploratory talk moves that were meaningful only in relation to the shared activity and the utterances of interactive partners. However, as children become developmentally more sophisticated, individual contributions become increasingly crucial to understanding the flow of interaction. By accounting for both verbal and nonverbal forms of interaction, ways of engaging with the activity, materials, and social partners were captured. Leaving out either dialogue or nonverbal forms of participation would have hidden key elements that are necessary for understanding how early elementary-aged children participate in playful learning activities. By combining qualitative and quantitative methods, behavioral indicators that reflect the principles outlined earlier in this chapter – response contingency, emergence, and multidimensionality – were captured. In addition, by assessing intersubjectivity and shared meanings along with evidence of collaboration, the model of collaborative competence was tested according to key indicators of each component. In order to find meaningful patterns without reducing the complexity that collaborations represent, it is necessary to develop principles that reflect this purpose. The next chapter will detail these principles and how they were exemplified during the study of preschooler free play.

CHAPTER 8

Principles for a Developmentally and Culturally Valid Methodology

As described in Chapter 1, research that attends to the social development of children enrolled in Head Start programs (e.g., Bulotsky-Shearer et al., 2008; Fantuzzo et al., 2004) often relies on a methodology designed to identify deficits in their language and cognition (Cole, 2013). The possibility that process-based methods can uncover capabilities among populations often deemed deficient is highlighted by a study wherein process-oriented methods were used to investigate the play of Australian Indigenous children. Over the course of the study, teachers shifted their perceptions of children's language use during play from deficient to creative and competent (Peterson et al., 2018).

Methods for assessing children's behavior are always based on multiple assumptions about the children who are the subjects of such research. The driving assumption behind the method proposed in this book is that young children seek out interactive partners primarily to create shared meanings with them together during play. Children are innately motivated to connect with their peers to solve problems and create new meanings that they could not do on their own. Intersubjectivity – an indicator of shared meaning – is therefore a tool that develops during interaction and functions in the service of collaborative competence. Therefore, although intersubjectivity reflects a goal of interaction, play interactions may occur without either intersubjectivity or collaborative competence. Although play during early childhood is the result of innate drives, the form of play that takes place during a given interaction is not universal; play in varied, culturally grounded forms occurs among all children and provides equal opportunity to give rise to intersubjectivity and collaborative competence.

Consistent with this set of assumptions, intersubjectivity may take the form of language, as has been well documented, or of coordinated action, or some other form of mutually adaptive participation and engagement in ways that include verbal and nonverbal elements and/or manipulation of objects. What comprises intersubjectivity is further clarified in the concept of "sociocultural activity-embodied" (SAE). This multidimensional definition points to a methodology that must allow for a similarly multidimensional operationalization of what types of behaviors are involved during an intersubjective interaction. Nonetheless, there are clear boundaries between what does and does not count as intersubjectivity during interaction. The key defining feature is the "mutual-ness" of the interaction – those moments when more than one child adapts their behavior, emotion, language, and/or use of materials to that of another, or the moments when people act in synch, or via synchrony, in varied forms.

The SAE view of intersubjectivity also defines when it occurs. The "when" of this form of intersubjectivity is emergence. Predicting the varied combinations of factors most likely to lead to the emergence of intersubjectivity can only occur once the intersubjective moments have been measured and their emergence traced backwards, retrospectively. Therefore, the method must be nimble enough to insert itself at any moment into an interaction that signals intersubjectivity. The method described in this chapter was designed to both scan a wide-ranging series of moments occurring in the micro-time of interactions and to be able to swoop in up close to identify the subtle details of an interactive exchange. This method provides both a broadly macro and intimately micro view of interactions simultaneously. To draw systematic conclusions about the nature of human interaction requires this micro/macro method. And yet such a methodology is often prohibitively complex, unusual, and untested, and thus is rarely attempted. Instead, interactions are flattened to serve the requirements of a convenient method. Instead of emergent, interactions are captured according to a predetermined time series. Instead of multidimensional, interactions are measured according to predefined elements. Instead of mutual, inter, occurring between children, interactions are based on only one part of the interaction – that which is observed as the response of the focal child, thereby removing the inter and redefining the behavior simply as action.

Case studies provide tremendous nuance and details of interactions that are so particular to the interaction under study that there is never the requisite zooming out to identify patterns, make predictions, or generalize. Alternatively, the method plays such a major role in framing intersubjectivity that it becomes the definition of the construct itself. The method described in this chapter allows for conclusions about trends in naturally occurring interactions to be drawn. The goal is to predict which factors are most likely to lead to high degrees of intersubjectivity and how this enables collaborative competence.

Measuring Social Complexity

Traditional research on play proceeded from the assumption that children engage in the type of play that corresponds to their individual capacities for social complexity (Rubin, 2001; Smilansky, 1968). American preschoolers from low-income families were historically the subjects of such research, with results showing that they participated in only the most rudimentary form, termed "functional play" (Parten, 1932; Rubin, 2001; Smilansky, 1968). However, more precise methods using naturalistic observation have shown low-income preschoolers to engage in constructive and imaginative types of play as well (Dyer & Monetta, 2006; Weinberger & Starkey, 1994). A new methodology that observed different forms of play over the course of naturally occurring play interactions revealed that children from varied income levels and backgrounds engaged in all categories of play complexity at equal rates across income groups, including over the course of a single play episode (Peterson et al., 2018; Robinson et al., 2003). These studies each used the Play Observation Scale, which combines cognitive and social categories (Rubin, 2001), from the least social and most cognitively simple (onlooker/functional) to the most complex (cooperative sociodramatic; Parten, 1932; Smilansky, 1968).

Howes and Matheson (1992) introduced a developmental sequence characterizing social interactions during play as beginning with imitation, becoming reciprocal, and finally developing into cooperative play. These three categories defined social complexity in terms of capacities for social engagement that individual children developed and demonstrated during play with peers. A later study with four-year-old children from both a high-socioeconomic status (SES) university preschool and a low-SES Head Start program found that among both populations of children "parallel aware" states, wherein children observe one another without interacting, predominated during play (Robinson et al., 2003). These play behaviors previously categorized as simpler and developmentally earlier served as bridges between cooperative (the most socially complex) forms of play, including those involving pretend (the most cognitively complex). By using methods that assessed the ongoing play episodes at multiple time points, the authors were able to track how different degrees of social and cognitive complexity emerged at different points among various play groups.

Mixed Methodology

Challenges to orthodoxies in psychology and developmental psychology often reject quantitative approaches as atomistic and mechanistic on their face, as described in Chapter 1. However, to understand general patterns of interactive functioning, it is necessary to find ways to identify trends without sacrificing the nuances and descriptive details provided by qualitative analysis. Quantifying behavior often requires decontextualization, which has been criticized for divorcing behaviors from their meanings (Burman, 2017; Valsiner, 2017). However, the methodology designed to capture collaborative competence during preschooler free play is derived from ethnographic details of the lives of children in Head Start classrooms and in particular their free play periods. The measures assess multiple levels of classroom functioning. Beginning with the overall layout of the classroom space and materials, the key features of each smaller activity setting are then measured. Finally, the method zeroes in on the play interactions occurring within those activity settings.

Qualitative analysis (as presented in prior chapters) of episodes from larger samples allow for the parsing of discrete interactive behaviors that can then be quantified as evidence of intersubjectivity. Observations of how interactions begin and end and differences in the extent to which children collaborate provide the details of what constitutes different types of collaboration. In this way, the ethnographic observations in Head Start classrooms and the qualitative analysis of select episodes provide the material for the quantitative measures and highlight the ways in which context is considered at various levels of analysis.

The method described later in this chapter was designed to capture patterns of collaborative competence that emerge in response to various factors both endemic and external to the play interaction. Previous research suggests that elements of the physical and social environment impact preschoolers' play. Social elements include group composition, such as group size and gender, wherein same-gender dyads were found to have longer peer interactions than larger and mixed-gender groups (Brownell et al., 2006), and smaller, longer-lasting play groups were associated with higher social competence (Veiga et al., 2017). The impact of the physical environment on preschoolers' play interactions has also been documented (Goncu et al., 2002; Howe et al., 2005; Li et al., 2016; Robinson et al., 2003; Shim et al., 2001; Veiga et al., 2017). For example, the space and materials of the play environment impact preschoolers' use of language and frequency and type of interactive play (Howe et al., 2005; Li et al., 2016; Shim et al., 2001; Veiga et al., 2017). Realistic in contrast to flexible objects influence the nature of children's play (Lloyd & Howe, 2003; Roskos & Neuman, 1998), and flexible objects elicited more complex fantasy play (Hogan & Howe, 2001; McLoyd, 1983). Similarly, more flexible physical arrangements, such as movable or varied-use rather than stationary furniture, have been related to greater complexity of play (Petrakos & Howe, 1996) and different play types (Li et al., 2016; Veiga et al., 2017).

Preschoolers have been shown to choose play partners based on a shared interest in activities and materials rather than individual traits (Hanish et al., 2007). Many long-standing research directions such as collaborative cognition (Bearison & Dorval, 2002; Rogoff, 1998), collaborative knowledge construction (Fischer et al., 2002), and socially shared cognition (Fawcett & Garton, 2005; Garton & Pratt, 2001), as well as more recent advances in studies of collaboration described in detail in prior chapters, focus on joint participation in shared activities that result in shared competencies. The unit of analysis in these approaches is expanded from a single person to socially interacting dyads or larger groups and, accordingly, to the interindividual processes underlying successful collaboration.

Methodological Principles

Along with measures of the interaction as the unit of analysis, the methods for studying collaborative competence reflect general principles that can be applied to different contexts. The overarching principle is that methods should be developed to suit the particularities of each interaction's process of interpersonal dynamics and salient contextual features. This reflects the goals for research on collaborative competence as detailing systematic processes as well as documenting the most impactful contextual influences on collaborations. Many of the procedures elaborated later in this chapter were designed specifically to be used to capture peer interactions during preschool free play periods. Therefore, examples of the specific methodology from the free play study are provided along with the principles that it reflects. A few of the methods used in the elementary playful learning research are noted as well. Given that the elementary-aged study is preliminary and not designed to depict systematic relationships that are generalizable, not all of the principles were applied in that study. The following is a numbered list of each methodological principle with examples of how each was applied:

(1) *An interactive context in which the participants freely choose their interacting partners along with the activities, materials, and space within which to engage.* The free play periods of preschoolers were selected as the ideal interactive context to assess collaborative competence among this age group. Each research site was a Head Start program located in 5 different neighborhoods within New York city. The program director selected 1 classroom to participate in the study. Each classroom had as part of its regular schedule a minimum of 45 minutes for free play in both the morning and afternoon. During these periods, children chose where they wanted to play and within each area made use of the provided space and materials. Most areas accommodated between three and five children, so they were also free to select their play partners. For elementary-aged children, activity stations with varied, open-ended materials were used, with the focus being on teacher-guided activities to reflect how collaborative competence can develop through play-based pedagogy.

(2) *Measures that are normed on the cultural groups for which they are intended to be used.* All of the participants in the Head Start study had family incomes below the federal poverty line (Head Start Bureau, 2006). All measures were developed, normed, and tested among preschoolers from low-income families and from majority Black and Latinx backgrounds. There was great cultural diversity in that children came from a variety of immigrant as well as nonimmigrant backgrounds and represented a variety of family cultures, such as African, Caribbean, African American, Mexican, Dominican, Puerto Rican, South American, and families of mixed ethnicity, race, nationality, and immigration status. The elementary-aged children attended a Title 1 school where 80 percent of families lived below the poverty line, with a similar mix of diversity among both children and teachers. The codes used for this study were developed based on observations of those classrooms. The racial/ethnic breakdown of the children and teachers is provided in Table 8.1.

(3) *Data collection procedures that capture naturally occurring behavior while minimizing observer impact.* During the taping of peer interactions in the Head Start program, the researcher positioned themself in the classroom and used a zoom lens in such a way that an observer could not tell where they were focusing. In this way, the children and teachers were not usually aware of their specific focus. However, at times, the researcher did approach children very closely. These children were almost never aware of being observed. If a child did become aware of being the focus of taping, the researcher quickly moved their gaze in the opposite direction. Although the camera remained trained

Table 8.1 *Demographic variables of children and teachers by classroom.*

	Race				Gender	
Classroom	Black	Latinx	Asian	White	Female	Male
1						
Teachers	2	0	1	0	3	0
Children	13	3	0	0	6	10
2						
Teachers	0	2	0	1	3	1
Children	4	11	1	0	9	7
3						
Teachers	0	2	0	0	2	0
Children	5	11	0	1	9	8
4						
Teachers	2	0	0	0	2	0
Children	8	9	0	0	9	8
5						
Teachers	2	1	0	1	3	1
Children	6	5	1	4	9	7

on the same focal children, this nonverbal signal was effective in dissuading the child that they were being observed, and they generally resumed their interaction without distraction. These procedures were possible because self-consciousness is not highly developed during early childhood. Prior research has shown that four- and five-year-old children are generally unaware of observer presence when engaged in activities (see Pellegrini, 2004 for a review). The teachers' awareness of being observed varied. Once the researcher made it clear that they were only interested in the children's behavior as it occurred naturally, the teachers seemed to become unaware of the camera. They also frequently commented to the researcher while they were taping with no apparent awareness of the taping itself. In this way, the researcher was able to establish a separation between their own presence in the classroom and the presence of the video camera. For both children and teachers, this split allowed for an objective record of classroom behavior while simultaneously allowing for the researcher to be integrated into the classroom community, thereby putting the participants at ease with their presence. For the elementary observations, the camera was propped up in a fixed position focused on the small focal group. The children were generally not aware of it and the teachers focused solely on the activities they were leading.

(4) *Teachers take a peripheral rather than central role during peer interactions.* For the Head Start study, peer interactions were the focus of data collection. Occasionally, a teacher would embed themselves in the children's play and/or begin directing the behavior of the children who were engaged in play. Once this happened, the episode was no longer video recorded and was excluded from analysis. However, this was a very rare occurrence.

(5) *Inclusion of the entire episode of interaction from start to finish during data collection.* Data collection procedures ensured that the entire episode was captured by the video camera. For the Head Start study, the steps in this process were as follows: (1) Locate an area of the classroom in which two or more children were playing near each other. (2) Zoom in on the children to determine whether they were indeed interacting with each-other. If no interaction was observed between the children after two minutes, survey the room until another activity area with children playing close to each other was found. (3) Repeat steps (1) and (2) until an episode of reciprocal interaction between children was observed. If no interaction occurred between the children in the area, a new activity area was selected for observation. (4) Once an interactive episode is identified, train the video camera to record it until all signs of interaction ceased for 20 seconds or more. (5) While keeping the camera focused on the interaction, visually scan the rest of the classroom for additional episodes. (6) If a new episode was identified while recording an ongoing episode, move to capture both episodes simultaneously or frequently shift focus back and forth between the two episodes.

(6) *Delineation of the interactive episode based on consistent participants.* The first step in coding the videotapes was to delineate discrete episodes of peer interaction from the stream of behavior on the videotape. Episodes were included based on two criteria: duration and participants. In terms of duration, it had been determined during the development of the measures that an interaction lasting less than 1.5 minutes could not be reliably coded. In addition, the theoretical definition of intersubjectivity as centered on shared activity required that interactions be adequately sustained so that some shared activity could be identified. A review of the tapes supported the notion that at least 1.5 minutes of interaction were

required to meet such a criterion. The second criterion for inclusion in the analysis was that episodes must be defined by continuity of participants. In other words, the interacting children who initially participated in the interaction must remain as the sole participants throughout the duration of the episode. If additional children joined in, the previously defined episode would be considered to be ending. This reflects the conceptualization of intersubjectivity as something that develops between interacting partners as a function of their particular interactive dynamics. In addition, this criterion allowed for increased reliability of coding and followed prior research assessing episodes of naturally occurring interactions among child peers (Pellegrini, 2004). If a new child participated interactively for at least 1.5 minutes, a new episode, inclusive of that child, was marked as beginning at the 1.5-minute mark on the coding sheet. In a situation in which participants were frequently entering and leaving the interaction, a determination was made as to whether any discrete episode within the changing of partners could be delineated. If this could not be reliably determined, the interaction was not included in the analysis.

(7) *Measures of mutual behaviors in which the interaction rather than the individual participants is the unit of analysis.* No individual child measures were used in the study, and all of the measures used were designed to assess interactive rather than individual behaviors. Each episode of play counted as a single case. This is consistent with the theoretical definition of intersubjectivity given in the previous section as emergent within the interaction. Given that intersubjectivity as a construct describes the nature of interactions rather than individuals, such a unit is necessary in any study attempting to define intersubjectivity as it functions in a given population.

(8) *Attention to group characteristics such as group size, gender, age, language, and culture.* Characteristics of each group's size, gender composition, and play type were considered. Size pertained to the number of children in the group and ranged from two (two children) to five (five or more children). The gender composition of the group was assessed using three types of groups: girls only, boys only, and mixed. The language and culture of interacting groups were depicted in the qualitative analysis.

(9) *Attention to environmental characteristics such as space, materials, and how they are used.* A measure of environmental flexibility assessed the extent to which materials could be used in a variety of ways and the

affordances of the physical environment. The term "affordances" refers to the opportunity for change to an object or a space's structure and function (Gibson, 1986). Each activity area in which the play episodes took place was scored for both material and space flexibility on a five-point scale, with those scoring 1 being the least flexible and those scoring 5 being the most flexible. The scoring of the materials and space within each activity area was based on both the data collected via videotapes and notes that had been taken on the materials and space of activity areas during data collection. Therefore, the scoring was based on an assessment of the materials and space as they appeared as well as being informed by how the children were observed to be using them. For example, if manipulatives were available on a large rug, it was helpful to know that the children used the rug space in many different ways, implying a high score of spatial flexibility for the area.

(10) *Attention to the type of activity in which children are engaged.* Play type was assessed using the three mutually exclusive categories of imaginative play, functional play, and constructive play. According to this coding scheme, children's use of materials determines the code given for play type. For example, if children are using blocks as part of pretend play, the play is coded as "imaginative play." If they are pushing the blocks around, it is coded as "functional play." And if they are building with the blocks, it is coded as "constructive play."

(11) *A measure of interactive behavior that includes multiple dimensions such as attentional, affective, and physical/embodied.* This measure was developed to reflect the dimensions of intersubjectivity defined as an embodied experience of joint participation, coordinated attention, and emotion that is centered on a shared activity. When applied to episodes of interaction, the measure is designed to assess both the nature and degree of the intersubjectivity that characterizes the interaction. This process captured variation between episodes in terms of both intersubjectivity level and type. Consistent with the view that intersubjectivity emerges among partners during interaction and reflects a high degree of alignment and coordination, behaviors were considered intersubjective when they: (1) occur simultaneously among all partners (e.g., children smile at each other simultaneously, coded as mutual positive emotion; or children observe the puzzle pieces simultaneously, coded as joint attention to materials); or (2) are reciprocally triggered by all interacting partners. For example, two

Principles for a Developmentally and Culturally Valid Methodology 147

children make eye contact and begin laughing, and within a few seconds a third child makes eye contact with the other two and joins in the laughter (coded as eye contact and mutual positive emotion); or four children take turns placing blocks in rapid succession on the same platform (coded as joint attention to task).

The intersubjectivity measure items were scored on the following four-point scale: 4 = constant; 3 = sustained; 2 = brief; 1 = none. These scores reflect both the length of the behavior and the number of times it was observed during the episode. The items were designed to capture moments of mutuality occurring within the behavioral stream rather than any individual behavior. The conflict items were included in order to provide an exhaustive measure of mutual engagement between peers. The following list provides short definitions of each item:

(1) Touching: Children touch each other's bodies (nonaggressive only).
(2) Eye contact: Children look each other in the eye simultaneously.
(3) Mutual positive emotion: Children show positive emotion simultaneously.
(4) Mutual negative emotion: Children show negative emotion simultaneously.
(5) Joint attention to task: Children are paying attention to the same task at the same time.
(6) Joint attention to materials: Children are paying attention to the same material(s) at the same time.
(7) Joint attention to conversation: Children are focused on the same conversation.
(8) Mutual focus: Children are concentrating for the same amount of time with the same amount of attention to the same activity.
(9) Reciprocal conversation: Children take turns and listen to each other speak, and they respond to what their partner said verbally or follow the other child's directions.
(10) Violation of property: Children take materials from each other without asking or destroy each other's work.
(11) Violation of space: Children touch each other in unwelcome ways, take over workspace, or push into each other's space aggressively.

(12) *A measure of collaborative complexity that allows for differing levels at different points in the interaction.* This measure assesses the extent to which the type of collaboration is observed over the course of the interaction. The definitions are listed from least to most complex as follows:

- Imitation: One child follows or mimics the actions of another. The leader/follower can change as long as there is only one idea guiding the activity at a time.
- Reciprocal: Children take turns; they respond to each other's actions or words back and forth only. They do not build on each other's ideas and do not create something new together.
- Cooperation: An interaction reaches the threshold of cooperation when something new is created as a result of collaboration by at least two children. This may be a new game, a new construction, or a new storyline for dramatic play.

Each of these behaviors is scored on a seven-point scale, reflecting the extent to which it characterized the collaboration. The scale definitions are as follows: 1 = none of the time; 2 = very small amount of the time; 3 = less than half of the time; 4 = half of the time; 5 = more than half of the time; 6 = most of the time; 7 = all of the time.

If cooperation received a score of 5 or greater, the type of cooperation was marked with one of the following definitions:

- Escalation: Children contribute to the same activity in a way that extends or expands on it in terms of intensity or duration.
- Negotiation: Children change the nature of an ongoing activity as a result of the words or actions of their interacting partners.
- Mutual goal-setting: Children discuss what they want to do and make a plan for how to proceed. They then carry out the plan together.

(13) *Measures that consider language as a tool along with nonverbal forms of communication.* As is apparent within the measure of intersubjectivity, children's use of language was coded for the extent to which it indicated joint participation in conversation rather than coding linguistic exchanges on their own. For the collaboration measure, verbal along with nonverbal behaviors were considered when scoring the level of collaborative complexity observed.

These examples are specifically applicable to capturing naturally occurring peer interactions with limited teacher intervention. Such methods could be applied to older children provided with self-selected activities and materials with which to interact using play-based pedagogy. However, as language becomes more central to children's collaborations, the incorporation of dialogic codes such as those described in the previous chapter could be added to the coding scheme. In the following section, details regarding reliably establishing the coding of the free play episodes are provided.

Reliability and Validity of Episodes and Measures

The boundaries of each interaction episode were reviewed three times: first alone by the primary investigator (PI), next by the coder for intersubjectivity items, and last by the coder for collaborative complexity items. In addition, the PI randomly selected a sample of episodes for joint coding. As a result of these reviews, 36 episodes were dropped from the sample due to low reliability, resulting in a final sample size of 277 episodes. Inadequate inter-rater reliability occurred evenly between all classrooms, and there was no evidence of systematic bias in the errors. The methods described earlier were each tested for indicators of both reliability and validity. The training of raters for the purpose of establishing inter-rater reliability as well as for the establishment of both face validity and factor validity of each measure is described subsequently.

Intersubjectivity Measure Coding and Reliability

The coding scheme for intersubjective behaviors was initially developed and tested during in situ observations of a bilingual Head Start classroom. This classroom was visited over a 1.5-month period for three to five days a week depending on the class and the PI's schedule. During this time, 80 discrete episodes were identified from the children's naturally occurring peer interactions during morning and afternoon indoor free play. To establish face validity of the intersubjectivity items, episodes were coded using the intersubjectivity measure once they had been identified. Minor changes to the definitions of items were made based on this process. A research assistant (RA) was identified at the beginning of data collection and trained on the intersubjectivity measure via joint coding with the PI in situ. The RA was an African American undergraduate psychology student who had experience working with young children. This RA was blind to the hypothesis of the study and the other measures. She was initially trained using in situ observations. Prior to beginning the in situ observations, she was given a copy of the codebook for review. The definitions were discussed with the PI and areas of confusion were clarified. Several episodes were then jointly coded for training purposes. The researcher and the RA sat near each other with separate coding sheets and observed peer interactions identified by the PI. Each code was discussed as it was observed during the interaction. Three separate episodes of interaction were jointly coded in this manner until it appeared that the RA had been adequately trained in the use of the measure. The researcher and RA then sat farther apart and coded eight episodes identified by the PI simultaneously without discussion. Scores were compared to assess agreement between the coders. Adequate (83 percent) absolute agreement was reached.

Following the in situ observations, the RA provided reliability coding for the videotaped episodes within five different classrooms/on the intersubjectivity measure. Thirty percent of video-recorded episodes (n = 32) were randomly selected to be joint coded from each classroom by selecting every 11th episode within each classroom. Ratings were compared and analyzed for agreement once all data had been coded. Cronbach's alpha was 0.90 and the intraclass coefficient was 0.83. The 352 scores on 11 items yielded an inter-rater reliability of 0.76 (Cohen's kappa). The remaining 68 percent of items were divided between the author and the RA and coded independently. The inter-rater reliabilities of each item are presented in Table 8.2.

Table 8.2 *Inter-rater agreement of the intersubjectivity measure across item and score.*

Item (n = 32)	Number agree	% agree
Touching	28	87%
Mutual positive emotion	29	90%
Mutual negative emotion	30	93%
Eye contact	27	84%
Joint attention to task	24	75%
Joint attention to materials	30	93%
Joint attention to conversation	29	90%
Mutual focus	29	90%
Reciprocal conversation	21	65%
Violation of property	31	96%
Violation of space	31	96%

Score	Never	Brief	Sustained	Constant	Total
n	143	103	96	32	374
% agree	84%	67%	89%	75%	80%
Number agree	121	70	86	24	301

Principal component analysis with Promax rotation was used to determine the dimensionality of the intersubjectivity measure. The three-dimensional model explained 78 percent of the variance of the items. The dimensions included (1) social (touching, eye contact, mutual positive emotion, joint attention to conversation, reciprocal conversation), (2) joint attention (joint attention to task, joint attention to materials, mutual focus), and (3) conflict (mutual negative emotion, violation of space, violation of property). The internal consistency of each dimension was assessed via scale reliability using Cronbach's alpha. Reliability for the social dimension was 0.80; for the joint attention dimension it was 0.85, and for conflict it was 0.75.

Collaboration Measure Coding and Reliability

The collaboration measure was initially developed during the in situ observations. At that time, it included four categories and was scored on a four-point scale. However, the category of "goal-corrected partnership," in which children changed their goals to reflect those of their interacting partners, was not observed consistently among the sample. In addition, the four-point scale did not adequately reflect the differences in collaboration type that were observed in a single episode. Therefore, the measure was changed to the current form of a seven-point scale and the "goal-corrected partnership" category was dropped from the measure.

Two new RAs were trained with the collaboration measure. The RAs were both Latinx undergraduate psychology students (Dominican American and Puerto Rican) who had experience working with young children. Any questions or requests for clarification were discussed with the PI prior to coding. Each RA then jointly coded three randomly selected episodes with the researcher and discussed scores and rationales. Three more randomly selected episodes were then coded until each RA reached 90 percent or higher agreement with the PI. The RAs coded the remaining episodes independently. At no time were both RAs coding the same classroom, and the RAs never conducted any coding together. The RAs were blind to the study's hypothesis and to all of the other measures.

After the coding of episodes on the collaboration measure for each classroom was completed, both RAs reviewed the codes and definitions with the PI separately and discussed how they would code a single randomly selected episode to ensure that they had retained their understanding of the measure. One of the RAs was the primary coder for three and a half of the classrooms and the other primarily coded one and a half classrooms.

Twenty-five episodes were joint coded by both RAs. Their ratings were compared after the last classroom had been coded on the collaboration measure. Cronbach's alpha was 0.87. The intraclass correlation coefficient was 0.78. Table 8.3 lists the inter-rater reliability of the collaboration measure by item. Table 8.4 lists the cross-tabulated agreement of both raters by score.

Group Characteristic Measures

Two measures assessed the social context of the interacting group. Size assessed the number of children in each episode as follows: 1 = two children; 2 = three children; 3 = four children; 4 = five or six children. Gender assessed the gender composition of the episode as follows: 1 = boys; 2 = girls; 3 = mixed. Play type assessed the type of activity occurring during the episode. Play type was assessed using the "Play Observation Scale" developed by Rubin (2001). Play type was coded as follows: 1 = dramatic play; 2 = functional play; 3 = constructive play. Adequate reliability has been established in prior studies (e.g., Coplan & Rubin, 1998). Inter-rater reliability for play type was high at 0.78 (Cohen's kappa).

The measure of length assessed the number of minutes in which children were engaged in a single episode of peer interaction according to the following categories: 1 = 1.5–5 minutes; 2 = 6–9 minutes; 3 = 10–14 minutes; 4 = 15 minutes or more

Table 8.3 *Inter-rater reliability for collaboration measure by item.*

	Cronbach's alpha	Intraclass correlation coefficient	Lower–upper bound
Imitation	0.80	0.67	0.36–0.85
Reciprocal	0.88	0.79	0.57–0.91
Cooperation	0.87	0.77	0.53–0.90
Total	*0.85*	*0.74*	*0.60–0.83*

Table 8.4 *Cross-tabulation of collaboration scores between two raters.*

Rater 2	Rater 1							
	1.00	2.00	3.00	4.00	5.00	6.00	7.0	Total
1.00	16	0	1	0	2	0	0	19
2.00	1	10	3	0	1	0	0	15
3.00	0	1	9	0	0	0	0	10
4.00	0	0	0	0	4	0	0	4
5.00	1	0	1	0	7	0	1	10
6.00	1	0	0	2	0	2	1	6
Total	19	11	14	2	14	2	2	

Activity Area Measures

Each classroom consisted of between six and eight distinct activity areas. The boundaries of the areas were designated by shelving units and by related materials being grouped together. In addition to areas with fixed boundaries created by shelves, there were areas that used tables or rugs to define them, as well as some areas that were only open when the teacher provided the materials. In addition, many of the areas were marked with signs, and in most of the classrooms only limited numbers of children were allowed to play simultaneously in each area. Therefore, within each classroom, children's free play was further segmented by the number of distinct activity areas. Classrooms varied in terms of the rules for moving between activity areas; however, all classroom teachers imposed some regulation regarding the responsibilities of children to clean up the area in which they had been playing. Every episode of peer interaction occurred within an activity area. During the initial delineation of episodes, descriptions of the materials and type of activity were listed on the coding sheet for each episode. This information was used to determine the activity areas in each classroom and to place the episodes into those areas accordingly. Each activity area was scored for both material and spatial flexibility on a five-point scale, as detailed in Principle (9) earlier in this chapter.

To determine the reliability of the environmental flexibility score, two professors of early childhood education with prior experience as preschool teachers scored 10 of the activity areas based on the list of materials and a written description of the spatial arrangement of each area. The scores and inter-rater agreement for each activity area are listed by flexibility ranking in Table 8.5.

Table 8.5 *Number, flexibility, and reliability of activity areas (n = 38) by classroom and percentage of scores given for flexibility across all activity areas and classrooms.*

Classroom	Number of activity areas	Material Flexibility		Spatial Flexibility		Range of intraclass correlation coefficients
		Mean	Range	Mean	Range	
1	9	2.8	1–4	3.7	2–5	0.82–0.90
2	7	2.4	2–5	3.7	2–5	0.85–0.91
3	7	2.2	1–4	3.4	2–5	0.86–0.90
4	9	3.4	1–4	2.6	2–5	0.85–0.91
5	6	3.16	2–5	3.0	2–5	0.82–0.91

Score	Activity areas given that score for material/spatial flexibility (%)
1	0%
2	25.8%
3	36.4%
4	9.8%
5	28.0%

Score	
1	13.5%
2	11.6%
3	31.6%
4	34.5%
5	8.7%

A teacher interaction measure was developed to exhaustively capture the ways in which the classroom teachers interacted with groups of children engaged in sustained peer interactions. The coding categories were developed after the tapes had been extensively reviewed for the coding of other measures. Prior research assessing the effect of teacher intervention on preschoolers' peer interactions also informed the development of the measure (Girolametto et al., 2004; Pursi, 2019; Ramani, 2012). However, the measure was too negatively skewed to be used in the study. There was very little teacher involvement in any of the episodes. The procedure was designed to capture solely child-directed and child-initiated interactions, so this likely contributed to the lack of teacher involvement in the sample.

The methods detailed here were designed to capture processes of how collaborative competence develops during naturalistic play among preschoolers. In addition, the methods allowed for analysis of the impacts of proximal space and materials during play and for a more distal comparison of classrooms and activity areas. No previous measure assessing nonverbal, activity-based dimensions of preschooler peer intersubjectivity or collaborative complexity exists. Furthermore, no measure of preschooler play uses interactive units of analysis for all behavioral indicators. The preexisting collaboration and play type measures were adapted from prior measures of individuals to a group-level assessment. Coding the episodes in their entirety enabled a holistic assessment of how the collaboration unfolded over its entire duration. The holistic coding of both the intersubjectivity and collaborative complexity measures precluded an event sampling approach and therefore departed from the more common and feasible systematic methods of observational coding. To account for the less systematic nature of the coding method, a robust inter-rater reliability procedure was implemented. The next chapter will demonstrate how the methods described here allowed for an investigation of both process and correlates of collaborative competence as they emerged during play. The operationalizations of variables described in this chapter allowed for systematic testing of relationships with implications for both theory and practice within the context of preschooler peer play.

CHAPTER 9

Analyzing Components of Collaborative Competence during Preschooler Free Play

The Unique Context of Play

The sociocultural activity-embodied (SAE) view argues that the context in which intersubjective interactions are most likely to occur are those that are collectively meaningful to the participants. This baseline of shared meanings provides a fertile starting point for the collective meaning-making that undergirds intersubjectivity and collaborative competence. For young children, free play provides the most obvious context in which to study intersubjectivity according to the SAE conceptualization. Prior research elaborates on why free play is an ideal context for investigating collaborative competence.

Collective Meaning-Making

Piaget (1971) and Vygotsky (1979b) both theorized play as the most developmentally salient activity for children between the ages of three and five. Vygotsky described play as providing the first zone of proximal development during which children were able to perform tasks and enact a range of social and cognitive abilities that were otherwise too advanced for them. The mechanism by which play enables developmental growth is both the nature of peer interaction during play and the role of imagination. Through stretching the boundaries of reality during play, young children experiment and make meaning of their own experiences and the world that they are coming to understand (Ferholt et al., 2019, 2020). Elkonin (2005) elaborated on these ideas by specifying sociodramatic play as requiring children to act according to the "social rules" of the play scenario rather than their own instincts. By taking on specific roles and adjusting those roles to the logic and patterns of their relationships with their play partners, they generalize their behavior, emotional expression, and a variety of other actions. This shifts their responses to the world from instinctual to those governed by general principles of social relations. Elkonin (2005) further elaborated upon the idea that developmental growth occurs during the early childhood period specifically because of engaging in sociodramatic play between the ages of three and five. Bodrova and Leong (2015) summarized the results of experiments that have tested this theory by various post-Vygotskian researchers and found that a host of physical, cognitive, and linguistic challenges were overcome by preschoolers within a sociodramatic play context that they could not achieve outside of play. They also found that play did not make a difference to children's capabilities under the age of three or over the age of six. Therefore, early childhood seems to be a sensitive period for the unique influences of play on developmental growth.

Vygotsky also contends that imagination arises out of play, as an outgrowth of using objects to make meaning with peers. This is consistent with the view of development as emergent from the play activity, mediated and motivated by social relations and the desire for shared meaning. Elkonin's (2005) leading activity theory of development more broadly implies that individual developmental growth is undergirded by socially mediated activities. In this way, individuals are both primed biologically for certain kinds of activities at different periods of development and simultaneously rely on those activities for promoting specific forms of development. However, as cautioned by Bodrova and Leong (2015), children do not automatically reap the benefits of play as soon as they enter the preschool period. Rather, support for the types of play that impact development is necessary. Elkonin's definition is referred to as "mature play" – a type that matches the descriptions given by Piaget and post-Piagetian researchers. This mature play has been termed "cooperative sociodramatic play" (Rubin, 2001). The various cognitive and social capabilities that are supported through play according to Vygotskian and Piagetian theoretical traditions include: decentration; acting in accordance with the intentions and perspectives of others rather than solely one's own; and symbolic thought, which extends to representational thinking and, more broadly, internal operations and the self-regulation required to adjust behavior according to the collectively determined logic of the play activity. Bodrova and Leong (2015) recommend specific support be provided for this type of play within school settings while simultaneously ensuring that the child-directed nature of free play is not lost.

This conception of the role of play in development is partially consistent with the SAE theory. However, the exclusive focus on sociodramatic play and the idea that play forms are characterized by different levels of complexity are at odds with the notion of collaborative competence. Rather than assigning complexity to the form of play, degrees of complexity characterize the collaboration and intersubjectivity that both support and emerge from a given play activity. The symbolic nature of pretend play does not in itself confer collective developmental benefit but rather it depends on the degree of social coordination combined with the mutual creation of an outcome connected to the play activity (as in a game, narrative, or structure) that connotes collective social and cognitive complexity. On this account, measures of intersubjectivity and collaborative complexity need not be tied to verbal interactions or to the fantasy element of the play activity. Rather, peer play in varied forms represents the socially significant activity of preschoolers, just as academic group projects or being on a sports team or musical ensemble represent socially significant activities of child and adolescent development. At each period of development, intersubjectivity and collaborative complexity develop from and determine the quality of those interactions that are most meaningful for those of a given age due to a complex mix of sociocultural and maturational factors.

Which forms of play predominate among children likely varies by culture, as has been shown in prior research (Trawick-Smith, 2010). Language-based sociodramatic play has been found to be most prevalent among higher socioeconomic status, European-heritage children (Edwards et al., 2006; Haight et al., 1999). More action-oriented types of parent–child play have predominated among Mexican American and African diaspora children (Fletcher et al., 2020; Roopnarine & Davidson, 2015).

By broadening the focus to all play forms, the present theorization removes the assumption that intersubjectivity is connected to a specific mental capacity – as in symbolic thought – and rather that it is tied to forms of collective engagement that are meaningful for particular age groups within a given sociocultural context.

The theorized relationship of play to preschoolers' development is parallel to that of intersubjectivity's relationship to the development of play among preschoolers. Socially complex play promotes social and cognitive development during early childhood, and intersubjectivity promotes socially complex play. Yet, socially complex play does not automatically occur during all preschooler peer interactions and is subject to contextual factors. Similarly, intersubjectivity does not automatically develop during all play activities and is equally sensitive to contextual factors. Intersubjectivity both supports and is supported by characteristics of peer interactions that are unique to play activities during early childhood. High degrees of intersubjectivity and collaboration constitute the most complex play activities, but these are lacking during more rudimentary play interactions. Intersubjectivity based in collective meaning-making characterizes peer play that has the greatest potential to promote collective development during the preschool period. Therefore, intersubjectivity that emerges during play is uniquely representative of the preschool age in terms of both constraints (relative to older children's intersubjectivity) and potential (relative to younger children). However, like "mature play," intersubjectivity does not automatically emerge from any play activity. Rather, particular conditions of the sociocultural context – both internal and external to the play interaction – either support or hinder intersubjective forms of relating.

Influences on Play Complexity

Researchers from a post-Piagetian tradition have investigated different types of play and whether the characteristics of the children and the play environment influence the social and cognitive complexity of the play. As discussed in the previous chapter, studies have consistently shown that individual measures of children's social pretend play are correlated with a host of other developmental capacities such as affective social competence (Lindsey & Colwell, 2013), theory of mind understanding (Lillard & Kavanaugh, 2014), language development (Thompson & Goldstein, 2019), and various cognitive capacities consistent with Piagetian theory (Lillard et al., 2011). However, criticism regarding a lack of consistent measurement of what constitutes pretend play has also challenged some of these findings (Thompson & Goldstein, 2019). In addition, evidence for a direct causal relationship between play and developmental achievements has been challenged (Lillard & Kavanaugh, 2014). Nonetheless, social pretend play has emerged as unique from all other play types in relating to individual developmental capacities.

The assumption that individual play behaviors derive from and support individual social skills (Fung & Cheng, 2017; Li et al., 2016) leads to interventions focused on strengthening peer play skills. Findings show that children who engaged in experimentally induced pretend play versus nonplay improved their peer play skills in later naturalistic settings (Fung & Cheng, 2017). Consistent with previously discussed research (Li et al., 2016), teacher reports were not reliable in this study, as teacher-reported social skills were not correlated with children's pretend play skills. Although these methods consider play individualistically, the finding that measures of interactive play across different contexts are related to one another suggests that the play activity itself is the site of development rather than decontextualized individual social skills.

The play activity as a unique context for developing collaborative competence is underscored by a study that sought to measure the impact of teacher support for group processes on individual children's collaborative play skills and individual children's social competence apart from the play activity (van Schaik et al., 2018). None of the expected relationships between group processes and individual social skills were found. Had the study looked at relationships between teacher support for group processes and the group dynamics – including collaborative competence – that emerged during the play activity, the results would likely have shown significant correlations.

As discussed in Chapter 2, the Western cultural commitment to assessing only the individual regardless of the psychological construct under study has made it difficult for developmental psychologists to uncover the collective social and cognitive competencies that underly collaborative play.

Research that diverges from mainstream developmental psychology has departed from individualistic assumptions to instead delineate moments of play interaction in which children's social, emotional, and cognitive development is collaboratively constructed with peers as well as adults (Ferholt et al., 2019; Hoey et al., 2018; Pursi, 2019; Pursi et al., 2018). These studies describe micro-processes by which adults and children develop shared meanings through play activities. This view of play as the central site for meaning-making among young children is consistent with Vygotsky's original conceptualization of the role of play in development (Connery et al., 2010). Accordingly, play is a fertile context for joint meaning-making that, in turn, leads to collaborative forms of cognitive and social development.

Play type and social complexity have each been found to vary with the play environment (Hogan & Howe, 2001; Shim et al., 2001; Weinberger & Starkey, 1994). In particular, the spatial arrangement of furniture and the materials available to children during play have effects on preschoolers' social interactions in terms of frequency and type of interaction (Howe et al., 2005; Weinberger & Starkey, 1994). Taken together, the research on young children's play suggests not only that free play is an ideal context for observing and capturing emergent collaborative competence but also that, for young children, play itself may be a necessary precondition for allowing the most complex forms of intersubjectivity and collaboration to develop among peers. More particularly, the research suggests that play must be defined in as expansive a way as possible to capture the broadest spectrum of conditions for emerging intersubjectivity. Play with a variety of materials, for a variety of purposes in different configurations, and with different forms of communication will thus allow for the most widely valid assessment of when, where, and how intersubjectivity develops among diverse groups of young children.

Investigating Collaborative Competence and Activity Areas during Play

The present study investigates all forms of peer play and characterizes the nature of the play activity (imaginative, constructive, functional) and the levels of intersubjectivity and collaborative complexity according to measures normed on the study's population as described in the previous chapter. These measures can accommodate the likely possibility that during ongoing peer interaction the play type and the degree of collaborative competence might change.

The quantitative methods used allow for systemic determination of patterns that are not intuitive or directly observable. The findings can reveal relationships between intersubjectivity and collaborative complexity, including specific forms and degrees of both components of interactions. In addition, the present study seeks to determine whether there are relationships between the material/spatial context, the play activity, and the type and degree of collaborative competence. Therefore, relationships between the variables defined in the previous chapter that occur over the course of play episodes will be explored at different levels. If higher degrees of collaborative competence are more likely to occur during specific types of activities and/or in relation to environmental features, direct implications for the structure of preschool classrooms and other play environments could be determined. Therefore, the first question addressed by this study is whether it is possible to apply systematic, quantifiable tools of measurement to interactive exchanges. If so, it is necessary to determine whether interaction episodes that include different combinations of individuals within different spatial and material contexts can produce unique cases, even if the same child participates in multiple episodes. If statistical tests of multicollinearity show that this is not possible, this will mean that the influence of an individual child's unique traits supersedes any emergent quality of an interaction. This would render the overall concept of collaborative competence ungeneralizable and measurable only via case study-type analysis. On the other hand, if statistical analysis confirms the hypothesis that the quality of interactions can be measured separately from individual traits and that these are highly influenced by the spatial, material, and interpersonal context, then it might be possible for collaborative competence to be assessed among a large sample of interacting groups.

More specifically this chapter addresses the following research questions:

(1) Do the dimension and level of intersubjectivity vary with group composition (gender/size) or play type?
(2) Are more intersubjective interactions longer lasting?
(3) What is the relationship between the two dimensions of collaborative competence: intersubjectivity and collaborative complexity?
(4) What is the impact of specific contextual factors on collaborative competence?
(5) What is the impact of contextual factors on the relationship between intersubjectivity and collaborative complexity?

Preliminary Results

In this study, the participants are groups rather than individuals. Therefore, the characteristics of interacting groups rather than individual cases comprise the sample. By describing the composition of child-selected play groups across 277 episodes of free play, information about individual children's propensity for types of groupings in which they choose to play is also revealed. The results depicted in Table 9.1 show that the majority of groupings had three children, and the least common group sizes were of five or more children. Most of the groups had a mix of boys and girls, whereas the fewest groups were made up of only boys. In terms of play type, most were characterized by functional play and the fewest were constructive. Most interactions lasted between 1.5 and 5 minutes (the shortest category), and the fewest interactions lasted the longest amount of time, at 15 minutes or more.

To verify the independence of the episodes, the Durbin–Watson test of multicollinearity was run. The Durbin–Watson statistic revealed no significant autocorrelation between the episodes. Therefore, each play episode was able to count as a unique case, supporting the idea that considering an interactive unit of analysis is possible using quantitative analysis. Descriptive statistics are reported in Table 9.2.

Among the interaction variables, imitation and cooperation were found to be slightly negatively skewed. This indicates that the groups scored more frequently at the lower end of both imitation (the simplest) and

Table 9.1 *Group characteristics and structural features of interaction episodes.*

Variable	Frequency	Percentage
Size		
2	10	37.0
3	105	37.5
4	56	20.0
5	15	5.0
Gender		
Boys	74	26.0
Girls	82	29.0
Mixed	124	44.0
Type of play		
Dramatic	93	33.0
Functional	114	40.0
Constructive	71	25.0
Duration in minutes		
1.5–5	115	41.0
6–9	77	27.5
10–14	54	19.0
15+	34	12.0

cooperation (the most complex) forms of collaboration. The mean score for imitation was the lowest, indicating that scores of imitation tended to be "none," "very small amount," or "less than half of the time." Cooperation tended to be scored low throughout the sample, but with more high scores than for imitation. However, no episode received the highest score for cooperation; that is, no group of children cooperated for the entire duration of the episode. Scores for reciprocal collaboration were evenly distributed throughout the sample. The social and joint attention dimensions of the intersubjectivity measure were normally distributed among the sample. However, the conflict dimension was found to be significantly negatively skewed, to the extent that there were almost no observations of conflict in the sample. This was therefore removed from further analysis.

Table 9.2 *Descriptive statistics of predictor and outcome variables.*

	Range	Mean	Standard deviation	Skewness
Intersubjectivity				
Social	5–20	12.85	4.01	0.038
Joint attention conflict	3–12	8.00	2.25	0.036
Collaboration				
Imitation	1–7	1.89	1.38	1.640*
Reciprocal	1–7	3.45	1.50	0.435
Cooperation	1–7	2.11	1.45	1.189*
Flexibility of areas				
Material flexibility	1–5	3.13	1.15	
Space flexibility	1–5	3.13	1.49	

*Significantly skewed to the left (majority of the sample scored on the lower end of the normal curve; i.e., 3 or below).

Relationship between Group Characteristics and Intersubjectivity

The findings showed that the dimension and level of intersubjectivity varied with group composition (gender/size) and play type. Smaller groups had more joint attention intersubjectivity, with the biggest difference existing between dyads and the largest groups. Girl-only groups had the highest degree of social/emotional intersubjectivity, differing the most from boy-only groups. Imaginative play groups scored significantly higher in social intersubjectivity than the other groups, and functional groups scored moderately higher than constructive groups on social intersubjectivity. On the other hand, imaginative play groups scored significantly lower than functional and constructive play groups on joint attention intersubjectivity. Interactions with higher joint attention and social-emotional intersubjectivity lasted longer regardless of group characteristics.

Relationship between Intersubjectivity and Collaborative Complexity

According to the formulation and hypothesis described here and in previous chapters, collaborative complexity emerges from intersubjectivity, with the two combined signifying collaborative competence. To support this theory, high levels of intersubjectivity should be consistently related to higher levels of collaborative complexity among interactive episodes. The results showed that social intersubjectivity was positively related to both reciprocal and cooperative collaborations and that joint attention intersubjectivity was negatively related to reciprocal collaborations only.

The role of context in shaping the relationships between intersubjectivity and collaboration must also be explored. The most distal environment that might have impacted the interaction variables was the classroom in which they occurred. There were significant differences between classrooms in joint attention and social intersubjectivity as well as in imitation and reciprocal forms of collaboration. The only interactive variable that did not differ between classrooms was the cooperative form of collaboration.

To understand what accounted for the between-classroom differences, the variables were compared within classrooms. The group composition and environmental variables were tested for their effects on the intersubjectivity and collaborative complexity variables. The results showed that each of the contextual variables except for gender composition contributed significantly to the between-classroom differences found in the interaction variables. The details are reported in Table 9.3.

More specifically, differences in the activity areas' flexibility of space and materials accounted for differences in intersubjectivity, imitation, and cooperative types of collaborative complexity. In other words, the flexibility of space and materials had a significant effect on all interaction variables

Table 9.3 *Multivariate analysis of covariance effects of contextual variables nested within classrooms on intersubjectivity and collaboration variables.*

Variable	Pillai's trace	F-statistic	Degrees of freedom
Classroom	0.2159	14.59***	5
Activity areas	0.3408	27.51***	5
Size	0.0505	2.84*	5
Gender	0.0050	0.27	5
Material flexibility	0.0971	5.72***	5
Space flexibility	0.0654	3.73**	5

*$p < 0.05$, **$p < 0.01$, ***$p < 0.000$.

except for reciprocal forms of collaboration. Classrooms with larger groups had greater levels of cooperation, whereas those with more material flexibility within activity areas had lower joint attention intersubjectivity, lower imitation, and higher cooperation. Classrooms with greater spatial flexibility within activity areas had lower joint attention intersubjectivity and higher cooperation. The full results are reported in Table 9.4.

Next, the analysis determined how interactions were affected by differences in activity areas across classrooms. Significant effects of all variables that differed between activity areas were found on all interaction variables except for social intersubjectivity. The specific effects of activity areas across classrooms were:

(1) Higher material flexibility was related to less imitation and less joint attention intersubjectivity, but more cooperation during play episodes.
(2) Higher spatial flexibility was related to more reciprocal and cooperative collaborations during play episodes.
(3) Larger groups had less joint attention intersubjectivity and more cooperative collaborations.

The full results of the models are reported in Table 9.5. The model explains 19 percent of the variance in the interaction variables.

The qualitative analysis provided in Chapters 4 and 7 is helpful for illustrating how the quantitative results function during play. For example, the following episode shows how a large group within a highly flexible environment is both collaboratively complex and has limited joint attention intersubjectivity during sociodramatic play:

> *Jorge circles around the "baby" talking loudly to no one in particular.*
> *Alessandro continues busily collecting materials from all over the classroom and piling them up beside the "baby."*
> *After a moment, Jorge approaches the other children to distribute the contents of a doctor's kit to each of them, saying, "The baby is sick, the baby is sick," "Give him medicine," "He needs a shot," alternating between Spanish and English.*
> *All four children simultaneously use the doctor's tools on the "baby" (another child), who begins crying loudly and squirming around.*
> *Jorge repeats his earlier refrain to quiet down.*
> *The children begin offering the "baby" the different foods that have been collected.*

Over the course of this episode, the children developed only brief moments of intersubjectivity among all of the members, and yet the shared activity was highly cooperative. The children participating in this episode spread

Table 9.4 Nested regressions for interaction variables by classroom characteristics.

	Social		Joint attention		Imitation		Reciprocal		Cooperation	
	b (SE)	t-ratio	b (SE)	t-ratio	b (SE)	t-ratio	b (SE)	t-ratio	b (SE)	t-ratio
R^2	0.24		0.10		0.18		0.03		0.04	
Classroom	5.71 (0.66)	8.65***	0.12 (0.39)	0.29	1.03 (0.24)	4.32***	−0.08 (0.28)	−0.27	0.08 (0.27)	0.32
Activity areas	−0.14 (0.01)	−9.53***	0.02 (0.01)	2.52*	−0.03 (0.01)	−4.84***	0.00 (0.01)	−1.23	−0.01 (0.01)	−2.25*
Size	0.11 (0.08)	1.27	−0.08 (0.05)	−1.68	0.02 (0.03)	0.49	0.03 (0.04)	0.76	0.07 (0.03)	1.98*
Gender	−0.09 (0.09)	−1.03	−0.04 (0.05)	−0.69	0.01 (0.03)	0.22	−0.01 (0.04)	0.42	−0.01 (0.04)	−0.17
Material	0.08 (0.06)	1.51	−0.07 (0.03)	−2.35*	−0.07 (0.02)	−3.67***	0.03 (0.02)	1.29	0.05 (0.02)	2.15*
Space	0.17 (0.06)	1.88	−0.07 (0.04)	−1.97*	0.01 (0.02)	0.483	0.03 (0.03)	1.26	0.06 (0.02)	2.39*

*p < 0.05, **p < 0.01, ***p < 0.000.

Table 9.5 Two-level model of the effect of activity area variables on interaction variables.

Fixed effect	Joint attention Coefficient (SE)	t-ratio	Imitation Coefficient (SE)	t-ratio	Reciprocal Coefficient (SE)	t-ratio	Cooperation Coefficient (SE)	t-ratio
Intercept (γ_{00})	7.98 (0.43)	18.59**	3.42 (0.27)	12.85***	3.24 (0.33)	9.97***	1.23 (0.36)	3.39***
Materials (γ_{01})	−0.23 (0.11)	−2.13*	−0.31 (0.07)	−4.58***			1.26 (0.07)	1.70**
Space (γ_{01})					0.18 (0.08)	2.30*	0.19 (0.08)	2.39*
Slope (γ_{10})	0.06 (0.02)	4.23***	−0.03 (0.01)	−4.21***	−0.02 (0.01)	−2.60*	−0.02 (0.01)	−1.99*
Size (γ_{11})	−0.01 (0.01)	−2.05*					0.01 (0.01)	1.89**

*p < 0.05, **p < 0.01, ***p < 0.000.

Note: Two-level models explained the variability in the slopes of the effects of activity areas on interactions.

out into different areas of the room, playing individually or in dyads, while still maintaining elements of the collaboratively constructed play theme. Toward the end of the episode, they reestablished intersubjectivity among all members as they came together to address their collectively construed task (soothing a crying baby). In this way, the spatial flexibility and large group size contributed to frequent lapses in intersubjectivity while simultaneously supporting a highly complex cooperative collaboration.

Lastly, the analysis revealed how the material and spatial flexibility of activity areas affected the relationship between intersubjectivity and collaborative complexity during play episodes. Across episodes, higher social-emotional intersubjectivity was shown to predict greater collaborative complexity, consistent with the theory of collaborative competence. The only significant relationship that was affected due to environmental flexibility was between joint attention intersubjectivity and reciprocal collaboration, with the former being negatively impacted by lower levels of the latter. Higher spatial flexibility weakened this relationship, in that groups were more likely to demonstrate reciprocal collaborations along with joint attention intersubjectivity within more flexible spatial environments than in less flexible spatial environments.

Collaborative Competence during Play

The findings suggest not only that children coordinate behavior with peers to varying extents during play but also that the type of behavior that is the focus of coordination varies with the type of shared activities in which children are engaged. For example, children participating in imaginative play coordinated their social, emotional, and conversational behavior, as evidenced by higher levels of social intersubjectivity during imaginative play as compared to during constructive and functional play. Children who were engaged in constructive play were more likely to have high levels of cognitive intersubjectivity based in joint attention and mutual focus. The methods of the present study demonstrated that collaborative competence requires social coordination that is tailored to both the social context of the interaction and the functional requirements of the shared play activity. This holistic view differs significantly from the definition of social competence as a set of skills that individual children bring to interactions. Instead, free play among preschoolers can be seen as a unique catalyst for collaborative competence as it emerges during a shared activity. Collaborative competence, as operationalized by the intersubjectivity and collaborative complexity measures, is thus a collective tool that extends children's shared activity during play.

Factor analysis of the intersubjectivity measure showed that the two language items were most strongly associated with the social items rather than with the attention items. Among the population assessed in the present study, the function of language was found to be primarily social and related strongly to shared emotion, eye contact, and other behaviors that connected the children socially and emotionally. Among episodes with high levels of joint attention intersubjectivity, the mutual focus on materials and tasks likely served as concrete referents to support children's nonverbal communication.

Characteristics of Play Episodes

Among the present sample of mixed-ethnicity, low-income preschoolers, the frequency and duration of play episodes are consistent with prior research (Weinberger & Starkey, 1994). For example, episodes of the shortest duration and of functional play were the most frequent. However, unlike prior research, the most socially complex play as defined by high levels of intersubjectivity was also the longest in duration. This finding may result from the present study's exclusive focus on interactive play episodes, whereas prior studies included the play of individual children. In the present study, once children got involved in a complex interaction with peers, they were able to sustain such play for an extended period. It is likely that high levels of intersubjectivity supported this ability.

Group Differences in Intersubjectivity

Differences in intersubjectivity found between groups suggest that the social composition and type of play relate to the dimensions of intersubjectivity. Groups made up exclusively of girls and groups that engaged predominantly in imaginative play were characterized by the highest levels of social intersubjectivity. This is consistent with research showing that girls are socialized to place more emphasis on social-emotional relating from a young age (Rose & Rudolph, 2006). In terms of play type, imaginative play has been shown to rely on verbal and social exchanges (Goncu et al., 2002), unlike play that is centered on materials, such as building with blocks, or on tasks, such as filling a bucket with sand or water (Rubin, 2001). Given that imaginative play interactions are based primarily in communication and social cohesion between children as opposed to play that is task-oriented, it makes sense that this type of play would engender a higher degree of social intersubjectivity than constructive or functional play.

Groups that were characterized as construction play groups and those that were smallest in size had the highest levels of joint attention intersubjectivity. Construction activities require sustained attention to the goal of the activity and the steps necessary to complete it. Therefore, it is reasonable to expect that interactions focused on constructive play would be associated with higher degrees of joint attention than those focused on the other types of play.

Contrary to prior research, larger groups showed more cooperation in the present study. This divergence from the literature was likely based in methodological differences, wherein prior research compared individual children's play behaviors with other measures (often via teacher report) of their social competence. Arguably, the relationship between what types of play groups individual children select and their performance on social competence measures may not relate to measures of emergent co-constructed group collaboration as described in the present study.

The findings showed that although girl-only groups had more imaginative play with higher social intersubjectivity than boy-only groups, gender composition had no significant impact on overall differences between classrooms in the degree of intersubjectivity or collaborative complexity variables. This finding suggests that although play type differs by gender composition and that levels of each intersubjectivity dimension differ by play type, the gender composition of groups does not explain differences in collaborative competence between episodes. This differs from prior research showing a positive effect of same-gender play groups on social complexity (Brownell et al., 2006). This prior study was done with a middle-class sample of young children using individual focal child measures of social complexity. Beyond the methodological differences discussed earlier, these findings suggest that gender might not function in the same way during play among different populations of children. Smaller groups were found to engage in more reciprocal and imitative collaborations. Given that these types of collaboration are characterized by social exchanges between group members, groups of five to six children might have been too large to maintain the participants' focus on social exchanges.

Interobjectivity and Intersubjectivity within Collaborative Competence

The functioning of the larger, highly cooperative groups can be understood through the concept of interobjectivity (Latour, 1996). Interobjectivity exists in a dialectical relationship to intersubjectivity. The latter is defined by interactive mutuality, synchrony, and reciprocity among participants that is focused on interpersonal dynamics. Interobjectivity, on the other hand, describes a group-level focus on the sharing of goals and objectives around common tools, activities, and situations (Latour, 1996; Talamo & Pozzi, 2011).

The qualitative analysis of the present study's subsample found that larger groups were more focused on shared goals in relation to the materials, space, and activity than triads and dyads (Garte, 2016). The following segment from one of these examples shows how the collective focus on a common goal for an activity was necessary for the development of interobjectivity-based collaborative competence:

> *Josh begins trying to rebuild the "bridge" using the same structure he did the first time.*
>
> MALCOLM: *watching Josh, says: "We have to make it so people don't knock it down."*
> JOSH: *"Cars need to go."*
> MALCOLM: *"They keep knocking it down," then, as he grabs two big column blocks, "We need these ones."*
>
> *Malcolm takes the columns to the inner corner of the block area and begins building a different type of structure.*
> *Josh follows him at first but soon returns to his previous position in the area playing with cars.*

This sequence shows an attempt to establish shared meaning and synchrony through a verbal exchange of ideas. However, with the focus on individual actions with materials, no shared meaning or intersubjectivity took shape.

> *Sarah and Mary reenter the area and join Josh in playing with cars.*
> *The three of them play with each of their cars near each other but without interacting.*

This signifies the potential for interobjectivity to develop through a shared focus and common use of materials. Yet, there is no collective activity and only brief joint attention. At this point, moments of collaboration based in imitation occur. This period of interaction reflects functional associative play.

> *Meanwhile, the structure made by Malcolm has gotten tall. The other three children see this and gather around it.*
> *Mary adds to Malcolm's structure using the small column blocks as she did in her earlier building.*
> *Malcolm takes each of her blocks down, saying "No, we need the big ones."*

> Mary goes to the shelf and brings back a big block saying, "Look I found one."
> Sarah, who has been driving her car over the structure, knocks down the columns. She quickly begins rebuilding the pieces and is joined by the other children who rebuild the structure together with highly coordinated actions.

Malcolm's structure triggers interobjectivity through the shared engagement in a collective activity with a common goal. This allows for coordinated actions characterized by high degrees of synchrony in relation to a shared task and mutual focus. Throughout this cooperative collaboration, the focus is outward on the shared task, materials, and goals (interobjective) rather than on interpersonal dynamics. This example is contrasted with a dyad using the highly structured material of a puzzle:

> The girls resume simultaneously taking pieces in and out. Another piece is matched by Zaria.
> Jessica smiles at the match and says, "Yeah," nodding her head.
> The girls take turns placing the other pieces, this time slowly and watching each other's placement before placing their own.
> After a while, Jessica begins banging two of her pieces together and laughing. Zaria does not respond to her and continues placing pieces.
> Jessica soon rejoins Zaria and takes turns placing the remaining pieces until the puzzle is completed.

This reciprocal collaboration with an inflexible material is primarily based in social intersubjectivity. Jessica's desire to use the puzzle pieces other than how they were intended is abandoned in favor of maintaining social intersubjectivity with Zaria. In this case, it is the focus on interpersonal dynamics that determines the collective goal and meaning of the activity via social intersubjectivity rather than an outwards focus on the task or material itself. This helps explain why high degrees of joint attention intersubjectivity that are focused on tasks and materials rather than social exchanges relate to lower levels of reciprocal collaboration.

Finally, a dyad working with a highly flexible material demonstrates components of both social and joint attention intersubjectivity during a highly cooperative collaboration:

> Julio mixes water in a bowl using a strand of plastic, stringy material.
> Marco walks up to the water table and bends over, looking up into Julio's face closely. He then points at the bowl and makes a stirring gesture, saying, "Alli, alli" (like this, like this).
> Julio smiles up at Marco and holds out the string in his direction.
> Julio reaches into the table and produces a much larger piece of the material, which he shows to Marco
> Marco smiles widely at Julio and the string; Julio matches his expression.

Here, the collective goal of a shared activity emerges through a combination of high social intersubjectivity and high joint attention intersubjectivity. The flexibility of the materials supports mutual exploration and joint attention and the dyadic group size supports social/emotional attunement.

> *Marco inspects the string, holding it up as Julio begins "plucking" it with a shovel.*
>
> *The two boys explore the material simultaneously, taking hold of large sections, pulling them apart, dividing the strings, dropping and scrunching them.*
>
> *While exploring, the two boys make eye contact, smile at each other, and nod whenever the other boy tries a new use of the material.*
>
> *Together they push the string into a bucket filled with water. Marco says in Spanish: "Drown it," then, "Now let's cut it."*
>
> *After some experimentation, they find it can be "cut" with the shovel while held taut.*
>
> *Both boys begin to "cut" their own pieces of string with the other water table materials.*

The combination of a highly flexible material with a high level of synchrony supports the collective exploration of innovative uses of the material. The catalyst and foundation for the activity was a combination of high social-emotional and joint attention intersubjectivity, which led to a highly cooperative collaboration.

Both the foursome with the blocks and the water table dyad had highly cooperative collaborations that produced something new as a result of collective efforts (a structure and a string game). However, the larger group's synchrony was based in an interobjective focus on shared tasks and use of materials, whereas the dyad's synchrony was based in an intersubjective focus on each other. Regardless of the primarily inner or outer focus, cooperative collaborations require high degrees of social-emotional and/or joint attention intersubjectivity to sustain their complexity. The findings of this study are consistent with prior research that shows that group members experience greater and lesser periods of coordination and joint focus during collaboration (Kozlowski & Bell, 2003; Robinson et al., 2003; Talamo & Pozzi, 2011). The positive relationship found between the synchrony-based measure of social–emotional intersubjectivity and all forms of collaboration is consistent with a previous study showing that dyads who experienced experimentally induced synchrony during an initial task demonstrated higher degrees of matched emotion and cooperation in a separate joint task than children who did not experience synchrony (Tunçgenç & Cohen, 2018).

The Impact of Context on Collaboration

Classroom-level differences affected all types of intersubjectivity and collaborative complexity except for cooperation, whereas activity areas had the greatest impact on cooperation. Children who engaged in cooperation the most complex and intense form were influenced by proximal factors that directly influenced the nature of interactions while being impervious to more indirect factors at the classroom level. Highly flexible activity areas were more likely to have groups of five to six children as opposed to smaller groups. The larger groups within the more flexible activity areas showed the highest levels of cooperation. Reciprocal collaborations require proximity and social monitoring among group members to allow for social exchanges. Therefore, cooperative collaborations are supported in highly flexible environments via "interobjectivity," as indicated by high degrees of joint attention intersubjectivity, whereas reciprocal collaborations are supported primarily by social intersubjectivity.

Conclusion

This chapter empirically tested the operationalization of young children's collaborative competence as emergent during peer play. The dual goal of this research, as outlined in Chapter 1, was to discover elements of collaborative processes that relate to group-level competence and to detail the contextual factors that contribute to collaborative competence during interaction. The findings discussed here provide new insights in both areas. The methodological principles used were consistent with culturally inclusive assumptions about how children demonstrate competencies at a collective level. This made it possible to show systematic relationships between components of interactions, intergroup functioning, and environmental variables.

Preexisting conceptualizations of social and play skills often reflect a pervasive individualistic bias in measures of psychological development. Research using the interaction as the unit of analysis for both the independent and dependent variables has produced innovative results (Kumpulainen & Kaartinen, 2003; Nieminen et al., 2022; Ricca et al., 2020; Yuill, 2021). As documented in this study, using the interaction as the unit of analysis provides directly observable processes of development rather than requiring researchers to infer internal mechanisms of individual functioning. This methodological approach reduces bias in measurement and increases validity. The operationalization of SAE intersubjectivity extends upon research that includes nonverbal contingent forms of relating along with the contingency of conversational turns (De Jaeger et al., 2016, 2017; Rakoczy, 2006; Schindler & Bakker, 2020). Such measures can capture the ways in which intersubjectivity functions more broadly than narrower definitions.

Given that the measures and results of this study are all tied to interactions rather than individuals, the implications must also be for the support of children in groups and support for interactions rather than interventions aimed at individual skill-building. Many psychologists and educators will find this challenging. We are so accustomed to assuming that the problem and the solution lie in individual skills, strengths, and deficits that it is hard to imagine a collective lens being applied so thoroughly to issues of psychological development. Yet, in school, children are rarely if ever alone. Although they may complete some individual work, this work is often an extension of a whole-group or small-group lesson. Although not fully explored in this chapter, the role of adults during free play as well as during more structured small-group activities should be investigated. In addition, multiple layers of the sociocultural and historical activity contexts in which children play and learn can and should be measured and investigated.

In the early elementary grades, teachers are constantly facilitating back-and-forth exchanges to promote children's learning. The study described in the following chapter shows how collaborative learning among early elementary-aged children can be researched according to the same methodological principles applied here.

Finally, by recognizing the importance of collaborative competence, teachers can be supported to use group interactions more effectively. Focusing on group-level competencies naturally highlights an area of strength for children who are typically referred to as "at risk," namely children from majority world cultural backgrounds, those whose parents have had little Western education, and those who are learning English in school. This pedagogical focus may lead to a broader valuing of collective ideals within the classroom, a shift in values that would more closely align with majority world racial and cultural groups than the current individualistic norms that define most of Western schooling. This shift could be an important factor in promoting the education and development of children who comprise a majority of public elementary school attendees. Indeed, by shifting methods of assessment to consider the collective as the unit of analysis more often, the strengths rather than the deficits of these populations might be highlighted for the first time in American education.

CHAPTER 10

Collaborative Competence during Early Elementary Playful Learning Activities

The purpose of this chapter is to apply principles of ideal collaborations to evaluate collaborative competence within the context of playful learning activities during early elementary school. This method is designed to demonstrate how collaborative competence as theorized in this volume functions during interactions that are more structured than free play. The relative roles of dialogue, materials, and student and teacher interactive dynamics are shown to differentially impact shared conceptual understandings and collective meaning-making. Extending empirical measures of collaborative competence into elementary school will create a framework for both research and practice to promote collaborative interactions for learning beyond preschool. Defining those group behaviors and dynamics that comprise ideal interactions will guide group-level pedagogical goals to the same extent that goals for individual learning and development have long driven educational research and practice.

This chapter attempts to synthesize methodologies from the study of collaborative cognition, dialogic education, and play-based pedagogy to provide a developmentally and culturally valid method for assessing collaborative competence among early elementary-aged students. As described in Chapter 7, the method was designed to analyze small-group interactions that include a mixture of child-directed and teacher-supported collaborative activities with a teacher-guided content focus. The observations selected for analysis focus on first graders and the teaching of two science concepts: "properties" and water filtration. The teachers use a combination of exploratory dialogue and hands-on experimentation to attempt to teach these concepts; however, the use of didactic instruction is very limited.

Measuring Collaborative Competence during Small-Group Pedagogical Activities

The previous chapters have shown how the ways in which researchers frame interactive data – what is included for analysis and how it is measured – have major impacts on how interactions are viewed and what conclusions are drawn from the results. This contention is supported by a large-scale literature review of coding schemes for classroom dialogue (Hennessy et al., 2020). This review suggests that, when analyzing pedagogical interactions, decisions about the level to code (micro, meso, or macro), the segment to code (turns, utterances, or word frequency), and the degree of nonverbal context to provide all impact the meaning that the analysis uncovers. This determines the implications that can be drawn regarding how different forms of talk affect student learning.

The intersubjectivity coding from different theoretical orientations detailed in Chapter 4 suggests that when analyzing interactions for the purpose of drawing conclusions about their patterns and meanings, a guideline for how much to include from the interaction and surrounding context can be stated as: "More is more." Consistent with the methodological principles outlined earlier in this section, measures should aim to get as close to the stream of interaction in its naturally occurring state as possible. The more distinct the analytic categories from the observed behavior, the more the lens of the researcher – their theoretical orientations, implicit biases, and cultural norms – influences the meanings that are assigned to interactive behavior and dialogue. In addition, details of the context in which the interaction occurs are crucial to grasping their meanings. However, without some reduction of data into theoretical categories, analysis is impossible. Similarly, interactive behavior must be assessed within a framework for analysis in order to draw conclusions. The analytical method for making sense of interactive data should therefore establish a balance between data reduction and providing enough naturalistic contextual information that the interactions can be understood on their own terms.

This chapter combines dialogic approaches to assessing collaborative complexity with nonverbal sociocultural activity-based embodied (SAE) dimensions that indicate intersubjectivity. Specifically, enacted intersubjectivity that includes the domains of nonverbal affective synchrony and mutual coordination of attention along with indicators of shared meaning and mutual adaptation comprise the elements of collaborative competence apart from dialogic components. The Scheme for Educational Dialogue

Analysis (SEDA), developed by Hennesy et al. (2020), provides coding schemes for teacher and child talk that emphasize the importance of exploratory or dialogic forms of communication for student learning. Indeed, numerous studies, as reviewed in prior chapters, show correlations between such talk and student achievement, in terms of both individual and group collective learning. More specifically, members of the SEDA research team have defined the following three key elements of dialogue as most crucial for improving student outcomes: building on ideas, invitations to build on ideas, and challenging or questioning ideas respectfully (Vrikki et al., 2019).

Therefore, the coding scheme used to measure collaborative competence during playful learning activities in early elementary school includes elements of the SEDA that have been significantly related to learning gains. This combination of dialogic, intersubjective, and collaborative indicators of collaborative competence can be applied to a broad range of interactions.

Drawing on the previous literature reviewed thus far, the most crucial decisions that must be made regarding observational methods include: determining the unit of analysis; deciding which types of behavior to code at which levels; and deciding how to reduce the data of the behavioral stream into manageable segments for analysis. This chapter charts a preliminary course for how to measure collaborative competence during small-group learning activities in early elementary school. The coding scheme is applied to three video-recorded small-group, teacher-guided activities that are child centered and include elements of play-based and dialogic pedagogy.

Unit of Analysis

As has been argued throughout this text, to capture the full range of collaborative dynamics, the unit of analysis should be the interaction. The definition of what comprises an interactive unit is informed by the concepts of "learning as a fluid ensemble," the SAE operationalization of intersubjectivity, and the constructs of distributed or collaborative cognition. The other consideration necessary for determining the unit of analysis is differentiating between macro- and micro-level measurement. The collaborative competence measure includes both a micro-level indicator of intersubjectivity and a macro-level indicator of collaborative complexity. These measures were applied to preschoolers' naturally occurring peer play without any teacher involvement. The present activity context is small-group explorations that are guided by a teacher and toward specific conceptual learning. Consistent with the methodological principles laid out previously in this section, the dimensions of the construct must reflect the particular context of the interaction – its goals, structure, and participants. In this case, the context now includes dialogic exchanges as focal points of analysis – especially those of teacher–student conversations.

Interactions among Early Elementary School Children

Kindergarten through second grade children have been shown to benefit from play-based learning (Portier et al., 2019; Weisberg et al., 2013). Despite being more capable with language than preschoolers, these older children continue to have limited perspective-taking ability and to require concrete experiences to make sense of ideas (Piaget, 1971). They also have limited control of attention and information processing and therefore benefit from activities that are directly and personally meaningful to themselves and relate to their own experience. Given these developmental traits, teachers facilitating learning experiences with this age group should adhere to the principles of exploratory talk while also supporting elements of children's play. As introduced in Chapter 7, the data that will be analyzed in this chapter are drawn from examples of first grade collaborative activities designed to teach science concepts through a mixture of dialogic and experiential engagement with shared materials. Although there is not a specifically delineated outcome measure to determine the extent of learning, the coding scheme is designed to determine the extent to which children demonstrate collaborative competence through dialogue and intersubjective engagement with the activity, their peers, and the teacher.

Dialogue

Dialogue can be coded with two different foci in early elementary pedagogical interactions. From a teacher's perspective, dialogue should serve two purposes. The first is to sustain collaborative engagement among the children with their interacting partners. This will ideally occur by following the principles of the CoEnact framework, (Yuill, 2021). The teacher acts as a facilitator to maintain group engagement, attention, contingency, and shared control. Specific "talk moves" used for this purpose include directing children to one another's contributions, asking for elaborations, and open-ended questioning (Hennesy et al., 2020; Vrikki et al., 2019).

The second purpose of coding dialogue is to determine the extent to which exploratory talk encourages children's critical thinking about content and concepts. This involves assessing the degree to which teachers embed vocabulary, scaffold reasoning, make connections between related ideas, and connect students' personal experiences to observations and known facts, as well as activating their prior knowledge and personal connections to content. These elements are equally relevant for coding student dialogue, with the added code for students of building on each other's ideas. Therefore, student dialogue provides both a process and an outcome measure of the extent to which students are learning over the course of the activity.

Social Coordination and Synchrony

In addition to dialogue, children use various nonverbal behaviors to signify the extent of their engagement and mutual coordination with their interacting partners and between themselves, the group, and the central activity. As elaborated in previous chapters, signs of social-emotional cohesion and synchrony include eye contact and mutual positive emotional expression, and joint attention signifies mutual engagement with shared materials. In addition, coordinating actions with one another and engaging in a common activity with equal participation indicate both intersubjectivity and collaborative complexity. Each of these items can be coded separately from dialogue by observing the extent to which children's actions with materials and tasks and their nonverbal communication and coordination with one another are reciprocal and mutually adaptive.

Shared Meaning

The closest approximation of an outcome variable in the following investigation is the measure of shared meaning or understanding. This indicator represents children demonstrating a collective understanding of the meanings of the common activity. Verbal and nonverbal mutual behaviors that demonstrate a new collective understanding of the meaning of the activity may be observed to determine whether this has occurred. This indicator of shared understanding should include both intersubjective and dialogic elements, as defined in the respective measures.

To test the applicability of this definition of collaborative competence to early elementary pedagogical activities, codes assessing the dimensions described earlier were applied to three video-recorded interactions.

Rather than testing linear relationships between aspects of the interaction and learning outcomes, the purpose of this exploration is to discover patterns of relationship between different elements of interaction: forms of teacher talk in relation to child behavior and the influence of different elements of the activity context on the collaborative competence that develops over the duration of the activity. More specifically, the coded interactions will be explored to address the following research questions:

(1) Does the nature of the dialogue change according to a change in the materials and/or children if the teacher is the same?
(2) How does teacher use of exploratory talk relate to children's use of exploratory talk?
(3) How do teacher's and children's references to internal states relate to exploratory talk?
(4) Is there a difference in intersubjectivity and exploratory talk between time segments of the activity – namely, introduction, exploration/application, and conclusion?

Each of these questions will be addressed via an initial exploration of the three videos. This preliminary analysis will be used to suggest future methods for assessing collaborative competence among early elementary school children and to establish formal coding procedures that will improve inter-rater reliability. A larger-scale investigation would include analysis at both the micro and macro levels. However, this preliminary exploration will focus on establishing micro-level codes. The micro level should enable analysis of two major components: nonverbal intersubjectivity and dialogic exchanges. The codes for joint attention to materials, eye contact, and mutual positive emotion from the preexisting intersubjectivity measure described earlier in this section will be used. The teachers' interactive behaviors are coded for intersubjectivity along with those of the children. In addition, to reflect the CoEnact framework and include concepts of synchrony and enactive coordination, codes entitled "children coordinate actions with one another," "coordinate activity," and "equally participate in shared task/activity" will be added to the intersubjectivity measure. Each of these codes has a slightly different emphasis (see the codebook provided in Table 7.1). The dialogic component will include indicators of exploratory talk used by all group members, including the teacher; however, each code is specific to either teachers or children, as defined in the codebook. This allows the dialogue codes to simultaneously indicate frequencies of teacher versus student talk. The only exception to this is the internal state code. This is the only item that is based on text frequency. Words associated with internal states were identified via a text search query and do not distinguish between speakers. In addition, the teacher directing peers to one another and peers responding to one another are added, as well as a code for demonstrating a shared meaning of the activity.

Procedure for Analysis of Videos

The adults in the videos were student teachers nearing the end of a semester-long practicum. Their activities had been preplanned in consultation with the classroom mentor teacher and using a template provided by their professor. Transcripts A1 and A2 featured the same student teacher teaching the same concept to different children and with slightly different materials, approximately two weeks apart. Transcript B1, previewed in Chapter 7, featured a student teacher from a different year paired with the same mentor cooperating teacher within the same classroom. This activity focused on a different concept within the same subject area, with different children and materials. Given that these student teachers were completing teacher training under the same mentor teacher, despite the two videos being recorded a year apart, the broader curriculum and the classroom environment were the same for both student teachers featured in the videos.

The videos were transcribed and the transcriptions along with the videos were entered into *NVivo 12*. The transcripts were each coded separately for exploratory talk and intersubjectivity. Code queries in *NVivo 12* were used to analyze the transcripts for the degree to which specific forms of exploratory talk were used. In addition, by using matrix coding and proximity coding, it was possible to identify when codes overlapped or occurred in a sequence. This was most useful for identifying the relationship between teacher and student exploratory talk. The first set of results compares dialogue within and between videos based on the analysis of transcripts. The second set includes a visual depiction of all of the codes as they occurred in real time within each video.

The full transcripts of Teacher A's episodes are provided in the following, which is followed by the answers to the questions:

Transcript A1: Total time: six minutes, verbal and nonverbal behaviors are depicted as coded from the videotape.

TEACHER: *So, do you guys know where clean water comes from?*
STUDENT 1: *Uhm I think it comes from places where people getting from, like lakes and then they clean it.*
TEACHER: *They do . . . does everyone agree with that?*
STUDENTS: *[shake head] Yes.*
Students and teacher talking overlap.
STUDENT 2: *And, and some.*
TEACHER: *Do you think they have to do something special to the water?*
STUDENT 3: *Maybe they like spill like a liquid in there so it can go back to the pee of the fish and all the stuff in the water.*
TEACHER: *Do you know what that's called? All that garbage, all that stuff that's in the water?*
STUDENT 3: *Stew?*
TEACHER: *It's called pollution.*
STUDENT 1 *excitedly raises hand: Yeah pollution! Pollution is garbage.*
STUDENT 2: *If you get some water in the garbage, it will . . .*
STUDENT 3: *So my mom got a video on her cellphone that was showing you a lot of garbage was in the sea, a lot, a lot.*
TEACHER: *Yes, so another way that we can clean the water is with a water filter.*
STUDENT 3: *Ooh, ooh [raising hand excitedly].*
Teacher and Student 3 overlapping.
TEACHER: *Do you have a water filter at home?*
STUDENT 3: *I have a filter for my fishtank, actually three water filters.*
TEACHER: *Who else has seen a water filter?*
STUDENT 2: *Well I had a water filter but it broke so we got a new one and we also used, like we put water in it, then we pour it, like a gallon.*
TEACHER: *So what happened when your water filter broke? Were you able to get clean water?*
Teacher, Students 2 and 3 talk overlapping.
TEACHER: *Yes, draw what you think a water filter is.*
STUDENT 3: *I'm just gonna draw the tubes.*
TEACHER: *[While students are drawing] I'm just going to show you guys something, be careful because I cut the top so it's a little sharp*
Puts a two-liter soda bottle cut in half on the table.
STUDENT 1: *I have an idea [takes the "filter part" out of the bottle], I see this really, it's not really cut.*
Teacher puts a small bottle of cloudy water on the table next to the "filter."
TEACHER: *This is dirty water, we're gonna try to clean this. How do you think you can use this [the bottle filter] to clean this water? What do you think a water filter needs?*
STUDENT 2: *Uhm, it needs some . . . like kind of or some thing that can.*

TEACHER: *Like something that can absorb . . . the nasty stuff.*
STUDENT 2: *Yeah like, I think when they bring the tubes into the water, and there's an opening and when it pours [using hands to demonstrate] it makes the pollution go into that tube and then the water that's clean now goes through the tube and . . .*
Teacher brings a bag of cotton balls to put on the table.
TEACHER: *So I have something here now, do you think you guys could use something like this, if we put it in here [pointing into the bottle filter], it will absorb the nasty stuff.*
STUDENT 2: *[Talk overlapping excitedly] Oh yeah, because cotton balls, they like get water.*
TEACHER: *Yeah, it's called absorption, absorbing is when something picks out another substance.*
STUDENT 4: *I don't want to touch that water.*
TEACHER: *It's ok, you don't have to touch the water, do you want to help with putting in the cotton balls?*
Students all nod yes.
TEACHER: *How many cotton balls do you think we should put in?*
STUDENT 1: *Ten.*
TEACHER: *Ten? OK.*
Students each take a handful of cotton balls from the bag.
TEACHER: *Put in as many cotton balls as you think we need.*
TEACHER: *Do you think this is enough? Do you think we need anything else?*
STUDENT 3: *Maybe something that [demonstrating with hands] sucks up.*
STUDENT 2: *Maybe a vacuum.*
Teacher asks students fill the filter with cotton balls.
TEACHER: *Let's see, let's see if cotton balls are enough to clean the dirty water.*
STUDENTS: *[Talking unintelligible]*
TEACHER takes "dirty water."
TEACHER: *This is just water with oil in it, you know the kind of oil you use to cook? Who wants to help me pour it.*
Student 2 helps.
EVERYONE: *Ooh, it's turning yellow [all are bending closely toward the water filter, watching intently].*
TEACHER: *Look up here, look at this – what color is this now?*
STUDENT 1: *So I know why the cotton balls are yellow on the top.*
TEACHER: *So up here? What do you think is happening?*
STUDENTS 1, 2, and 3: *It's yeah. The oil . . . [overlapping talking].*
Student 4 helps pour, the other students watch the inside of the filter.
STUDENT 2: *Ooh, ooh, it's coming out – clean water.*
TEACHER: *You see clean water?*
STUDENTS: *[Unintelligible]*
TEACHER: *Do you see all this stuff on the top?*
Student 4 finishes pouring the water in.

STUDENT 4: *Ooh, clean water.*
TEACHER: *So what do you guys observe here?*
STUDENT 1: *I see ... the dirty water, the cotton balls were yellow, and it stopped [pointing at the bottom of the filter with the clean water], the cotton balls blocked the dirty water so it could be clear.*
TEACHER: *Do you guys think we might need something else to clean this water?*
STUDENT 2: *I think we need some more water, how 'bout lets pour some clean water.*
TEACHER: *What if the water had pieces of garbage in it?*
STUDENT 1: *Oh I have an idea.*
TEACHER: *Do you think the cotton balls would be able to stop the garbage or would we need something else?*

The students did not respond to the last question and the activity ended.

The second transcript is depicted with time stamps according to when each utterance occurred in the videotape. Only verbal content is presented.

Transcript A2: Total time: 4 minutes and 45 seconds.

Speaker	Time	Content
Teacher	00:01	How do we get clean water, do you guys know? What do you guys know about clean water?
Child	00:02	We have to filter it.
Teacher	00:03	How come we have to filter it?
Child	00:05	Like we have to ... and it's still not very clean.
Teacher	00:15	Yeah, right so we're gonna try to make – we have this today and we also have gravel, what do you think the gravel can do to the water? Remember what happened with the cotton balls last time? Do you want to tell your friends what happened with the cotton balls?
Child	00:30	We put the cotton balls here and then we put the yucky water here and then it came out in the funnel over here because it did not look like clean.
Teacher	00:45	Does the water look clean?
Children	00:46	No ...
Teacher	00:48	No, right? So what do you think we should add to our water filter? You think it will make it clean? What should we put first? What do you think will make it clean?
Child	00:55	Put the cotton balls and then, and then.
Teacher	00:58	How come? How come should we put the cotton balls first?
Children	01:01	I don't know, maybe to filter ...
Teacher	01:02	To filter them? So let's all try to put the cotton balls first?
Children	01:03	Yeah.
Teacher	01:04	We will try the cotton balls first. What do you think the cotton balls will do?
Children	01:05	Um, well, they're gonna get clean the water.

(cont.)

Speaker	Time	Content
Teacher	01:07	How? How will they make it clean? Do you guys know what that's called? What is it going to do to the water – the cotton balls?
Children	01:08	I don't know.
Teacher	01:09	It's gonna absorb, it's gonna absorb the nasty stuff.
Child	01:10	What does that mean?
Teacher	01:12	Absorb means to suck out – to take away, like a sponge, you guys know what a sponge is?
Children	01:28	Yeah.
Teacher	01:31	No don't put that much we need room for our gravel remember? Do you guys think we should add in our rocks? Don't put too much.
Child	01:34	Don't put too much! Is that much good?
Teacher	01:38	I think that's good . . . Do you think we should add some gravel to it?
Children	01:49	Yeah, yeah. Can I pour it?
Teacher	01:50	We're gonna put a little bit.
Teacher	01:57	Really, really tiny, really tiny . . . We're gonna pour it in, we're actually gonna pour it, help me pour it in, let's see what happens when we pour it in . . . Careful, careful . . . let's see . . .
Child	02:00	It feels good.
Teacher	02:01	It feels good?
Child	02:02	Can I test it?
Teacher	02:03	You wanna test it out – see how well our filter works?
Child	02:21	Yeah.
Teacher	02:22	OK.
Child	02:23	Can you just put the water in? The yucky water in?
Child	02:29	Put the yucky water in.
Teacher	02:38	OK, who wants to try putting the yucky water first?
Children	02:39	Me! Me!
Teacher	02:50	OK, try – let's see what happens . . .
Children	02:51	Ew . . .
Teacher	02:52	Let's just give it a minute.
Teacher	02:56	Let's see what happens – is the water coming out yet? Do you think we put too much?
Child	02:58	It's absorbing the yucky water.
Teacher	02:59	Who else wants to try putting in the water?
Children	03:12	Me! Me!
Teacher	03:13	OK . . . Put it . . .
Child	03:20	It's dripping a little bit.
Child	03:30	I wanna also put it in . . . Can I put it in?
Teacher	03:44	You can try. Do you see the water coming out?
Child	03:58	It's clean! It's clean.
Teacher	04:04	You think so? We're gonna see right now. You wanna try, Cielo? Let's let Cielo do it.
Children	04:05	Woah, it's getting clean.

(cont.)

Speaker	Time	Content
Teacher	04:06	You think so? Let's see, let's give it a minute ... What does the water look like?
Children	04:07	Cleeean ... cleeeean ... Can we drink that water? Can we drink that water?
Teacher	04:08	Nooo [laughing], you can't drink that water. This is just the first part of filtering. First we have to get all that yucky stuff out. Do you think we should add something else to the filter to make it even more clean or do you guys think we have enough?
Child	04:11	Yeah ... salt.
Teacher	04:12	Salt? [Laughing] ... So what do you guys think happened? Tell me what happened? What did we do? What did we do?
Child	04:27	First we put in cotton balls ...
Teacher	04:28	Ummhmm, cotton balls.
Child	04:29	Then we poured in.
Teacher	04:30	Gravel ...
Child	04:31	Yeah gravel ... then we poured in the water.
Teacher	04:32	OK, what happened to the water?
Child	04:33	Then it got like a little bit more clean.
Teacher	04:34	A little more clean? How come? What did the cotton balls and the gravel do?
Child	04:35	It just get off, get off the yucky things.

Do the Types of Exploratory Talk Change Because of a Change to the Materials and/or Children If the Teacher Is the Same?

There was a difference in exploratory talk codes between the activities with Teacher A. In Activity A1, without the extra material of gravel, the most common utterances were children's "content connection" at 8.5 percent, followed by teacher "eliciting ideas" at 8.0 percent. In Activity A2, with extra materials, the most common utterances were teacher "eliciting ideas" at 16 percent, followed by teacher "prompting for elaboration" at 12 percent. Children's highest-frequency utterance was "content connection" at 5 percent. Overall, the proportion of child talk to teacher talk was higher in the first video, with fewer materials. Figures 10.1 and 10.2 show the frequencies of exploratory talk in Teacher A's Activities A1 and A2.

Collaborative Competence during Early Elementary Playful 189

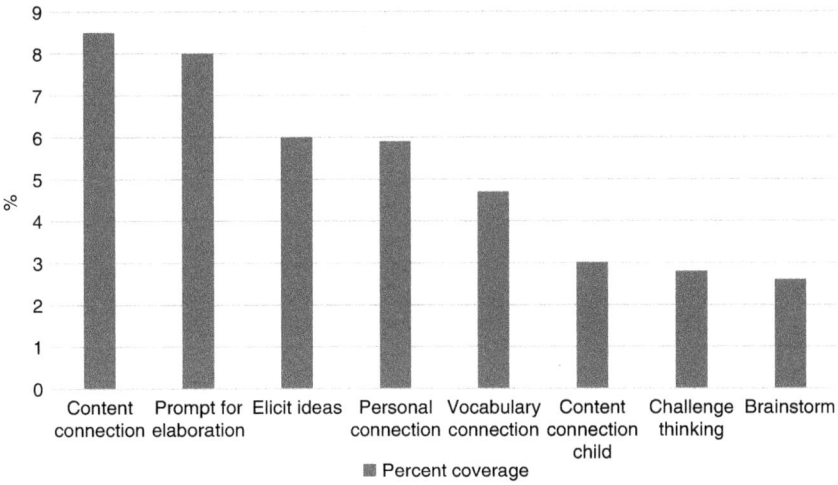

Figure 10.1 Teacher A's Activity A1 – frequency of dialogue.

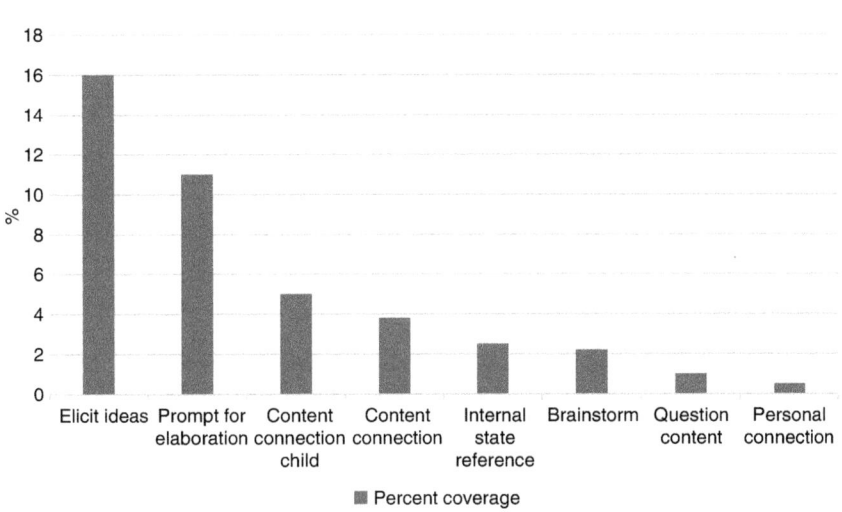

Figure 10.2 Teacher A's Activity A2 – frequency of dialogue.

The following is the full transcript of dialogue between children and Teacher B, which is presented with the time stamps of when the statements were made over the course of the 15-minute video recording.

Speaker	Time	Content
Teacher	00:26	So we're scientists and we're going to an experiment with the Play-Doh and the clay and the Doh that I showed you guys earlier that I got for the science area and before I start I need to ask you a very big and important question: Does one of you know what it can mean or have you ever heard of the word "property"? Uh, Mako?
Child	01:02	Uhm ... its like – your stuff.
Teacher	01:03	Your stuff, yes it can be like your personal belongings.
Child	01:04	A property is like a place, like in something that you rent.
Teacher	01:05	Yes, it can be someplace that you are.
Child	01:06	It can be like your house.
Teacher	01:28	Yes, your house.
Teacher	01:30	So if you think of all those things that you just mentioned, those are things that people own, right? All those kind of things you have. So Doh and clay kind of have properties in them kind of like things that they own or have. So before going to start off, so properties are different qualities of an object. It could be like its color, its texture, its weight. It could be other things and properties help us identify the kind of materials that we're seeing or touching right? So we're going to today, we're going to identify the properties of clay and some before we sort of I'm going to give you guys a little piece of each of them. You can feel the texture of it before we start.
Child	02:31	It's sticky.
Teacher	02:32	It's sticky?
Child	02:33	It's hard.
Teacher	02:34	It's hard? Those are kind of like the two words that describe it right, see that's the clay.
Child	02:35	And squishy
Teacher	02:38	And squishy?
Child	02:41	This time of when.
Child	02:50	And you can take it apart and put it back together.
Teacher	02:51	You can take it apart and put it back together, kind of different from other things, right? 'Cause this table you can't do that with it right, it's a different material.
Teacher	03:06	What about the Doh, do you think it would feel the same?
Child	03:10	No.
Teacher	03:11	Or do you think it will feel different?
Child	03:13	The same.
Teacher	03:14	You think it will feel the same?
Child	03:15	With that?
Teacher	03:22	That's the Play-Doh.
Child	03:23	No, it feels different, different.

(cont.)

Speaker	Time	Content
Teacher	03:24	It feels different? How?
Child	03:25	It's soft and it's something and it's squishier.
Teacher	03:26	One at a time, and it's squishier than the?
Child	03:29	Than the green clay.
Teacher	03:30	Than the green clay? What were you saying? The same thing? So it's more, squishier?
Teacher	03:50	And what about you, Sophia?
Child	03:55	This is more squishier and more moist.
Teacher	03:58	So it feels different, right?
Child	04:01	Uhm, well, I was, um, seeing if the red would be lighter and the green would be heavier but for me it feels like they're the same.
Teacher	04:14	It feels like they're the same, 'cause they're kind of similar, even though one feels squishier, they're the kind of kind of the same, right, so you feel like the weight is the same?
Child	04:28	Uh-huh.
Teacher	04:29	Maybe we should think about that, I never thought of that before . . .
Teacher	04:30	So what do you think?
Child	04:31	Now it's smooth.
Child	04:32	This one's a little heavier.
Teacher	04:33	You think that one's heavier? Oh, we should've gotten a weight. So I think.
Teacher	04:47	So I have a question for you: Do you think that texture and properties that you identify will be the same after we add water to it?
Child	04:55	Nooo.
Teacher	04:56	How would it changed? Oh, I want you guys to be able to predict what will happen first.
Child	05:05	I think the red might . . . maybe the red will switch and the red will get harder and stickier like the green will get squishier.
Child	05:27	I think the red one will get slimier.
Child	05:36	I think that the red one will get more wet and dry, and this one will get like the red one.
Teacher	05:43	Why do you think it will get slimier?
Child	05:51	Because one time I tried to put some of my Doh in water and it got slimier.
Teacher	05:58	So you did this before, you're familiar with this . . .
Child	06:08	I put Play-Doh in the water when it gets dryer.
Teacher	06:18	So when it gets dry you put water on it and it changes.
Teacher	06:19	Let's put the clay over here and the Doh here.
Child	06:20	Uhm, once I mixed water paint and slime together and it made a really slimy slime and so slime kind of turned into like a liquid.
Child	06:50	Wow.
Child	06:51	So I put, uhm, clay in water.
Teacher	06:52	So you noticed that things get changed when you add water to it. This is similar to other things, so that's what you guys are saying, right? So let's try to add water to each of them to see if the same thing will happen like the slime like you guys were telling me. But move your chair up. OK, I'm just going to do a little bit.

(cont.)

Speaker	Time	Content
Child	07:24	*Ohhhh.*
Teacher	07:27	*Do you think that I should add more?*
Child	07:28	*Yeah . . .*
Child	07:29	*Yes, that's good.*
Child	07:38	*I think you should fill it until there's water on top.*
Teacher	07:41	*Oh so it's like covered in it. How will that change it?*
Child	07:48	*Maybe it would just get squishier because there will be water all around it.*
Teacher	07:54	*So you absorb the water.*
Child	08:02	*Yeah, and then you could fill it again so the red.*
Teacher	08:05	*So it's covered again? Right?*
Child	08:06	*No, like, like.*
Teacher	08:07	*I'm going to need more water after this.*
Child	08:11	*Yeah, I know.*
Teacher	08:12	*That is a lot of water.*
Teacher	08:18	*How does this feel? But this is the clay, right?*
Child	08:20	*Hmhm, yeah, you might want to squish it so that you don't.*
Teacher	08:22	*Somebody wants to squish it? You want to squish it?*
Child	08:25	*Yeah, it's getting harder.*
Teacher	08:30	*It's getting harder than it was?*
Child	08:32	*Yeah, less now it feels a little stickier.*
Teacher	08:38	*This feels stickier?*
Child	08:40	*No, it feels less stickier.*
Teacher	08:41	*It feels less stickier? You think the in the end, it feels less. Yeah, it feels less stickier. You think the water made it feel less stickier? It felt softer, right?*
Child	08:50	*At first when I touched it, it felt a little sticky, and then when I touched it again, it didn't feel any more sticky.*
Teacher	08:58	*It got harder? You think it got harder? Some people say it feels softer, some people say it feels harder.*
Child	09:03	*I say it feels a little harder.*
Child	09:07	*I say you should put the rest of the water.*
Teacher	09:08	*Do you think we should shape the Doh?*
Child	09:11	*Yeah. Yeah.*
Teacher	09:12	*To see if it would be similar? Yeah, I'm going to I'm going to need more water.*
Child	09:19	*That's a lot – every time I squish it is gets harder.*
Teacher	09:23	*The more you squish it, you're the harder it gets, right.*
Child	09:30	*I'm just taking it apart so that I want some water.*
Teacher	09:32	*OK. OK, let's check, let's put the clay back, let's check the Doh.*
Child	09:38	*Wait, that's red Doh?*
Teacher	09:41	*Yeah, that's red Doh. Now I see, like it's changing a little bit, it's changing faster, right? I don't know if you guys agree with me.*
Child	09:52	*This one is slimier.*
Child	09:53	*It's slimier, slimy, it's like so slimy.*

(*cont.*)

Speaker	Time	Content
Child	09:54	Slime, slime, slime.
Teacher	09:55	So listen to what Mako said, she said.
Child	09:58	It was so slimy.
Child	09:59	This is so slimy, I felt like.
Teacher	10:10	When you touch this one, you feel like it's almost stays the same, right?
Child	10:14	Yeah.
Child	10:15	And I wonder what happens if you put that one in this and then you put this in this water.
Child	10:20	My hands are getting really red.
Teacher	10:21	Really, if you look, let's listen to your friend. What happened, Tom?
Child	10:26	I wonder if you put that that one in the same jar as this this one.
Teacher	10:31	How do you think?
Child	10:32	Like I think that if you combined it, it will get more different.
Teacher	10:36	It will be more different if you combine it because it's like if you're combining the properties of the clay and Doh together, right? It's like changing, right?
Teacher	10:49	So I feel like we should do what Devon said.
Child	10:52	This one's even slimier.
Teacher	10:53	This is gonna get messy. So Devon said we should mix it together to see what happens.
Child	10:59	Mix it?
Teacher	11:02	You said to put it together, wasn't that what you said?
Child	11:06	Uh-huh.
Teacher	11:07	Is it changing?
Child	11:08	No.
Teacher	11:09	Mako said it's not changing.
Child	11:16	It's still hard and now put it in water.
Teacher	11:24	Oh, Devon's getting a little absorbent more here. So I feel like we should put it back and kind of leave it there for a minute and see if this changes the longer we leave it. All right. But we should let it sit there for a minute. So let's wash our hands because our hands are like …
Child	11:54	I think it's doing that, because I think that that one is more soft and it has more space inside.
Teacher	12:05	It has more space inside?
Child	12:06	That one's getting more red.
Child	12:07	I think that one is absorbing the water more because it's like softer and it's like the texture helps it to absorb water.
Teacher	12:29	So you're saying it's because the texture's different, therefore the changes were different, right? Exactly what is right?
Child	12:36	That water is red.
Teacher	12:37	This water is red, right, so it's like changing the color too.
Child	12:44	That one changed to green.
Child	12:48	No, this one's in the water, still, and the water and.
Child	12:52	Looks like …

(cont.)

Speaker	Time	Content
Teacher	12:53	Because remember what Arrow said, he said: They both have different textures. Therefore, when you add water, they're going to change differently, right? So I want to end this activity. And I want to know what you learned. Arrow?
Child	13:11	I learned that the softer things are the more the like squishier they get, and also I want to say something and also. So. In the red and the green is still like the green in this one.
Teacher	13:42	Even if we put it on, the other one it's still the same, right? Michael?
Child	13:48	I learned that even if you put one thing that's squishy and one thing that's hard, it's still going to be the same.
Teacher	14:03	It's still going to be the same, right, because the texture is still the same, even if you put it together right there, still. Sophia?
Child	14:11	I learned that if you put clay in water it does not change.
Teacher	14:16	It does not change much, right? Compared to the. Maybe we should try like softer clay, right?
Child	14:24	Yeah. I learned that you can put that in the water the water turns red.
Teacher	14:42	Yes, right, Mathew? He said that if you put the Doh in this in water, the water turns red, right? But if you put the clay in it stays the same. But what happens if the Doh was yellow, do you think the water would turn yellow too?
Child	14:56	Yeah.
Teacher	14:57	So it's not only because of the color, its more because of the texture.
Child	15:02	I think if it was yellow and it was soft the water would turn yellow.
Child	15:05	I think if both of them were soft that water would turn green and that water would turn red.
Teacher	15:12	Yeah, so you agree.
Child	15:15	We agree.
Teacher	15:18	So those things that you guys just described to me, like the color, you guys are saying that some of them are softer, others are saying, harder, like you guys say, one is more slimy, right? Those are the properties of the materials, right? So next thing, next time you think about something, you might think about the properties, right? So this table right here. If you put water on it, it would just get wet, right? But it wouldn't get like softer like the Doh, right. Because it has different properties, right? Which is the texture. And all the things that make up the table, right.

How Does the Teacher's Use of Exploratory Talk Relate to Children's Use of Exploratory Talk?

The teacher talked more than the children in all three activities. The close sequential relationships between teacher and child talk are depicted in Table 10.1. Teachers eliciting ideas produced the most responses from the

Table 10.1 *Teacher talk directly preceding child response, comparing Teacher A and Teacher B activities.*

	Child responses										
	Brainstorm		Content connection		Personal connection		Question content		Vocabulary	
	TA	TB	TA	TB	TA	TB	TA	TB	TA	TB
Teacher talk										
Challenge thinking	2	3	2	3	0	3	0	2	0	1
Content connection	0	3	4	3	2	3	2	2	2	1
Direct to peer	0	0	0	2	0	0	2	2	0	1
Elicit ideas	2	3	10	3	5	5	0	2	2	1
Prompt for elaboration	4	3	6	3	2	3	2	2	0	1

TA = Teacher A; TB = Teacher B.

children – for Teacher A, children responded with a content connection 10 times and a personal connection five times. Teacher B's eliciting ideas led to a personal connection from children five times and a content connection three times.

The rest of the response sequence frequencies differed by teacher. Teacher A had differing degrees of child responses to each teacher dialogue move, whereas Teacher B had a consistent response pattern for all other talk moves except "direct to peer." For Teacher B, each additional type of teacher talk was followed most frequently by an equal response of "brainstorm," "content connection," and "personal connection" and an equally less frequent response of "question content" and one child response for each teacher code of "vocabulary connection." This shows that Teacher B's exploratory talk was most often followed by different forms of children's exploratory talk.

Teacher A, on the other hand, had varying responses to each form of dialogue. After eliciting ideas, prompting for elaboration was most frequently followed by children responding with every form of dialogue, most commonly "content connection" followed by "brainstorm." Teacher content connection was followed by each of the forms of child dialogue except for "brainstorm." These results suggest that dialogue does not function in isolation but is related to multiple factors of the interaction – from the relationships between the participants to the materials and content of the shared activity, among infinite others.

How Do Teachers' and Children's References to Internal States Relate to Exploratory Talk?

Coding the dialogue for internal state references showed that the teachers used more internal state language than the children. Teacher A used more internal state language than Teacher B overall, and much more during dialogue that showed the greatest use of internal state language, with the most frequent being eliciting ideas, followed by prompting for elaboration. The children in Teacher A's groups also used more internal state language than those in Teacher B's group. Among the children, the greatest use of internal state language occurred when making a content connection – six instances for Teacher A's group and four instances for Teacher B's group. All of the instances of internal state language are depicted in Table 10.2.

Table 10.2 *Forms of dialogue that included references to internal states by teacher.*

	Brain storm	Challenge thinking	Content connection	Content connection child	Direct to peer	Elicit ideas	Personal connection	Prompt for elaboration	Question content	Vocabulary connection
Teacher A	3	3	8	6	2	13	0	10	3	1
Teacher B	3	3	5	4	2	3	0	3	2	1

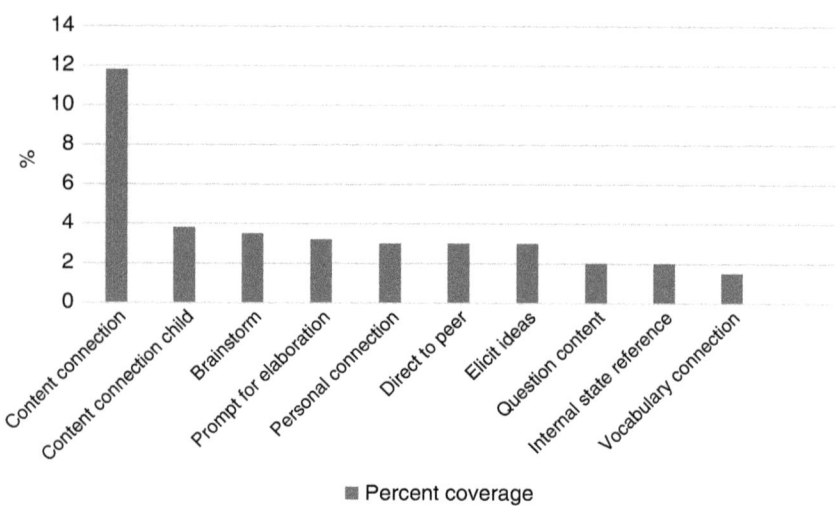

Figure 10.3 Teacher B's activity – frequency of dialogue.

Dialogue Frequencies between Teachers A and B
The activity with Teacher B involved different children and a different topic but the same grade level, classroom, head teacher, and content area (science) as those of Teacher A. These two teachers used very different forms of exploratory talk from one another. Teacher B used more than twice as many "content connections" as Teacher A. "Content connection" was the most frequent dialogic code for Teacher B, whereas this was among the least common for Teacher A's two activities. Teacher B used "prompt for elaboration" and "elicit ideas" the least often, whereas Teacher A used them the most often. Teacher B used "challenge thinking" as the second most common type of dialogue, whereas teacher A used "challenge thinking" the least. In summary, Teacher A favored more open-ended, child-centered types of dialogue, whereas Teacher B used more content- and concept-focused dialogue. Figures 10.1, 10.2, and 10.3 show the dialogue frequencies of Teacher A's first and second activities and Teacher B's activity, respectively.

For child talk, "content connection" was the most common form of dialogue used by both teachers. Children questioning content and making vocabulary connections were the least common across all activities. However, the children in Teacher B's activity used "brainstorm" and "personal connection" at a much higher rate than those in Teacher A's

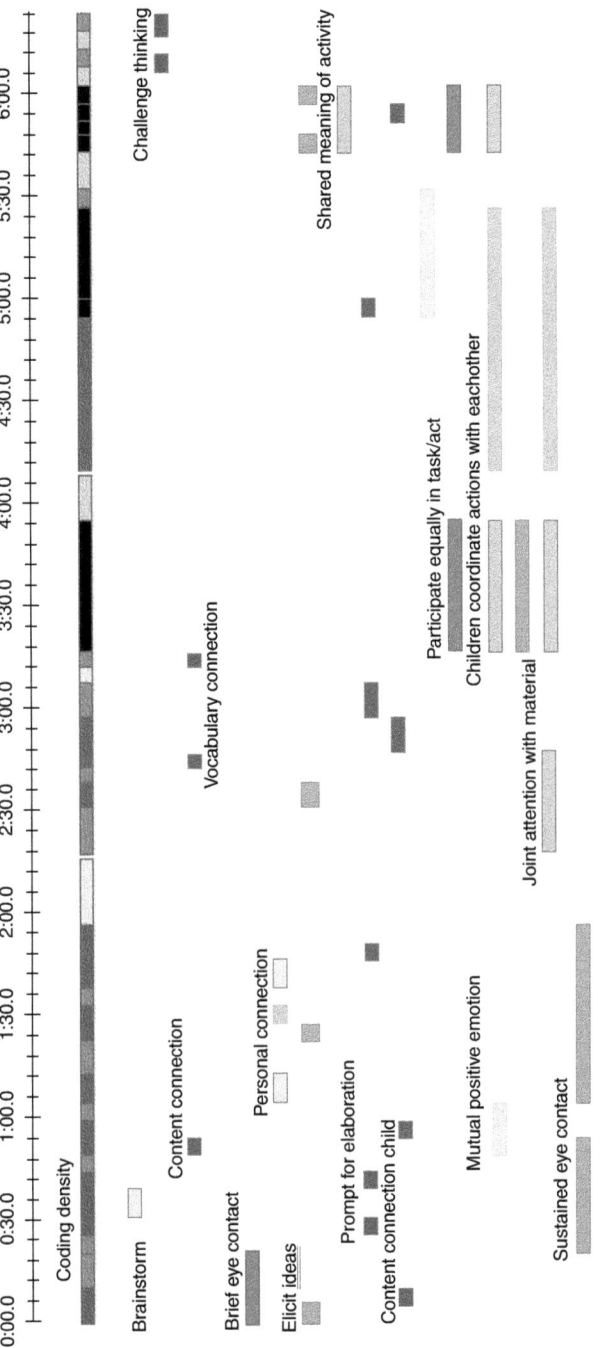

Figure 10.4 Coding of Teacher A's Activity A1.

activities. This might have been due to the greater focus on the content modeled and encouraged by Teacher B.

Is There a Difference in Intersubjectivity and Exploratory Talk between Time Segments of the Activity, Namely Introduction, Exploration/Application, and Conclusion?

Teacher A's first activity codes are shown in Figure 10.4.

The most densely coded segment was characterized by high intersubjectivity, especially joint attention, mutual participation, and coordination of activity toward the middle of the activity. There was a brief moment of "content connection" by the teacher leading into this segment, but no other exploratory talk overlapped with the intersubjectivity codes. Children's "brainstorming," "content connections," and "personal connections" were concentrated toward the beginning of the activity and overlapped with sustained eye contact and mutual positive emotion. Teacher A's "prompting for elaboration" and "eliciting ideas" were spread evenly throughout the activity. Another densely coded segment occurred toward the end of the activity, which was characterized by a mixture of intersubjectivity and exploratory talk. Teacher A "elicited ideas" and "prompted for elaboration," whereas the children made a "content connection." They also demonstrated a shared meaning of the activity, participated equally, and coordinated their actions. This segment directly preceded one in which there was mutual positive emotion and joint attention with the material. Finally, the teacher challenged thinking at the end of the activity, but this was not followed by any response. There was no vocabulary connection or questioning of content by the children and no direction to peers by Teacher A during this activity.

Teacher A's second activity involved different children and a similar activity with one additional material as compared to their first activity. The codes for the second activity are depicted in Figure 10.5.

Similar to Teacher A's first activity, the most densely coded segments were in the middle of the activity and had high intersubjectivity characterized by participating equally in an activity, children coordinating actions with one another, sustained eye contact, and joint attention to the material. Teacher A eliciting children's ideas directly preceded children making content connections. Teacher A's exploratory talk in terms of prompting for elaboration and eliciting ideas was concentrated at the beginning of the activity before the children were engaged in coordinating activity with one another. The use of internal state language occurred only during teacher

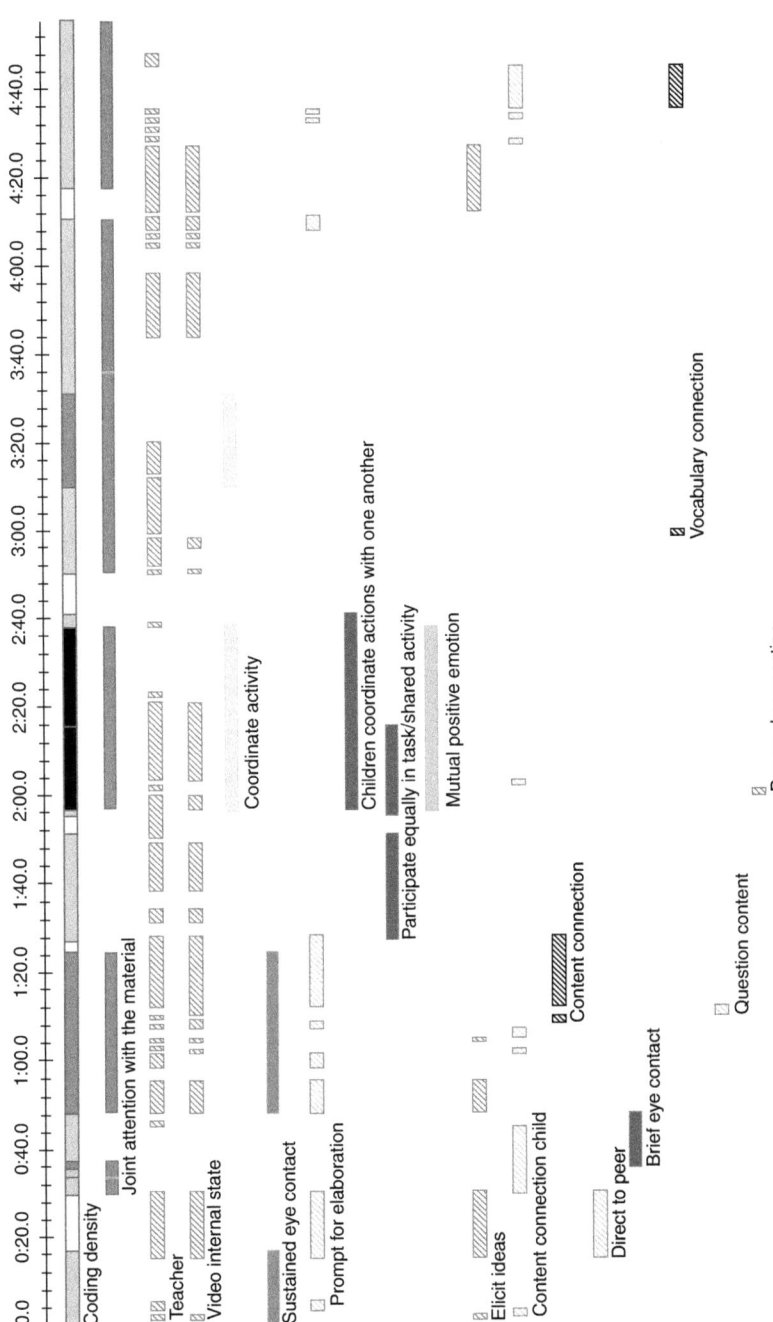

Figure 10.5 Coding of Teacher A's Activity A2.

talk, and teacher talk predominated during the activity. Mutual positive emotion, children's personal connection, and coordinated actions occurred only at the midpoint and corresponded with less teacher talk and more intersubjectivity.

Both videos showed that exploratory talk and active engagement with the activity occurred separately. Intersubjectivity was highest during activity engagement when there was less talk. These high-engagement periods occurred in the middle of the activity and followed a greater period of exploratory talk. Teacher A's second activity had only one period of high intersubjectivity and mutual engagement, whereas their first activity had two such periods. Additionally, the first activity had a more densely coded segment toward the end that included a mixture of intersubjectivity and exploratory talk. This was the only segment across both activities during which the teacher challenged the children's thinking and the children demonstrated a shared meaning of the activity.

Teacher B's activity, introduced in Chapter 7, was conducted during a different year. However, the regular classroom teacher (who worked with the student teacher in the video) and the classroom environment were the same. This video was three times longer than those capturing either of Teacher A's activities. Every single code was applied at least once to Teacher B's activity. The coding is depicted in Figure 10.6.

There were three high-density segments. The first was toward the end of the introduction and the next two were in the middle of the active engagement period. The first third of the video – or the introduction – was characterized by a mixture of intersubjectivity and exploratory talk among both children and teachers. One key difference between the two teachers was that Teacher B used far more content connections than eliciting ideas and prompting for elaboration. Prompting for elaboration was one of the least used forms of exploratory talk by Teacher B.

Another key difference is that there was more intersubjectivity characterized by joint attention, eye contact, and mutual positive emotion during the introduction, separate from the mutual engagement with the activity. Children's participation trailed off during the final third of the activity. At the very end, the teacher used a large amount of exploratory talk, but there was no coded response from the children or signs of intersubjectivity. However, during and immediately after the shared engagement in the activity, children used exploratory talk that was not seen in Teacher A's videos, namely "vocabulary connection" and "questioning content." Teacher B also directed children to their peers during and after the shared engagement with materials segment of the activity, and this was followed

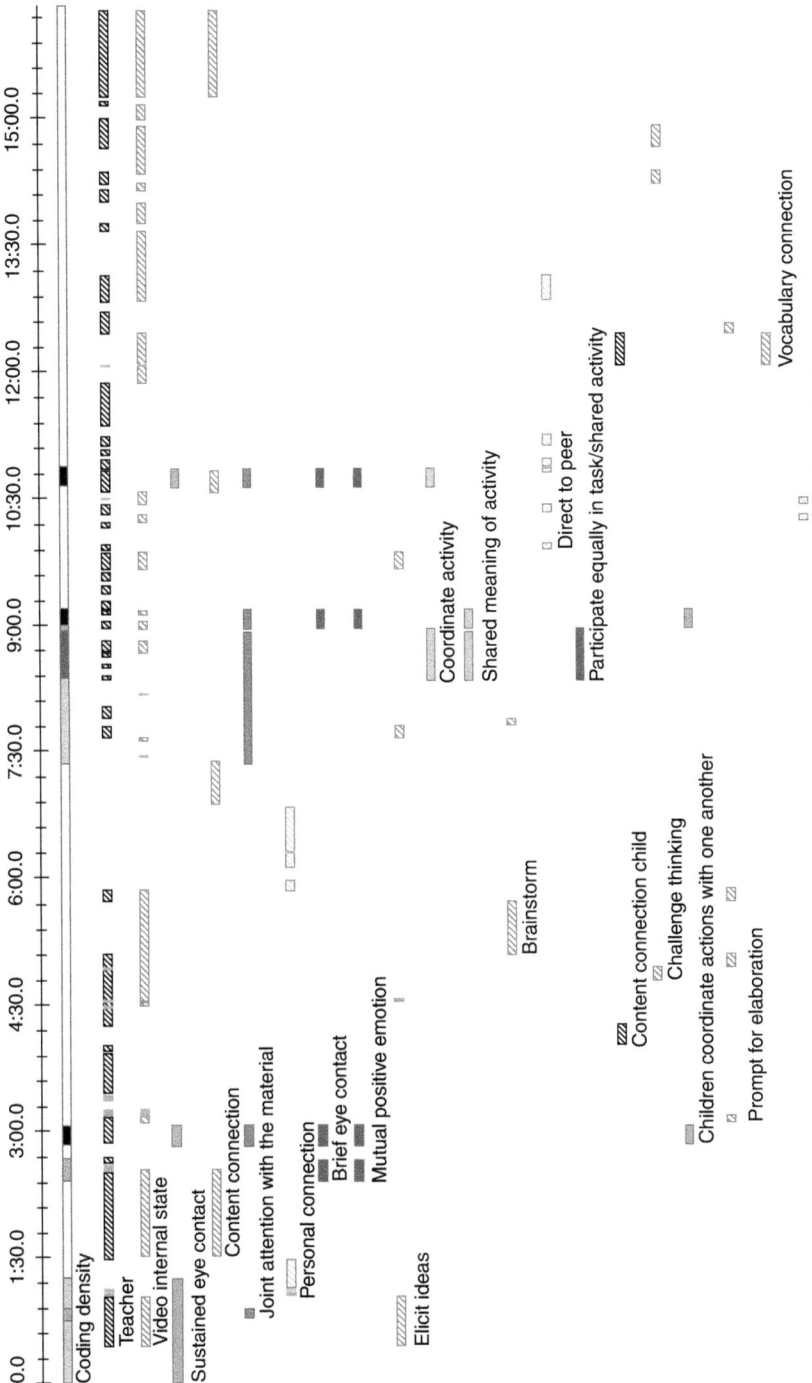

Figure 10.6 Coding of Teacher B's activity.

immediately by children making a content connection. Unlike Teacher A's activities, there were some moments when children used internal state language during Teacher B's activity.

Summarizing the Results

From this analysis, we can see that intersubjectivity corresponded most frequently with active engagement in activities when dialogue was less extensive, and that these moments typically fell in the middle of the teacher-facilitated learning activities. We also can see that activities with the same teacher showed similar patterns regarding the forms of exploratory talk used most often as compared to those of a different teacher. Given that we are only looking at three activities from two teachers, these are simply emerging patterns that might not persist within a larger sample. The goal of this chapter is to suggest some ways in which we can begin to conceptualize the functioning of intersubjectivity and exploratory dialogue as components of collaborative competence within the context of teacher-facilitated, playful learning activities. By examining both talk and nonverbal engagement and by analyzing pedagogical, conceptual, affective, and synchronous elements of collaborative competence simultaneously, this method has the potential to offer new insights into how the components that characterize productive free play during preschool can be expanded and adapted to characterize collaborative playful learning in early elementary school.

Finally, these short activities were designed to teach a specific concept using child-centered, teacher-guided methods. This provides one example of how play-based pedagogy could be used in early elementary school to facilitate collaborative learning. However, these activities were highly structured by the teacher-selected space and materials and by teacher guidance. As a result, children participated within teacher-determined constraints. As described in the literature earlier in this chapter, this type of activity might benefit some aspects of learning in early elementary school; however, peer collaborations that are child-directed wherein children apply knowledge and skills to collective problem-solving should also be included in early elementary approaches to collaborative competence. As shown in the transcripts and coding, limited peer-to-peer interaction occurred during the activities, despite the teachers minimizing didactic instruction. To fully engage with the concepts presented, children need to explore and discuss the ideas and applications with their peers outside of the management of an adult. In addition, by experimenting further with materials on their own, children might fully make sense of the related concepts as a group through a collective form of accommodation. In all of the transcripts provided, the children appear to have just begun to grasp the meanings of the concepts at the center of the activities. The closest they come to fully comprehending either the idea of "properties" or methods of water filtration is during peer dialogue and joint engagement with the material. A follow-up child-led activity using the same materials could generate new information about how dialogic and activity-based forms of intersubjectivity and collaborative competence interact to produce new collective understandings of science concepts among first graders.

In conclusion, the methodology used to analyze these teacher-guided activities could be applied to child-directed collaborative learning activities during early elementary school. It would be interesting to see the forms of exploratory talk that would emerge from child-directed explorations without adult guidance and whether intersubjectivity would peak during similar points in an ongoing child-directed activity.

PART IV

Implications for Theory, Research, and Practice

CHAPTER 11

Making the Shift to Interactivity in Education and Psychology

The previous chapters suggest that the exclusive focus on individuals has stymied the fields of both psychology and education. Developmental psychology has been unable to produce significant new research insights that could improve developmental outcomes among children placed at risk. The most robust findings within developmental psychology have come from investigating dyadic processes as they occur within the constructs of attachment, synchrony, and mutual responsive orientation among other relationally construed psychological phenomena. On the other hand, repeated attempts to find significant and consistent correlations between various independent variables and individual measures of children's social functioning have been limited. Within education, attempts to connect measures of teacher quality to individual student outcomes have been equally lacking. Indeed, despite decades of research and policy devoted to the issue, academic achievement among American children from low-income families and from Black and Latinx racial groups has not risen to match that of their white middle-class peers as assessed via standardized tests (Henry et al., 2020). Educational scholarship has focused almost exclusively on either boosting individual achievement scores, testing the efficacy of interventions via individual outcome measures, or targeting support to enhancing the skills of individual teachers and students. Yet the studies that have identified significant predictors of student outcomes are more often found within the literature investigating interactive methods such as dialogic education, cooperative learning, and interventions aimed at shifting classroom culture at the group level.

We Are Not Measuring What Matters

What if most of the social capacities that children demonstrate while interacting with peers are more the result of peer dynamics than the child's individual traits? What if all of the interventions aimed at addressing individual social and intellectual "deficits" would have been better aimed at addressing group dynamics? Such a possibility frees up teachers and researchers to investigate a broader swath of the social contexts in which children interact with peers and adults. To do such research requires significant changes to how educational and psychological scholarship defines competence, growth, and development. As detailed in the previous section, methods and measures must proceed from theoretically grounded operationalizations in order to be valid and meaningful. The change advocated in this book would not only shift from individual to collective notions of achievement but also from static outcome measures to dynamic assessments of process.

Despite conclusive evidence that social context has significant influence on test performance and other individual outcome measures via the impact of stereotype threat (Desombre et al., 2019; Steele, 2021), education research continues to rely solely on individual student measures that ignore social context. These measures have become imbued with tremendous power, as they represent a proxy for instructional quality in American schools and are the sole indicators of how American students fare academically. Attempts to counter the impact of stereotype threat on students who are disproportionately affected by it have been documented through self-affirmation theory (Steele, 2021). This entails embedding methods of self-affirmation into instruction. However, to be effective, these methods must reflect the cultural values of the students, including the values of interdependence and social cohesion (see Steele, 2021). This research on adolescents shows that both negative and positive effects on achievement occur due to sociocultural elements such as group-level appraisals and intergroup functioning, particularly among majority world student populations. Such research shows developmental continuity with findings that preschoolers' behavior is influenced by their teachers' perceptions of them (Mantzicopoulos & Neuharth-Pritchett, 2003) and that elementary students' school success in multiple domains is highly influenced by classroom composition (Sutton et al., 2021). This research suggests that for achievement measures to be culturally valid for minoritized populations they must first be socially contextualized. Yet, measures of educational achievement used to influence local and national educational policy within the US continue to reflect a solely individualistic account of learning and development.

Collaborative Problem-Solving

Despite the stubborn adherence to individualistic measures of learning in school within the US, the international world recently acknowledged the crucial role of collaborative capacities in educational achievement. In 2015, the Programme for International Student Assessment (PISA) declared collaborative problem-solving (CPS) to be one of the key twenty-first-century skills that it would assess internationally. The PISA's definition of CPS derived in part from that of the work of an international team that included the US entitled the "Assessment and Teaching of 21st Century Skills Project" (AT21SP). The AT21SP was informed by the technology industry and designed to focus on the collaborative skills necessary for the workforce in the education of 11–15-year-olds. The conceptual definitions consider collaborative and problem-solving skills as two separate yet necessary components of CPS (Scoular et al., 2017). One of the key components is shared understanding of ideas and meanings and another is collaborative decision-making. Both the PISA and the AT21SP approaches assess the individual subskills necessary to effectively contribute to group functioning.

The PISA assessment prioritizes group over individual functioning in terms of demonstrating success but tracks only individual skills during the problem-solving process. Alternatively, the AT21SP assessment framework defines collaborative skills such as "participation," "interaction/action," and "social regulation," among others, that can be coded at the group level (see Graesser et al. 2018 for more details).

The results of the PISA assessment showed that only 8 percent of 15-year-old students showed high levels of CPS competencies (as per their definition) worldwide. As a result, a new emphasis on developing collaborative skills has been suggested as a crucial task for psychology and education (Graesser et al., 2018). Although much research has used the paradigm of individual subskills comprising group functioning during CPS tasks, the fields of cognitive science and organizational psychology have developed the construct of macrocognition in teams that provide an alternative, holistically collaborative approach. This construct attempts to model group-level processes and microinteractions using concepts such as entropy while simultaneously accounting for individual contributions. The in-task assessment framework (Andrews-Todd & Forsythe, 2020; Andrews-Todd & Kerr, 2019) moves the outcome variable from an assessment of the final result to assessments of different points in the CPS process. This allows for a definition of competence as occurring at multiple time points as part of dynamic processes.

Developmental Issues in CPS

These initiatives have brought theories and methods from cognitive science and human–computer interaction (HCI) into educational and developmental psychology, introducing concepts such as emergence and entropy to the study of interactive dynamics. However, as mentioned earlier in this text, there are concerns that using paradigms from the area of industry teamwork while failing to consider the social and cognitive development that students must undergo in order to master such skills at different ages leaves theories incomplete and will not allow for the development of such skills at earlier ages (Gauvain, 2018). Implicit in Gauvain's (2018) critique is the idea that a developmental approach to CPS requires attention to the individual development of the requisite collaborative skills at different ages and stages. Although she acknowledges that individuals learn within and through a social context, she does not consider emergent group processes to be developmental, nor the possibility that development can be studied at the micro level as it occurs over the course of a collaboration. These notions require separating the concept of development from an individual unit of analysis. Doing so would allow for measures of achievement that center on collective processes.

Cukurova et al. (2018) echo the importance of recognizing age-based differences in forms of CPS and the types of learning that groups can extract from it. By focusing on the nature of shared tasks and the contexts surrounding them, Cukurova et al. (2018) acknowledge that group-level processes and outcomes are highly relevant to understanding and promoting learning and collaboration in schools. An example of how a developmental characteristic such as self-regulation can be reformulated as a collective competency is suggested by Hakkinen et al. (2017). They show how the effectiveness of CPS is predicated on socially shared regulation (SSR) and then apply those collaborative skills from SSR to inquiry-based learning formats. They argue that teacher education must begin developing CPS skills in preservice teachers using the parallel process of scaffolding education students' own experiences with SSR and CPS while they are developing pedagogical approaches to support future students in developing these capacities. Their work offers a concrete example of how to connect prior pedagogical approaches such as inquiry-based, project-based, or problem-based learning to highly refined definitions of collaborative competencies that can be developed and assessed at the group level.

While the Western world is discovering the importance of collaboration for meeting twenty-first-century employment needs, the handbook edited by Nsamenang and Tchombe (2012) for African educators and psychologists has long described collaborative structures of education as culturally relevant and educationally transformative for African schoolchildren. Indeed, the PISA results of CPS assessment showed cultural diversity within learning settings as positively predictive of greater CPS competency. Although this finding has not been explored in depth, it is possible that students from majority world cultures contributed to the development of the collaborative skills of classmates for whom sophisticated collaborations are less common.

In addition to addressing problems collaboratively, the authenticity of the problem that the group is attempting to solve is key in majority world learning settings such as apprenticeships and participation in a community of practice (Lave & Wenger, 1991; Nsamenang & Tchombe, 2012). This element of authenticity has also been recognized as crucial for effective CPS (Nieminen et al., 2022). Although the CPS literature gives little explicit reference to either developmental psychology's or cultural psychology's treatment of collaborative learning, there is significant conceptual overlap. For example, synchrony is included as a measure of group cohesion and is shown to be a significant predictor of collaborative effectiveness. Similarly, the concept of SSR is reminiscent of the coregulation literature within developmental psychology. Finally, although Vygotsky, Piaget, and Erikson are only occasionally mentioned in articles focused on CPS, the methods of project-based learning, reciprocal teaching, culturally mediated cognition, and discovery-based learning that derive from these theories are all consistent with the components of CPS identified by both the PISA and the AT21SP (see the literature cited earlier for meta-analyses and reviews of CPS).

Despite the theoretical and empirical convergence of both Western and majority world educators and scholars on how authentic, meaningful activities undertaken in relation to socially and culturally valued goals lead to learning and broader psychological development, these components are rarely considered within educational policy. Interventions for children deemed educationally at risk almost never account for any of these social or sociocultural dimensions. When social context is considered by education researchers or policymakers, it is usually in terms of describing the home environment as inadequately preparing children for school. This view of the at-risk child assumes that a deprived home environment imposes a set of strengths and weaknesses on each child that remain fixed regardless of differences in the social and cultural contexts that they encounter. Evidence that children's behavior changes significantly due to social context (Robinson et al., 2003; Roncacino-Moreno & Branco, 2017) debunks this stereotypical picture of a minoritized child from a low-income family.

Imagining a Different Way

Given the current individualistic paradigm of educational assessment and policy, it is not possible to determine whether an interactive, socially contextualized approach to learning would help to close the so-called achievement gap. Testing this would require new outcome measures of growth, development, and learning, along with new methods of instruction. What would an interactive measure of academic achievement look like? Within this new paradigm, would it be possible to consider achievement apart from social development? Or, as in the majority world, would intelligence become redefined as intrinsically related to social responsibility, describing a child's ability to contribute to collective efforts, replacing the current view of intelligence as a static, internal trait disconnected from social activity? Would a focus on collaborative competence allow for universal guidelines as to what children should learn when? If intelligence was redefined as being useful and responsive to one's community and achievement was measured by effective communal participation in collective problem-solving, would it be possible to define knowledge and skills apart from the authentic needs of particular communities? With this approach, would it be possible for anyone to determine which culturally valued practices should be taught without being a part of that community?

These questions point to the power redistribution that would be necessary for a vision of development and achievement centered on collaborative competence. Current achievement measures are standardized and imposed by policymakers who do not need detailed knowledge of the cultures and communities in which the students they are assessing live. To enable support for collaborative competence to be widespread in schools, it is necessary for educators local to the school community and the students themselves to decide what collective goals to focus on. The Child-to-Child (C2C) program described in Chapter 2 demonstrates an example of this. The Classroom Assessment of Sociocultural Interactions (CASI) measure described in Chapter 5 provides another example of how culturally specific pedagogy can be assessed on a large scale without losing what is most relevant to a particular group of students.

To begin to shift education toward an interactive rather than individual endeavor, education policymakers and researchers must first acknowledge that processes of teaching and learning are never linear or one-dimensional. As described in ecological and dynamic systems theories, developmental change occurs as an outgrowth of an infinite variety of potential catalysts aligning in endlessly varied ways. Learning as a form of developmental change is a prime example of the dynamism of development. To recognize that development and, by extension, learning can occur in collective forms via interactive dynamics would change the current paradigms of both psychology and schooling. If collective growth is considered equally valid to individual growth, the focus of classroom teaching must also expand. Teaching goals focused exclusively on meeting the intellectual, social, and emotional needs of individual students would expand to include meeting those needs of groups of various sizes and configurations who engage with one another for a variety of shared purposes. Rather than solely scaffolding individual children's understandings and skills, instruction would address scaffolding the skills and concepts of a dyad, triad, or other sized group while simultaneously considering how to best support interindividual processes and peer scaffolding as they emerge from group dynamics. Teachers would learn to structure facilitation to support multiple possible outcomes of group interaction. Such a focus for education would create an infinitely more complex pedagogy with unlimited potential for accelerating learning and social development than the current individualistic approach.

Ideally, teacher support for peer scaffolding and group-level development can provide a multiplying effect of instruction in that the growth of both the group and of the individual as a group member will be simultaneously spurred on by the combination of teacher and peer support. Ideally, this dual-dimension support for children in groups would amplify the impacts of instruction beyond what traditional teaching without the added benefit of peer support can have. This model will also mean that the outcomes of any given pedagogical interaction would be highly unpredictable, being subject to the vicissitudes of evolving group dynamics. Among adult working groups, this process is ultimately related to high degrees of innovation. As has been shown in the examples of preschooler play episodes and teacher-facilitated playful pedagogy of a first grade science experiment, the path toward growth is highly nonlinear. These models of collaborative competence among groups involve peaks and lows of intersubjectivity and shared understandings along with plateaus of engagement, as well as conflicts and periods of disengagement from the shared activity.

As highlighted in the preschool play study, social-emotional intersubjectivity plays a crucial role in maintaining collaboration. Similarly, the first grade groups showed more engagement with materials and conceptual understanding during periods of heightened nonverbal intersubjectivity rather than dialogue. These findings of young children's collaborative competence being contingent on interactive synchrony – especially social-emotional forms – are consistent with findings of collaborative group work among older children, adolescents, and adults. The group-level sense of solidarity and shared purpose along with individual members' beliefs in the efficacy of their group have consistently been shown to predict group effectiveness far more strongly than the skill levels of individual group members. The role of collectively meaningful activity in supporting collaboration has also been highlighted for different ages. As detailed via the sociocultural activity-embodied (SAE) depiction of intersubjectivity in action, increases in the collective meaning of the shared activity are related to increased levels of intersubjectivity, which in turn enabled the complexity of the collaboration to grow. On the other hand, whenever the activity lost its shared meaning to the participants, each of the elements in the model quickly decreased or dissolved. Among the first grade science activities, the children's engagement with the materials and personal connections to the content were highest during moments of heightened intersubjectivity. Therefore, regardless of age, the shared activity at the center of the interaction must be authentically collectively meaningful to the groups themselves as a prerequisite for any collaborative competence or learning.

As highlighted by the CoEnact framework (Yuill, 2021), the design of shared materials and the immediate environment must support collaboration, just as the flexibility of space and materials was shown to support more complex collaborations among preschoolers. This evidence that the material environment provides crucial support for collaborative competence and problem-solving is suggested by numerous studies of social complexity during play, and collaborations among elementary-aged children, These findings are consistent with the example of first graders' provided in the previous chapter wherein their moments of experimentation with open-ended materials were the only time when they indicated conceptual understanding. The role of the physical environment in learning has long been documented by classic theorists such as Montessori and Piaget and via the cultural tools concept of Vygotsky. The design function of classroom space and materials for promoting effective collaboration was illustrated by research showing how a multiuser tablet table supports coordination of actions and enables mutually adaptive behavior. Schools need to recognize that these contextual elements are key to optimizing group learning and development, especially in younger children, who rely more heavily on supports and concrete referents for collaborative interactions.

In addition, the role of space and materials as cultural tools must be carefully considered to enable the establishment of an inclusive setting and shared knowledge base for collective learning and development. Teacher support should facilitate children's attention to one another's actions and increase their awareness of others' internal states while simultaneously providing key information, content, and connections to content that engender personal and group-level interest and meaning. As depicted in the early elementary learning activities, teachers and students exhibited the most dialogue when making personal connections with content, which then framed direct engagement with the materials as a personally and collectively meaningful shared activity. The episode that featured the greatest degree of shared meaning in relation to the activity was the one in which the teacher devoted a significant amount of dialogue to making content connections. This aspect of schooling is best reflected in the CASI measure (Jensen et al., 2020), which emphasizes the teacher's ability to draw meaningful cultural connections between students' home cultures and personal experiences and classroom learning. As a characteristic of classroom culture, learning groups made up of children who share some aspects of culture and differ in others will nonetheless find activities that are collectively meaningful to them through commonalities both of culture and of a common developmental period. This dual salience of cultural and developmental features is key to the concept of collaborative competence and the SAE theory of intersubjectivity. Self-chosen free play activities that were characterized by high collaborative competence reflected these dual components. This was also found in abundance within the child-directed play-crafting activity, which depicted high degrees of shared meaning-making and intersubjectivity; yet this was lacking in the science and math activities that were absent of intersubjectivity, in which the teacher failed to create a bridge between the cultures of home and school, as detailed in Chapter 4.

Playful learning activities offer a means by which teachers can create authentic connections between children and content, as demonstrated in the examples of first grade science activities. The method used to assess collaborative processes offers a potential starting point for how to create measures that assess interactive units such as dialogue and intersubjectivity while simultaneously capturing learning. Applying these methods to children's self-directed exploration and experimentation with peers around science concepts could provide insights into both collaborative competence and conceptual and content-related learning as well as the relation between the two.

Redesigning Education

Incorporating a focus on collaborative competence in every aspect of schooling requires a significant redesign of American education. The structure of schools would change to reflect an emphasis on group-level learning processes. The arrangement of teachers would mirror that of students in that, rather than working alone, multiple adults with complementary skills and knowledge would work together with heterogeneous groups of children to support, facilitate, and, in some cases, model the skills, knowledge, and conceptual understandings necessary to meet shared goals. Teachers would also work together in groups to establish common, broadly defined goals for children's learning and psychological development that reflect what is meaningful for their student population.

A change from outcome to process measures would mean that elements of school that were designed to support a focus on end results would change to allow educators to gain insights into elements of process. This focus on process would also introduce uncertainty and ambiguity into plans for learning. Rather than aspiring to structured plans, procedures, and routines, creating environments to support open-ended group responses would become the goal of teaching. At the school level, some practical features that would change to reflect this include age-based grouping, the pacing of the curriculum, school and class daily schedules, and the use of textbooks and curriculum guides. Within the classroom, learning outcomes would need to be redefined to reflect the principle of equifinality: many paths to the same goal. Therefore, rather than segmenting a scope and sequence through which students master specific knowledge and skills, concepts would be defined broadly so that collaborative groups could engage with them in multiple ways. The methods by which groups can demonstrate learning would be equally broad. In addition, opportunities for innovation as a product of collaboration would be built into the structure of curriculum. In this way, the curriculum would be emergent rather than fixed. Constraints on what could be learned from any given activity would be limited only by the nature of the subject area. This would require teachers of early elementary students to be subject matter experts beyond what current training provides. Higher levels of expertise in math, science, social studies (history/economics/geography), and literature would allow elementary school teachers to recognize when students were mastering a concept in unexpected ways.

Policy-Level Change

Assessments that focus on the progress and development of groups and that include assessments of different configurations, structures, materials, and methods for group learning would necessarily replace the current system of high-stakes standardized tests. Rather than using such assessments for evaluating the merits of individuals, methods of measurement would assess what works best for whom and under what circumstances. This would require a restructuring of the school system nationwide. Policymakers would no longer be able to draw conclusions based on aggregated data of achievement disconnected from social learning contexts. Instead, experts in pedagogy, group dynamics, cultural psychology, and content areas would work together with teachers in classrooms. In-depth studies of group learning would be shared and reported. Scholars and teachers would share the same questions, investigations, and roles rather than the current siloing of research and practice.

Reconceptualizing risk and resilience as tied to interactive dynamics that occur between the child, peer group, and teacher would invalidate assessment measures that presume teachers can report on individual child behavior as separate from the ongoing classroom dynamics of which they are a part. Instead, relational constructs of social and emotional challenges and strengths would reflect intersubjective and dialogic processes. To capture these dynamics, innovative methods from cognitive science, conversation analysis, and HCI would be used. These methods would replace the assumption that children bring risk factors and deficits with them into the classroom with an understanding of how psychological challenges and resources among groups of children and adults intersect. Investigations would center on what contextual elements shape interactions in positive or negative directions.

Teacher Training

A shift toward the interaction as the focus for pedagogy and assessment in education requires a change in the way in which teachers are trained and the nature of professional development. Parallel to the shifts in policy, teachers and student teachers would use their own pedagogical interactions with their students and colleagues as the basis for developing their practice.

Observing microprocesses of interactions, designing materials and environments most conducive to peer collaboration, and exploratory dialogue would make up the bulk of teacher training. Rather than designing a priori universal strategies and methods for teaching, teachers would use their own cultural frameworks and personal backgrounds to establish intersubjectivity and authentic relationships with students. From this starting point, they would learn details of their students' home cultures in order to find overlaps as well as distinctions in relational styles and norms. This inside-out approach to developing culturally sustaining practices would be honed during real-time interactions in classrooms, allowing for an experientially derived basis for culturally responsive pedagogy. Preservice teachers would learn to identify the strengths and needs of children in relation to their interactions and shared goals with their classmates as well as the shared goals of the classroom culture. Rather than learning how to handle "classroom management," teachers would work with colleagues to develop classroom cultures that reflect the home cultures of the school community and to establish authentic methods for resolving conflicts. A greater emphasis on recruiting teachers who share cultural backgrounds with the students that they teach would be a focal point for policy.

This approach reflects that of play-based pedagogy, in that there is a balance between the student and teacher directions of learning processes. The challenge is the scope and sequence of the curriculum. Currently, play-based activities and group projects must connect to the learning goals of the curriculum regardless of student interests or the dynamics of the collaborative activity. In an interaction-based pedagogy, group dynamics will influence the nature and focus of the activity. Teachers will document the learning that emerges during the process and tie it to content areas. Scaffolding will support moving group-level learning toward increasing complexity. As in the play-crafting activity depicted in Chapter 4, the teacher's role will be to facilitate effective collaboration without imposing the direction of the activity. In this way, assessment will focus on collaborative competence and its development among groups as much as it will focus on skill and content learning.

CHAPTER 12

A Theoretical Home for the Role of Collaborative Competence in Education

This final chapter offers a theoretical paradigm for connecting the various methodological approaches and empirical findings that support collaborative competence as a primary driver and unit of analysis for human development. The first set of empirical and theoretical claims was developed by Michael Tomasello, who contends that – more than any other feature – what makes humans unique from all other species and provides our greatest advantages is our instinct toward collaboration. The second framework provides an alternative view of both psychology and education via the transformative activist stance (TAS) theory within the broader theoretical paradigm of cultural historical activity theory (CHAT). This framework argues for an emancipatory form of education that acknowledges the inherently collaborative nature of learning and development. Each will be elaborated in this chapter to offer overarching conceptual frameworks for how to move the agenda of collaborative competence forward at multiple levels of theory and practice within both education and psychology.

Development as Inherently Collaborative

Tomasello (2014, 2016, 2019) has developed a theory that bridges the ontogenetic claims of nativist and sociocultural developmental theorists. The premise of this view is that humans are innately predisposed to collaborate. People are enculturated into the particular ways of their given culture. Into Culture is perpetuated via collaborations that lead to it's transmission and dissemination of said culture. Tomasello (2019) describes numerous experiments comparing the social behavior of great apes – the closest relatives to humans – showing how they diverge at each point in development. Siposova et al. (2018) shows how joint attention based infant intersubjectivity with their caregiver persists across cultures, including those with limited to no face-to-face contact. This dual-level analysis of ontogeny and phylogeny across diverse cultures shows that there are universals of collective intentionality and collaborative creation of culture. Despite these universals, wide cultural variations exist in the methods, content, styles, and goals of collaboration. The nature of human interactions and that of what comprises "culture" are just as varied across the world. In other words, all humans are genetically predisposed to participate in creating and transmitting culture, yet each culture has its own values, norms, goals, and roles that exist in infinite variation as a reflection of human cultural diversity.

In an earlier work, Tomasello et al. (2005) asserted that language acquisition and development are embedded within the capacity for collaboration. However, his later works (e.g., Tomasello, 2019) include cross-cultural research in which nonlinguistic forms of communication are posited as the primary means of social coordination. Perspective-taking is at the center of this theory, explaining how collaborative peer interaction during early childhood gives rise to a dual form of perspective-taking in which the individual considers both their own and the perspective of their interacting partner(s) simultaneously. This dual perspective-taking ability allows humans to adapt and coordinate behavior with the goals of others while maintaining their own perceptions of shared phenomena. Therefore, the individual coexists with the collective during social interaction. Nonetheless, the bulk of evidence for this theory suggests a subsuming of the individual within the sociocultural. Examples include studies of conformity, imitation, and moral decision-making that show how throughout the lifespan people engage in behaviors such as imitation to demonstrate allegiance and affinity with group members rather than to learn instrumental skills from others (Engelmann & Tomasello, 2019). Accordingly, much of human behavior is driven by social affiliation goals rather than individual pursuits.

Tomasello (2016, 2019) argues that the evolutionary shift that allowed for human language and culture – mutually constitutive components of our unique species – was the divergence from competition. Initially focused only on individual acquisition of food, shelter, mates, and dominance, even among one's own kinship group, ancient humans instead began to cooperate with others and to live close to each other, allowing for a cooperatively oriented species to develop that is driven to work together with members of their group to solve common problems. Tomasello credits the cooperative turn with establishing the basis for all behavior that is unique to humans: transmission of culture to the young by elders, conformity as a basis for a uniquely human morality, and of course the abstract thinking and technological development that have arisen over the course of human history. Rather than crediting language or complex tool use as a precursor for culture, he posits that the ability to establish collective intentionality – merging one's own perspective with those of others while maintaining one's own individual perception – gave rise to both human language and culture.

Collective intentionality derives from joint attention, shared goals, and common culturally based meanings. This dual perspective-taking enables attention to be given not only to the task at hand but also to recursive thinking about the appraisals of others. The nature of language is used as evidence for the ways in which recursive thinking and dual perspective-taking are innately embedded within human development. A prime example of the interaction between language, recursive thinking, and collective intentionality is the concept of prolepsis (described in Chapters 3 and 4), whereby a speaker always speaks with some expectations regarding the knowledge and understanding of the listener. Tomasello argues that the human emphasis on cultural groups and the extent to which shared lifeways are transmitted to children are driven by the telos of effective collaboration. The definition of collaboration that follows from this account is dependent on collective intentionality, wherein the roles and perspectives of multiple individuals are ideally coordinated for the purpose of accomplishing a shared task that benefits the group.

Tomasello's argument is not merely descriptive. He also reviews research supporting the value of collaborative interactions, as they lead to more sophisticated cognition and problem-solving than individual endeavors, regardless of context (e.g., Warneken et al., 2014). Tomasello's evolutionary explanation for what makes us uniquely human ties together varied evidence of how we diverge from great apes in our behavior (Tomasello & Hermann, 2010). He connects these clues to show that the difference lies in the complexity and subtlety of our collaborative skills. In a series of experiments, he claims that our ability to collaborate as a species is also the basis for our uniquely human moral, cultural, child-rearing, and social institutions. Language is both an outcome and a catalyst of our collaborative abilities. The ways in which we use language as humans are concrete representations of our intersubjective minds. However, Tomasello argues that the effectiveness of our collaborations and the extent of our skills in this area vary with experience. The human child develops a sophisticated theory of mind during early childhood but does so through their experience of interacting and relating within a uniquely human culture. Although the primary ingredients for intersubjectivity and collaboration are present during infancy, the sharpening of intersubjective and collaborative skills, further supported by language in use, occurs via increasingly complex social interactions during ontogeny. On this account, language is both evidence of and necessary for the ubiquity of intersubjectivity throughout human development.

Support for this theory comes from research showing that when children collaborate, they focus more on maintaining the social interaction than completing the task, even when there is a reward for task completion. At each stage, children strive to maintain social engagement and to ensure that interacting partners share in task rewards (Tomasello, 2020). Collaborations based in intersubjective relating are preferred over individual work by children of various ages (Brennan & Enns, 2015). Highly effective collaborations have also been shown to lead to optimal outcomes in problem-solving, innovation, and conceptual learning – all representing higher-order thinking. The place to hone these skills is within the particular culture that a child shares with their relatives – the one they are born into and surrounded by. All cultures promote positive social interactions within their society and among their "in group." Yet different cultures prioritize different forms of learning, skills, and behavior in distinct ways. Tomasello's argument clearly implies that humans should be promoting collaborative skills throughout the lifespan but especially during childhood when cultural transmission occurs (Packer & Cole, 2019). Raising highly skilled collaborators will benefit all of society. Tomasello's argument is consistent with the research summarized here documenting the importance of collaborative forms of development.

Tomasello's account, like the one put forward in this book, makes the case that not only is the individualistic conception of society and child development an exclusively Western paradigm not shared with the majority of cultures around the world, but also that we are at our best as a species when we use our greatest strength – namely our capacity for collaboration and cooperative endeavors – to achieve shared goals.

Nonetheless, the prevailing Western models of schooling, learning, and intelligence are each based in individualistic, competitive notions. Although human adults compete, they often compete in groups to meet goals that are shared by the larger culture of which they are apart. To be celebrated by human society, talented individuals must reflect a given set of values that are shared with the broader culture. Yet children's development and achievements within the Western world are treated as primarily individual. For example, learning math in school is viewed as resulting from the individual's capacity, although math concepts are the basis for technological and scientific advances that are used to solve societal problems.

Philosophical analysis has revealed how culture and cultural institutions are established and maintained by social relations at the micro and macro levels (Searle, 1995, 2005). Nonetheless, scholarship in developmental psychology and education reifies the Cartesian idea that thinking, learning, and feeling are all individual, internal states, private and disconnected from social relations (Stetsenko, 2016). Given that psychology was founded by detaching the study of the psyche from philosophy and religion, scholars have suggested that these assumptions should be interrogated as to whether the constructs of the field accurately reflects the human experience (Castro & Lafuente, 2007). The first step in this would be to critically examine the methods used to analyze and measure human behavior. Beyond this, subdisciplines of psychology that influence education, such as developmental science, must ask whether our research paradigms are providing insights to allow children to realize their greatest potential. Within the confines of an exclusively individualistic methodology, the question becomes whether more can be learned without changing the current methodological paradigm (Valsiner, 2017).

Reconsidering the Unit of Analysis

The most efficient way to recenter psychology's emphasis from the individual to the collective is to shift the unit of analysis. To date, every field of psychology – from clinical to developmental – begins and ends with the individual. Group processes, when they are explored, are still often tied to a dependent variable that assesses individual-level outcomes. Accepting psychological results that do not land within some measure of individual behavior means recognizing the value of collective achievements as a psychological outcome. Yet this does not mean that our individual perspectives are completely subsumed within the group. As explained by Tomasello, adapting individual- and group-level perspectives to one another is what enables the complexity and evolution of human endeavors. However, artificially extracting the individual perspective from the social context and assessing it as static removes the complexity, fluidity, and dynamism of human subjectivity and intersubjectivity.

Our methods of assessment reflect our unit of analysis. The outcomes of these measures guide our society, especially in pedagogy. Although everything children learn is deeply embedded in culture, we do not make those cultural connections explicit in either research or pedagogical practice. We do not ensure that individual children learning in particular schools are learning the lifeways of their home and community cultures. Instead, many children learn in a disconnected fashion; the basis for the knowledge and skills being imparted by teachers is artificially separated from what would otherwise be a natural process of cultural transmission (Hale, 2016). As a result, children whose home cultures are most distant from the cultures reflected by the institution of school are least likely to fully engage with such "learning" (Delpit, 2006, 2012). To undo this, we must begin with new models and methods for understanding human development. A few possible steps for beginning such a transformation are outlined in the following subsections.

Decentering Eurocentric Principles

The first necessary step is to disentangle notions of hierarchy and status from different cultural forms of relating. In the present field of psychology, Eurocentric principles are valorized as "mainstream" while all other forms of child-rearing, developing, and interacting are deemed to be located in the separate field of "cultural psychology." This is the result of psychology's origins as a modern European field of study. The Western European intellectual tradition has perpetuated a cultural hegemony in which Western culture is considered normative, whereas "foreign" cultures are used to test comparisons with the norm (Hwang, 2023; Tomacic & Berardi, 2018). To disrupt the Eurocentric bias that currently infiltrates every aspect of psychological science, new assumptions, theories, and methods that have already been developed from within the majority world must be fully integrated into mainstream psychology. As described in Chapter 2, a fundamental basis for Eurocentric bias is the individualistic, atomistic way of viewing the human psyche. Expanding this to include relational ontologies will reveal a world of new concepts and methods for understanding the full breadth of human psychology. This has already been shown within Indigenous psychologies.

Clinical psychology is similar to developmental psychology in that both subdisciplines determine how a population of vulnerable people is understood, assessed, and treated. Within developmental psychology the population is children, and especially children designated as "at risk," whereas in clinical psychology the subjects of research and practice are those experiencing psychological and emotional distress. The Diagnostic and Statistical Manual of Mental Disorders (DSM) defines all psychological disorders as disorders of individuals. Accordingly, most research into abnormal psychology uses the individual as the unit of analysis. Much like the educational interventions prescribed by developmental and educational psychology, psychiatric interventions are almost exclusively targeted to individual deficits, challenges, and needs. This individualism in both measurement and treatment persists despite the evidence that dysfunctional systems, such as families, operate to create and maintain emotional imbalances among groups, according to interactive dynamics often based in group-determined roles and relationships (Nicols, 2010). Similarly, social experiences form the basis for trauma, and individual responses to such trauma are exhibited within relational dynamics (e.g., Allen et al., 2014; Conger et al., 2015; Wüsten & Lincoln, 2017). Many well-established treatments for psychological disorders are relational and dynamic, involving dyads as well as larger groups (Bradley et al., 2014; Carrera et al., 2016). These treatments specify that efficacy is contingent on interactive rather than individual factors – that psychological disorders cannot be treated in isolation from the sociocultural contexts in which people live. Despite a growing consensus that the causes and cures for psychological disorders are irreducibly collective and tied to social interactions, the diagnoses – and therefore the constructs that comprise the field of clinical psychology – are exclusively limited to the individual.

This mirrors developmental psychology, in which, despite a recognition that ontogenetic processes are interactive, the outcome is measured at the individual level. The question becomes: What of the actual psychological phenomenon remains when it has been stripped of its social, relational quality? This question has not been addressed within psychology, although it has been extensively discussed in fields like philosophy, sociology and cultural studies. Many of the most prominent thinkers within these fields describe the individual self as an illusion, being merely a reflection of the myriad social relations that comprise the existence of an individual.

Rethinking Outcomes

To reconcile the extensive evidence of the primacy of the social with research and interventions that privilege the individual, psychology must shed its stubborn allegiance to the individual in the form of outcome variables. Designing group-level outcomes means taking the importance of group-level functioning seriously. Beginning with an acknowledgment of the supremacy of culture – the shared baseline that frames each social activity in automatic and unseen ways – we must ask: What is the best possible outcome of any given endeavor? Collaborative competence could be recognized as a major goal of development, with the same status as abstract thinking or moral development. Most studies that do investigate interactive skills do so for the purpose of relating them to later or concurrent individual achievements. To shift this paradigm, we must devote research to modeling ideal group processes and outcomes for different purposes and at different ages.

As demonstrated in the studies of preschoolers and first graders as well as innovative research from the fields of cognitive science, human–computer interaction and collaborative problem-solving, research delineating a developmental progression of microinteractions that detail how groups best relate both verbally and nonverbally at different ages, in different social contexts and material environments, and for specific purposes would allow for the creation of group-level outcome variables. Descriptions of intersubjectivity as it appears at different stages are the closest that developmental psychology has come to a literature of ideal interactive processes. However, the varied ways in which intersubjective forms of relating can be applied to different group goals at different points in ontogeny and within different contexts are needed.

Maintaining a Developmental Approach with an Interactive Unit

Perinat and Sadurni (1999) have shown that among infants the meaning of objects is embodied within the actions of their interacting partner, such as a parent. According to their model, meanings are transmitted socially from parent to infant until the infants become themselves the "narrators" of meaning in later infancy. The SAE account of intersubjectivity presented in this book may be seen to continue this ontogeny of meaning into the preschool period, during which peers reconstruct meanings out of the social context of their interactive play. During imaginative play, the meanings of objects and tasks are reimagined beyond what was transmitted earlier. This time, the social coordination of actions in relation to objects in the environment occurs between equals, as a negotiation of meaning. The sociocultural and historical context influencing the negotiation of meanings given to objects and activities includes the adult-prepared environment as the background while simultaneously being created by the constantly changing meanings of preschoolers' own play activities. The unique developmental traits of the preschool period give rise to an intersubjectively constituted reality that emerges from shared activity beyond the "givens" of adult society. In this way, the "transmission" of meanings from adult to child as described by traditional theorists is replaced by an intersubjective transformation of meaning, in which the unique subjectivities of the children emerge as they cocreate the meanings of their shared activity together. This view of development as inherently transformative rather than transmissive depicts early childhood as a time when children become coauthors of their reality together with their peers during play.

Uniting the Subject with Collaborative Activity

Such a view is conceptually consistent with Stetsenko's (2016) Transformative Activist Stance (TAS) paradigm of development within the broader CHAT perspective. Consistent with this view, children continuously engage in collectively changing the world during play while they themselves are changed by their collaborative actions. Stetsenko argues for a repositioning of human activity, society, and transformation as components of development that are co-occurring and in continuous dynamic and dialectical relation. On this view, human agency, sociohistorically and collaboratively constructed, is at the center of both development and the nature of society (as a constantly evolving phenomenon). A value-neutral form of acting on the world is impossible according to the TAS, as human agency always reflects striving that is imbued with values and goals. This perspective acknowledges the cultural and historical dimensions of systems of socially shared activity and how those dimensions are implicated in every developmental process. By highlighting the role of agency and the inherently activist nature of human transformation of the world, it extends CHAT. Thereby, agency and activism simultaneously produce development at both individual and collective levels.

This perspective requires a conception of individual, collaborative, social, and historical change wherein each component is mutually constitutive, equally dynamic, and with no fixed points of origin or end. Yet the activist stance does imply goal-directedness and a telos of "making the world/ourselves better," as people are made better by the world as they make it better.

Assessing a collaborative interaction from this perspective requires new methods that acknowledge the ways in which human agency is enacted during a process that is simultaneously cocreating the meanings of that agency in relation to the ongoing collaboration. Ricca et al.'s (2020) use of a measure of entropy overlaid with indicators of states of collaboration provides a useful example of how to analyze change and stability in human collective striving at various levels while also acknowledging the micro-interactive behaviors that influence those states. Matusov's (1996) depiction of play-crafting in which interactants coconstructed goals and identities in relation to a dynamically emergent collective project is another example that includes language and moments of cohesion and dissolution.

Stetsenko (2016) concludes her account with a prescription for education. Again, she expands on the notions of learner-centered, inquiry-based methods to argue that learners do not enter a learning situation with their interests and questions already determined, but that discovering those interests and questions is embedded in the learning process, as is the search for the identity of the learner. Students must be supported through the provision of tools and collaborative structures to engage in processes of collective striving as they simultaneously cocreate themselves and their expanded knowledge. In other words, teachers cannot attach a set of problems or questions to a fixed set of interests and goals among learners a priori because learners must discover and pursue their interests and goals as part of their process of coconstructing their identity by posing problems and authoring their own activist projects. This view of collaborative learning as primarily about problem-posing, wherein learners collectively identify what matters to them, create shared meanings, and explore new understandings, is reminiscent of Schindler and Bakker's (2020) description of the affective field during processes of collaborative problem-posing. Teacher-learners are embedded within historical and social contexts while they are cocreating new futures and their versions of a better world as collectively imagined and strived for. This process, tied to the pursuit of identity and led by collective striving, can never be ethically or affectively neutral. Instead, Stetsenko (2016, p. 329) writes: "Knowing then is a deeply personal, passionate, and ethically evaluative process achieved from a position of struggle, care and concern, a desire to move forward and beyond the present, in transcending its status quo."

This depiction of knowledge as an example of human development requires a restructuring of education into a space where teachers and learners together grapple with the meanings of history and society for the purposes of enabling learners' identities to emerge dynamically. The learners' identities are a component of knowledge creation and of supporting the collective project of imagining and remaking the world in more ethical and just ways as a product of engaging with it.

A Theoretical Home for the Role of Collaborative Competence 231

To tie this approach to a developmental sequence joins together peer play as a site of children's collective authoring of their reality (Perinat & Sadurni, 1999) during early childhood with emergent forms of collaborative problem-posing and problem-solving during late childhood and adolescence. Between these developmental periods, methods that assess dynamic emergent capacities for both social coordination and shared conceptual meaning-making are found in diverse research and pedagogical frameworks. These include collaborative competence, play-based pedagogy, and dialogic education within the CoEnact framework. These approaches offer a way for learners to collectively pursue their own identities and knowledge construction in relation to authentically meaningful and dynamically and constituted shared goals. As described earlier, each of these aspects combines research scholarship with a methodology for teaching and learning, which are inextricably linked. These forms of pedagogy are designed to be emancipatory, as the TAS is about striving against any form of oppression or barrier to human agency and development. In this way, TAS theory requires methods for applying it within educational contexts that are inherently political, ethical, and grounded in a telos of social justice.

The TAS provides a broad framework wherein subjectivity and human agency function with varying degrees of intersubjectivity. This intersubjectivity occurs at two levels: with coactors who are engaged in collaborative undertakings and simultaneously with the broader cultural and historical meanings that, in turn, provide a common cultural standpoint for collaborations.

If two-year-olds jointly create socially defined meanings of objects (i.e., status functions) with the adults in their proximity (Rakoczy, 2006), preschoolers collaboratively enact shared realities out of intersubjectivity with peers (as shown in this volume; Goncu, 1993), and adults collectively create innovative work products that go far beyond what any individual could have imagined, then school-aged children can build on their ability to construct collective conceptual understanding within a variety of disciplines. School should provide opportunities for children to make use of their uniquely human capacities for intersubjectivity. As they to create and develop shared meanings with their peers and teachers and in so doing to they simultaneously create their own identities as agents who are actively engaged in creating a better world together.

Conclusion

This book has argued for a rethinking of psychology and education that challenges the Eurocentric biases inherent in individualistic assumptions and approaches. Tomasello makes a compelling case for the idea that, as humans, we are at our best when we function in the way that we are uniquely evolved for – cooperatively. His theory has strong evidential support, and there does not seem to be much counterevidence to challenge it. The question thus arises as to why developmental psychology has maintained its individualistic bias so comprehensively despite related fields and even research within the field providing challenges. Social psychology has convincingly demonstrated that our behavior is more easily predicted by our relationships with others or our allegiances to groups than any individual trait. It is time for the field of developmental psychology to consider that, by failing to recognize the inherently social, collaborative nature of human development, we are ignoring the answers to many questions that the field has long sought to answer, especially regarding the most vulnerable populations of children. It is simultaneously time for our education systems to rethink the cultures that they were built to reflect. Perhaps by learning from those cultures whose children have the greatest skills in collaborative competence we could better ensure the learning and development of all children.

References

Achenbach, T. M. (1966). The classification of children's psychiatric symptoms: A factor-analytic study. *Psychological Monographs, 80*, 1–37.

Ackerman, B. P., Brown, E. D., & Izard, C. E. (2004). The relations between contextual risk, earned income, and the school adjustment of children from economically disadvantaged families. *Developmental Psychology, 40*, 204–216.

Ainsworth, M. D. S., & Bell, S. (1970). Attachment, exploration, and separation illustrated by the behavior of one year-olds in a strange situation. *Child Development, 41*, 49–67.

Alcalá, L., Rogoff, B., & López Fraire, A. (2018). Sophisticated collaboration is common among Mexican-heritage US children. *Proceedings of the National Academy of Sciences of the United States of America, 115*(45), 11377–11384.

Allen, J., Balfour, R., Bell, R., & Marmot, M. (2014). Social determinants of mental health. *International Review of Psychiatry, 26*(4), 392–407.

Andrews-Todd, J., & Forsyth, C. M. (2020). Exploring social and cognitive dimensions of collaborative problem solving in an open online simulation-based task. *Computers in Human Behavior, 104*, 105759.

Andrews-Todd, J., & Kerr, D. (2019). Application of ontologies for assessing collaborative problem solving skills. *International Journal of Testing, 19*(2), 172–187.

Ansari, A., & Gershoff, E. (2015). Learning-related social skills as a mediator between teacher instruction and child achievement in Head Start. *Social Development, 24*(4), 699–715.

Artut, P. D. (2009). Experimental evaluation of the effects of cooperative learning on kindergarten children's mathematics ability. *International Journal of Educational Research, 48*(6), 370–380.

Ashitaka, Y., & Shimada, H. (2014). The cultural background of the non-academic concept of psychology in Japan: Its implications for introductory education in psychology. *International Journal of Psychology, 49*(3), 167–174.

Atkinson, L., Beitchman, J., Gonzalez, A., Young, A., Wilson, B., Escobar, M., Chishold, V., Brownlie, E., Khoury, J. E., Ludmer, J., & Villani, V. (2015). Cumulative risk, cumulative outcome: A 20-year longitudinal study. *PLoS ONE, 10*(6), e0127650.

Avnet, M. S. (2016). A network-based analysis of team coordination and shared cognition in cooperative learning groups. *Journal of Educational Research*, *105*(5), 329–335.

Bakhtin, M. (1981). *The dialogic imagination*. M. Holquist (ed.). Austin: University of Texas Press.

Ball, D. L., & Forzani, F. M. (2009). The work of teaching and the challenge for teacher education. *Journal of Teacher Education*, *60*(5), 497–511.

Barajas-Gonzalez, R. G., Ursache, A., Kamboukos, D., Huang, K.-Y., Dawson-McClure, S., Urcuyo, A., Huang, T. J. J., & Brotman, L. M. (2022). Parental perceived immigration threat and children's mental health, self-regulation and executive functioning in pre-kindergarten. *American Journal of Orthopsychiatry*, *92*(2), 176–189.

Bardack, S., Herbers, J. E., & Obradović, J. (2017). Unique contributions of dynamic versus global measures of parent–child interaction quality in predicting school adjustment. *Journal of Family Psychology*, *31*(6), 649–658.

Bateman, A., & Fonagy, P. (2004). *Psychotherapy for borderline personality disorder: Mentalization based treatment*. New York: Oxford University Press.

Bearison, D., & Dorval, B. (2002). *Collaborative cognition: Children negotiating ways of knowing*. Westport, CT: Greenwood Press.

Beraldo, R. M, Ligorio, M. B., & Barbato, S. (2018). Intersubjectivity in primary and secondary education: A review study. *Research Papers in Education*, *33*(2), 278–299.

Berg-Nielsen, T. S., Solheim, E., Belsky, J., & Wichstrom, L. (2012). Preschoolers' psychosocial problems: In the eyes of the beholder? Adding teacher characteristics as determinants of discrepant parent–teacher reports. *Child Psychiatry & Human Development*, *43*, 393–413.

Bernstein, V. J., Harris, E., Long, C., Iida, E., & Hans, S. (2005). Issues in the multicultural assessment of parent–child interaction: An exploratory study from the starting early starting smart collaboration. *Journal of Applied Developmental Psychology*, *26*, 241–275.

Bertucci, A., Johnson, D., Johnson, R., & Conte, S. (2012). Influence of Group Processing on development of young children: a systematic review. *Journal of Educational Research*, *105*(5), 329–335.

Birk, S. L., Stewart, L., & Olino, T. M. (2022). Parent–child synchrony after early childhood: A systematic review. *Clinical Child & Family Psychology Review*, *25*, 529–551.

Bodrova, E., & Leong, D. J. (2015). Vygotskian and post-Vygotskian views on children's play. *American Journal of Play*, *7*(3), 371–388.

Bostock, L., & Koprowska, J. (2022). "I know how it sounds on paper": Risk talk, the use of documents and epistemic justice in child protection assessment home visits. *Qualitative Social Work*, *21*(6), 1147–1166.

Bradley, R., Drummey, K., Gottman, J., & Gottman, J. (2014). Treating couples who mutually exhibit violence or aggression: Reducing behaviors that show a susceptibility for violence. *Journal of Family Violence*, *29*(5), 549–558.

Bradley, R. H., & Caldwell, B. M. (1979). Home observation for measurement of the environment: A revision of the preschool scale. *American Journal of Mental Deficiency, 84*(3), 235–244.
Brennan, A., & Enns, J. (2015). When two heads are better than one: Interactive versus independent benefits of collaborative cognition. *Psychonomic Bulletin & Review, 22*, 1076–1082.
Brownell, C. A., Geetha, R. B., & Zerwas, S. (2006). Becoming a social partner with peers: cooperation and social understanding in one- and two-year olds. *Child Development, 77*, 803–821.
Bruner, J. (1978). The role of dialogue in language acquisition. In A. Sinclair, R. Jarvella, & W. J. M. Levelt (eds.), *The child's conception of language* (pp. 241–256). Berlin: Springer-Verlag.
Buell, M., Han, M., & Vukelich, C. (2017). Factors affecting variance in Classroom Assessment Scoring System scores: Season, context, and classroom composition. *Early Child Development and Care, 187*, 1635–1648.
Bulotsky-Shearer, R. J., Bell, E. R., Romero, S. L., & Carter, T. M. (2012). Preschool interactive peer play mediates problem behavior and learning for low-income children. *Journal of Applied Developmental Psychology, 33*, 53–65.
Bulotsky-Shearer, R. J., Fantuzzo, J. W., & Mcdermott, P. A. (2008). An investigation of classroom situation dimensions of emotional and behavioral adjustment and cognitive and social outcomes for Head Start children. *Developmental Psychology, 44*, 139–154.
Bulotsky-Shearer, R. J., Fernandez, V. A., Bichay-Awadalla, K., Bailey, J., Futterer, J., & Qi, C. H. (2020). Teacher–child interaction quality moderates social risks associated with problem behavior in preschool classroom contexts. *Journal of Applied Developmental Psychology, 67*, 101103.
Burchinal, M., Vandergrift, N., Pianta, R., & Mashburn, A. (2010). Threshold analysis of association between child care quality and child outcomes for low-income children in pre-kindergarten programs *Early Childhood Research Quarterly, 25*(2), 166–176.
Burchinal, M., Xue, Y., Auger, A., Tien, H., Mashburn, A., Peisner, F. E., Cavadel, E. W., Zaslow, M., & Tarullo, L. (2016). Testing for quality thresholds and features in early care and education. *Monographs of the Society for Research in Child Development, 81*(2), 46–63.
Burlaka, V., Bermann, E., & Graham-Bermann, S. (2015). Internalizing problems in at-risk preschoolers: Associations with child and mother risk factors. *Journal of Child & Family Studies, 24*(9), 2653–2660.
Burman, E. (2017). *Deconstructing developmental psychology* (3rd ed.). London: Routledge.
Butler-Barnes, S. T., Leath, S., Williams, A., Byrd, C., Carter, R., & Chavous, T. M. (2018). Promoting resilience among African American girls: Racial identity as a protective factor. *Child Development, 89*(6), e552–e571.
Buyse, E., Verschueren, K., Verachtert, P., & Van Damme, J. (2009). Predicting school adjustment in early elementary school: Impact of teacher–child

relationship quality and relational classroom climate. *Elementary School Journal, 110*(2), 119–141.

Cabello, V. M., & Topping, K. J. (2018). Making scientific concepts explicit through explanations: Simulations of a high-leverage practice in teacher education. *International Journal of Cognitive Research in Science, Engineering & Education (IJCRSEE), 6*(3), 35–47.

Cappa, K. A., Begle, A. M., Conger, J. C., Dumas, J. E., & Conger, A. J. (2011). Bidirectional relationships between parenting stress and child coping competence: Findings from the pace study. *Journal of Child and Family Studies, 20*, 334–342.

Carra, C., Lavelli, M., & Keller, H. (2014). Differences in practices of body stimulation during the first 3 months: Ethnotheories and behaviors of Italian mothers and West African immigrant mothers. *Infant Behavior & Development, 37*(1), 5–15.

Carrera, M., Cabero, A., González, S., Rodríguez, N., García, C., Hernández, L., & Manjón, J. (2016). Solution-focused group therapy for common mental health problems: Outcome assessment in routine clinical practice. *Psychology & Psychotherapy: Theory, Research & Practice, 89*(3), 294–307.

Cassidy, J., Jones, J., & Shaver, P. (2013). Contributions of attachment theory and research: A framework for future research, translation, and policy. *Development and Psychopathology, 25*(4 pt. 2), 1415–1434.

Castro, J., & Lafuente, E. (2007). Westernalization in the mirror: On the cultural reception of Western psychology. *Integrative Psychological & Behavioral Science, 41*(1), 106–113.

Cazden, C. B. (2001). *Classroom discourse: The language of teaching and learning.* Portsmouth, NH: Heinemann.

Chaiklin, S. (2019). Units and wholes in the cultural-historical theory of child development. In Edwards A., Fleer M., Bøttcher L. (eds.), *Cultural-historical approaches to studying learning and development* (pp. 263–277). Singapore: Springer.

Chang, H., Shelleby, E. C., Cheong, J., & Shaw, D. S. (2012). Cumulative risk, negative emotionality, and emotion regulation as predictors of social competence in transition to school: A mediated moderation model. *Social Development, 21*(4), 780–800.

Chou, H.-W., Lin, Y.-H., & Chou, S.-B. (2012). Team cognition, collective efficacy, and performance in strategic decision-making teams. *Social Behavior & Personality: An International Journal, 40*(3), 381–394.

Christie, S., Gao, Y., & Ma, Q. (2020). Development of analogical reasoning: A novel perspective from cross-cultural studies. *Child Development Perspectives, 14*(3), 164–170.

Chua, R. Y., Kadirvelu, A., Yasin, S., Choudhry, F. R., & Park, M. S. A. (2019). The cultural, family and community factors for resilience in Southeast Asian Indigenous communities: A systematic review. *Journal of Community Psychology, 47*(7), 1750–1771.

Clegg, J. M., Wen, N. J., DeBaylo, P. H., Alcott, A., Keltner, E. C., & Legare, C. H. (2021). Teaching through collaboration: Flexibility and diversity in caregiver–child interaction across cultures. *Child Development, 92*(1), e56–e75.

Cole, M. (2013). Differences and deficits in psychological research in historical perspective: A commentary on the special section. *Developmental Psychology, 49*(1), 84–91.

Cole, M., Gay, J., Glick, J., & Sharp, D. (1971). *The cultural context of learning and thinking: An exploration in experimental anthropology.* New York: Basic Books.

Conger, R. D., Martin, M. J., Masarik, A. S., Widaman, K. F., & Donnelan, M. B. (2015). Social and economic antecedents and consequences of adolescent aggressive personality: Predictions from the interactionist model. *Development & Psychopathology, 27*(4 pt. 1), 1111–1127.

Connery, M. C., John-Steiner, V., & Marjanovic-Shane, A. (eds.). (2010). *Vygotsky and creativity: A cultural historical approach to play, meaning making, and the arts* (vol. 5). Lausanne: Peter Lang.

Coplan, R. J., & Rubin, K. H. (1998). Exploring and assessing nonsocial play in the preschool: The development and validation of the Preschool Play Behavior Scale. *Social Development, 7*(1), 75–91.

Coppens, A. D., Silva, K. G., Ruvalcaba, O., Alcalá, L., López, A., & Rogoff, B. (2014). Learning by observing and pitching in: benefits and processes of expanding repertoires. *Human Development, 57*(2/3), 150–161.

Correa-Chávez, M., & Roberts, A. L. D. (2012). A cultural analysis is necessary in understanding intersubjectivity. *Culture & Psychology, 18*(1), 99–108.

Correa-Chávez, M., & Rogoff, B. (2009). Children's attention to interactions directed to others: Guatemalan Mayan and European American patterns. *Developmental Psychology, 45*(3), 630–641.

Creavey, K. L., Gatzke-Kopp, L. M., & Fosco, G. M. (2018). Differential effects of family stress exposure and harsh parental discipline on child social competence. *Journal of Child & Family Studies, 27*(2), 483–493.

Cukurova, M., Luckin, R., & Baines, E. (2018). The significance of context for the emergence and implementation of research evidence: The case of collaborative problem-solving. *Oxford Review of Education, 44*(3), 322–337.

D'Ambrosio, U. (2006) *Ethnomathematics: Link between traditions and modernity.* Rotterdam: Brill.

Dasen, P. R. (1984). The cross-cultural study of intelligence: Piaget and the Baoule. *International Journal of Psychology, 19*(4/5), 407.

Davidson, K., & Roopnarine, J. L. (2021). Ethnic–racial socialization in early childhood: Effects of parent–teacher congruency on children's social and emotional development. *Early Child Development and Care, 192*, 1–15.

Dayton, A., Aceves-Azuara, I., & Rogoff, B. (2022). Collaboration at a microscale: Cultural differences in family interactions. *British Journal of Developmental Psychology, 40*, 189–213.

De Jaegher, H., & Di Paolo, E. (2007). Participatory sense-making: An enactive approach to social cognition. *Phenomenology and Cognitive Sciences, 6*, 485–507.

De Jaegher, H., Peräkylä, A., Stevanovic, M. (2016). The co-creation of meaningful action: Bridging enaction and interactional sociology. *Philosophical Transactions of the Royal Society B: Biological Sciences, 371*, 20150378.

De Jaegher, H., Pieper, B., Clénin, D., & Fuchs, T. (2017). Grasping intersubjectivity: An invitation to embody social interaction research. *Phenomenology and Cognitive Sciences, 16*, 491–523.

de la Osa, N., Granero, R., Trepat, E., Domenech, J., & Ezpeleta, L. (2016). The discriminative capacity of CBCL/1½–5–DSM5 scales to identify disruptive and internalizing disorders in preschool children. *European Child & Adolescent Psychiatry, 25*(1), 17–23.

Delpit, L. D. (2006). *Other people's children: Cultural conflict in the classroom.* New York: The New Press.

Delpit, L. D. (2012). *"Multiplication is for white people": Raising expectations for other people's children.* New York: The New Press.

Desmond, M., & Lopez Turley, R. N. (2009). The role of familism in explaining the Hispanic–white college application gap. *Social Problems, 56*(2), 311–334.

Desombre, C., Jury, M., Bagès, C., & Brasselet, C. (2019). The distinct effect of multiple sources of stereotype threat. *Journal of Social Psychology, 159*(5), 628–641.

Diaz-Loving, R. (2005). Emergence and contributions of a Latin American Indigenous social psychology. *International Journal of Psychology, 40*(4), 213–227.

Ding, Y., Xu, X., Wang, Z., Li, H., & Wang, W. (2014). The relation of infant attachment to attachment and cognitive and behavioural outcomes in early childhood. *Early Human Development, 90*(9), 459–464.

Domenech-Rodriguez, M. M., Donovick, M. R., & Crowley, S. L. (2009). Parenting styles in a cultural context: Observations of protective parenting in first generation Latinos. *Family Process, 48*(2), 195–210.

Dyer, S., & Moneta, G. B. (2006). Frequency of parallel, associative, and co-operative play in British children of different socio-economic status. *Social Behavior and Personality, 34*, 587–592.

Ebersöhn, L. (2019). *Flocking together: An Indigenous psychology theory of resilience in Southern Africa.* Cham: Springer International Publishing.

Edwards, A., Fleer, M., & Bøttcher, L. (eds.). (2019). *Cultural-historical approaches to studying learning and development.* Singapore: Springer.

Edwards, C. P., de Guzman, M. T., Brown, J., & Kumru, A. (2006). Children's social behaviors and peer interactions in diverse cultures. In X. Chen, D. French, & B. Schneider (eds.), *Peer relationships in cultural context* (pp. 23–51). New York: Cambridge University Press.

Edwards-Groves, C., & Davidson, C. (2020). Special Issue: Talk and interaction in the dialogic classroom: Pedagogy, practice and change. *Australian Journal of Language and Literacy, 43*, 4.

Eisenberg, N. (2001). The core and correlates of affective social competence. *Social Development, 10*(1), 120–124.

Elkonin, D. B. (2005). Chapter 1: The subject of our research: The developed form of play. *Journal of Russian and East European Psychology*, *45*(1), 22–48.

Engelbrecht, P., & Natzel, S. G. (1997). Cultural variations in cognitive style: Field dependence vs field independence. *School Psychology International*, *18*(2), 155–164.

Engelmann, J. M., & Tomasello, M. (2019). Children's sense of fairness as equal respect. *Trends in Cognitive Sciences*, *23*(6), 454–463.

Engeström, Y. (2007). Enriching the theory of expansive learning: Lessons from journeys toward co-configuration. *Mind, Culture and Activity*, *14*(1–2), 23–39.

Erikson, E. (1963). *Childhood and society*. New York: Norton.

Evans, G. W., Li, D., & Sepanski Whipple, S. (2013). Cumulative risk and child development. *Psychological Bulletin*, *139*(6), 1342–1396.

Fantuzzo, J., Sekino, Y., & Cohen, H. L. (2004). An examination of the contributions of interactive peer play to salient classroom competencies for urban Head Start children. *Psychology in the Schools*, *41*, 323–336.

Fauth, B., Atlay, C., Dumont, H., & Decristan, J. (2021). Does what you get depend on who you are with? Effects of student composition on teaching quality. *Learning & Instruction*, *71*, 101355.

Fauth, B., Decristan, J., Decker, A.-T., Büttner, G., Hardy, I., Klieme, E., & Kunter, M. (2019). The effects of teacher competence on student outcomes in elementary science education: The mediating role of teaching quality. *Teaching & Teacher Education*, *86*, 102882.

Fawcett, L. M., & Garton, A. F. (2005). The effect of peer collaboration on children's problem-solving ability. *British Journal of Educational Psychology*, *75*, 157–169.

Feldman, R. (2007). Parent–infant synchrony: Biological foundations and developmental outcomes. *Current Directions in Psychological Science*, *16*(6), 340–345.

Feldman, R., & Masalha, S. (2010). Parent–child and triadic antecedents of children's social competence: Cultural specificity, shared process. *Developmental Psychology*, *46*, 455–467.

Feldman, R., Bamberger, E., & Kanat-Maymon, Y. (2013). Parent-specific reciprocity from infancy to adolescence shapes children's social competence and dialogical skills. *Attachment & Human Development*, *15*(4), 407–423.

Ferholt, B., Guarrasi, I., Jornet, A., Nardi, B., Rajala, A., & Williams, J. (2020). Humanity's leading activity: Survival, of the humanity of our species. *Mind, Culture, and Activity*, *27*(2), 95–98.

Ferholt, B., Nilsson, M., & Lecusay, R. (2019). Preschool teachers being alongside young children. In S. Alcock & N. Stobbs (eds.), *Rethinking play as pedagogy* (pp. 15–31). London: Routledge.

Fernald, A., Marchman, V. A. & Weisleder, A. (2013). SES differences in language processing skill and vocabulary are evident at 18 months. *Developmental Science*, *16*(2), 234–248.

Fernández, M., Wegerif, R., Mercer, N., & Rojas-Drummond, S. (2002). Re-conceptualizing "scaffolding" and the zone of proximal development in the

context of symmetrical collaborative learning. *Journal of Classroom Interaction*, *36*(1/2), 40–54.
Fernyhough, C., Wainwright, R., Gupta, E., & Tuckey, M. (2002). Maternal mind-mindedness amd attachment security as predictors of theory of mind understanding. *Child Development*, *73*, 12.
Finegood, E. D., & Blair, C. (2020). Relating poverty and parenting stress to emerging executive functions in young children. In K. Deater-Deckard & R. Panneton (eds.), *Parenting stress: Adaptive and maladaptive consequences for developmental well-being of children* (pp. 181–207). New York: Springer.
Fischer, F., Bruhn, J., Graesel, C., & Mandl, H. (2002). Fostering collaborative knowledge construction with visualization tools. *Learning and Instruction*, *12*, 213–232.
Fish, J. (2022). Towards a Haudenosaunee developmental science: Perspectives from the two row wampum. *Infant and Child Development*, *31*(1), e2279.
Fleer, M. (2006). The cultural construction of child development: Creating institutional and cultural intersubjectivity. *International Journal of Early Years Education*, *14*(2), 127–140.
Fletcher, K. K., Cates, C. B., Mendelsohn, A. L., & Tamis-LeMonda, C. S. (2020). Play in Mexican-American mothers and toddlers is frequent, multimodal, and rich in symbolic content. *Infancy*, *25*(5), 535–551.
Forman, E. A., Minick, N., & Stone, C. A. (eds.) (1993). *Contexts for learning: Sociocultural dynamics in children's development.* New York: Oxford University Press.
Fuchs, T., & De Jaegher, H. (2009). Enactive intersubjectivity: Participatory sense making and mutual incorporation. *Phenomenological Cognitive Science*, *8*, 465–486.
Fung, W., & Cheng, R. (2017). Effect of school pretend play on preschoolers' social competence in peer interactions: Gender as a potential moderator. *Early Childhood Education Journal*, *45*(1), 35–42.
Gage, N. A., Adamson, R., MacSuga-Gage, A. S., & Lewis, T.J. (2017). The relation between the academic achievement of students with emotional and behavioral disorders and teacher characteristics. *Behavioral Disorders*, *43*(1), 213–222.
Gamberini, L., & Spagnolli, A. (2004). The "presence of others" in a virtual environment: Different collaborative modalities with hybrid resources. *Cognition, Technology and Work*, *6*, 45–48.
Garcia-Carrion, R., López de Aguileta, G., Padrós, M., & Ramis-Salas, M. (2020). Implications for social impact of dialogic teaching and learning. *Frontiers of Psychology*, *11*, 140.
Garner, P. W., & Mahatmya, D. (2015). Affective social competence and teacher–child relationship quality: Race/ethnicity and family income level as moderators. *Social Development*, *24*(3), 678–697.
Garner, P. W., Shadur, J. M., & Toney, T. (2021). The effects of teacher–child racial congruence, child race, and emotion situation knowledge on

teacher–child relationships and school readiness. *Psychology in the Schools*, *58*(10), 1995–2016.

Garte, R. (2015). Inter-subjectivity as a measure of social competence among children attending Head Start: Assessing the measure's validity and relation to context. *International Journal of Early Childhood*, *47*, 189–207.

Garte, R. (2016). A socio-cultural, activity-based account of preschooler intersubjectivity. *Culture and Psychology*, *22*(2), 264–275.

Garte, R. (2019). Collaborative competence during preschooler's peer interactions: Considering multiple levels of context within classrooms. *Integrative Psychological and Research*, *54*(1), 30–51.

Garton, A. F., & Pratt, C. (2001). Peer assistance in children's problem solving. *British Journal of Developmental Psychology*, *19*(2), 307–318.

Gauvain, M. (2018). Collaborative problem solving: Social and developmental considerations. *Psychological Science in the Public Interest*, *19*(2), 53–58.

Gee, K. A., & Asim, M. (2019). Parenting while food insecure: Links between adult food insecurity, parenting aggravation, and children's behaviors. *Journal of Family Issues*, *40*(11), 1462–1485.

Gesell, A. (1933). Maturation and the patterning of behavior. In C. Murchison (ed.), *A handbook of child psychology* (pp. 209–235). New York: Russell & Russell/Atheneum Publishers.

Gevers, J. M. P., Li, J., Rutte, C. G., & Eerde, W. (2020). How dynamics in perceptual shared cognition and team potency predict team performance. *Journal of Occupational & Organizational Psychology*, *93*(1), 134–157.

Gibson, J. J. (1986). *The ecological approach to visual perception*. Hillsdale, NJ: Lawrence Erlbaum Associates.

Gielen, U. P., & Roopnarine, J. L. (eds.). (2016). *Childhood and adolescence: Cross-cultural perspectives and applications*. Santa Barbara, CA: ABC-CLIO.

Gilkerson, J., Richards, J. A., Warren, S. F., Montgomery, J. K., Greenwood, C. R., Oller, D. K., Hansen, J. H. L., & Paul, T. D. (2017). Mapping the early language environment using all-day recordings and automated analysis. *American Journal of Speech–Language Pathology*, *26*(2), 248–265.

Gillespie, A., & Cornish, F. (2010). Intersubjectivity: Towards a dialogical analysis. *Journal for the Theory of Social Behaviour*, *40*(1), 19–46.

Gillies, R. M. (2014). Developments in cooperative learning: Review of research. *Anales de Psicología: Revista de La Facultad de Filosofía y Ciencias de La Educación*, *30*(3), 792–801.

Girolametto, L., Weitzman, E., & Greenberg, J. (2004). The effects of verbal support strategies on small-group peer interactions. *Language, Speech & Hearing Services in Schools*, *35*(3), 254–268.

Gobeil-Bourdeau, J., Lemelin, J.-P., Letarte, M.-J., & Laurent, A. (2022). Interactions between child temperament and family environment in relation to school readiness: Diathesis-stress, differential susceptibility, or vantage sensitivity? *Early Childhood Research Quarterly*, *60*, 274–286.

Goncu, A. (1993a). Development of inter-subjectivity in social pretend play. *Human Development*, *36*, 185–198.

Goncu, A. (1993b). Development of intersubjectivity in the dyadic play of preschoolers. *Early Childhood Research Quarterly*, *8*(1), 99–116.

Goncu, A., & Gaskins, S. (eds.). (2007). *Play and development: Evolutionary, sociocultural, and functional perspectives* (1st ed.). London: Psychology Press.

Goncu, A., Mistry, J., & Mosier, C. (2000). Cultural variations in the play of toddlers. *International Journal of Behavioral Development*, *24*(3), 321–329.

Goncu, A., Patt, M. B., & Kouba, E. (2002). Understanding young children's play in context. In P. K. Smith & C. H. Hart (eds.), *Blackwell handbook of childhood social development* (pp. 417–437). Oxford: Blackwell.

Gone, J. P. (2019). Considering Indigenous research methodologies: Critical reflections by an Indigenous knower. *Qualitative Inquiry*, *25*(1), 45–56.

Graesser, A. C., Fiore, S. M., Greiff, S., Andrews-Todd, J., Foltz, P. W., & Hesse, F. W. (2018). Advancing the science of collaborative problem solving. *Psychological Science in the Public Interest*, *19*(2), 59–92.

Inspiring Mathematics: Lessons from the Navajo Nation Math Circles. (2019). United States: Mathematical Sciences Research Institute.

Kochanska, G. (2017). Reflections on the legacy of early relationships. *Developmental Psychologist*. www.apadivisions.org/division-7/publications/newsletters/developmental/2017/07/early-relationships

Greenfield, P. M., Keller, H., Fuligni, A., & Maynard, A. (2003). Cultural pathways through universal development. *Annual Review of Psychology*, *54*(1), 461–490.

Haight, W. L., Wang, X. L., Fung, H. H. T., Williams, K., & Mintz, J. (1999). Universal, developmental, and variable aspects of young children's play: A cross-cultural comparison of pretending at home. *Child development*, *70*(6), 1477–1488.

Häkkinen, P., Järvelä, S., Mäkitalo-Siegl, K., Ahonen, A., Näykki, P., & Valtonen, T. (2017). Preparing Teacher-Students for Twenty-First-Century Learning Practices (PREP 21): A framework for enhancing collaborative problem-solving and strategic learning skills. *Teachers & Teaching*, *23*(1), 25–41.

Halberstadt, A. G., Denham, S. A., & Dunsmore, J. C. (2001). Affective social competence. *Social development*, *10*(1), 79–119.

Hale, J. E. (2016). Thirty-year retrospective on the learning styles of African American children. *Education and Urban Society*, *48*(5), 444–459.

Hamamura, T., Xu, Q., & Du, Y. (2013). Culture, social class, and independence–interdependence: The case of Chinese adolescents. *International Journal of Psychology*, *48*(3), 344–351.

Hamre, B. K., Hatfield, B., Pianta, R., & Jamil, F. (2014). Evidence for general and domain-specific elements of teacher–child interactions: Associations with preschool children's development. *Child Development*, *85*(3), 1257–1274.

Hamre, B. K., Pianta, R. C., Downer, J. T., & Mashburn, A. J. (2008). Teacher's perceptions of problems with young students: Looking beyond problem behaviors. *Social Development*, *17*, 115–136.

Hanish, L. D., Barcelo, H., Martin, C. L., Fabes, R. A., Holmwall, J., & Palermo, F. (2007). Using the Q Connectivity method to study frequency of interaction with multiple peer triads: Do preschoolers' peer group interactions at school relate to academic skills? *New Directions for Child and Adolescent Development, 118*, 9–24.

Harkness, S., & Super, C. M. (1996). *Parents' cultural belief systems: Their origins, expressions, and consequences.* New York: Guilford Press.

Harkness, S., & Super, C. M. (2020). Culture and human development: Where did it go? And where is it going? *New Directions for Child & Adolescent Development, 173*, 101–119.

Harrist, A. W., & Waugh, R. M. (2002). Dyadic synchrony: Its structure and function in children's development. *Developmental Review, 22*, 555–592.

Head Start Bureau. (2006). *Policy statement.* www.acf.hhs.gov

Healey, D. M., Gopin, C. B., Grossman, B. R., Campbell, S. B., & Halperin, J. M. (2010). Mother–child dyadic synchrony is associated with better functioning in hyperactive/inattentive preschool children. *Journal of Child Psychology and Psychiatry, 51*(9), 1058–1066.

Heiphetz, L., & Oishi, S. (2022). Viewing development through the lens of culture: integrating developmental and cultural psychology to better understand cognition and behavior. *Perspectives on Psychological Science, 17*(1), 62–77.

Hennessy, S., Howe, C., Mercer, N., & Vrikki, M. (2020). Coding classroom dialogue: Methodological considerations for researchers. *Learning, Culture and Social Interaction, 25*, 100404.

Hennessy, S., Rojas-Drummond, S., Higham, R., Márquez, A. M., Maine, F., Ríos, R. M., & Barrera, M. J. (2016). Developing a coding scheme for analysing classroom dialogue across educational contexts. *Learning, Culture and Social Interaction, 9*, 16–44.

Henrich, J. P. (2020). *The WEIRDest people in the world: How the West became psychologically peculiar and particularly prosperous* (1st ed.). New York: Farrar, Straus and Giroux.

Henrich, J. P., Heine, S. J., & Norenzayan, A. (2010). The weirdest people in the world? *Behavioral and Brain Sciences, 33*(2–3), 61–83.

Henry, D. A., Betancur Cortés, L., & Votruba-Drzal, E. (2020). Black–white achievement gaps differ by family socioeconomic status from early childhood through early adolescence. *Journal of Educational Psychology, 112*(8), 1471–1489.

Heyman, M., Poulakos, A., Upshur, C., & Wenz-Gross, M. (2018). Discrepancies in parent and teacher ratings of low-income preschooler's social skills. *Early Child Development and Care, 188*(6), 759–773.

Hill, T., & Palacios, N. (2021). The influence of parental warmth and stress on reading through approaches to learning: Racial/ethnic variation. *Infant and Child Development, 30*, e2210.

Ho, D. Y., Peng, S. Q., Cheng Lai, A., & Chan, S. F. F. (2001). Indigenization and beyond: Methodological relationalism in the study of personality across cultural traditions. *Journal of Personality, 69*(6), 925–953.

Hoey, E. M., DeLiema, D., Chen, R. S. Y., & Flood, V. J. (2018). Imitation in children's locomotor play. *Research on Children & Social Interaction, 2*(1), 1–24.

Hogan, C., & Howe, N. (2001). Do props matter in the dramatic play center? The effects of prop realism on children's play. *Canadian Journal of Research in Early Childhood Education, 8,* 51–66.

Holding, P., Abubakar, A., Obiero, E., & Van Baar, A. (2011). Validation of the Infant–Toddler HOME Inventory among households in low income communities at the Kenyan coast. In F. Deutsch, M. Boehnke, U. Kühnen, & K. Boehnke (eds.), *Rendering borders obsolete: Cross-cultural and cultural psychology as an interdisciplinary, multi-method endeavor: Proceedings from the 19th International Congress of the International Association for Cross-Cultural Psychology.* https://scholarworks.gvsu.edu/iaccp_papers/71/

Howe, C., & Abedin, M. (2013). Classroom dialogue: A systematic review across four decades of research. *Cambridge Journal of Education, 43*(3), 325–356.

Howe, N., Petrakos, H., Rinaldi, C., & Lefebvre, R. (2005). "This is a bad dog you know": Constructing shared meanings during sibling pretend play. *Child Development, 76,* 783–794.

Howes, C., & Matheson, C. C. (1992). Sequences in the development of competent play with peers: Social and social pretend play. *Developmental Psychology, 28,* 961–975.

Hurley, E. A., Boykin, A. W., & Allen, B. A. (2005). Communal versus individual learning of a math-estimation task: African American children and the culture of learning contexts. *Journal of Psychology, 139*(6), 513–527.

Hutchins, E. (1995). *Cognition in the wild.* Cambridge, MA: MIT Press.

Hutchins, E. (2014). The cultural ecosystem of human cognition, *Philosophical Psychology, 27*(1), 34–49.

Huwaë, S., & Schaafsma, J. (2018). Cross-cultural differences in emotion suppression in everyday interactions. *International Journal of Psychology, 53*(3), 176–183.

Hwang, K. K. (2011). Reification of culture in indigenous psychologies: Merit or mistake? *Social Epistemology, 25*(2), 125–131.

Hwang, K. K. (2012). *Foundations of Chinese psychology: Confucian social relations.* New York: Springer SBM.

Hwang, K. K. (2023). An epistemological strategy for initiating scientific revolution against WEIRD psychology. *Integrative Psychological and Behavioral Science, 57*(2), 361–380.

Hyun, S., McWayne, C. M., & Smith, J. M. (2021). "I See Why They Play": Chinese immigrant parents and their beliefs about young children's play. *Early Childhood Research Quarterly, 56,* 272–280.

Jensen, B., Mejía-Arauz, R., Grajeda, S., Toranzo, S. G., Encinas, J., & Larsen, R. (2020). Measuring cultural aspects of teacher–child interactions to foster equitable developmental opportunities for young Latino children. *Early Childhood Research Quarterly, 52,* 112–123.

Jensen, B., Valdés, G., & Gallimore, R. (2021). Teachers learning to implement equitable classroom talk. *Educational Researcher, 50*(8), 546–556.

Johnson, D. W., & Johnson, R. T. (2002). Learning together and alone: Overview and meta-analysis. *Asia Pacific Journal of Education, 22,* 95–105.

Johnson, D. W., Johnson, R. T., Roseth, C., & Shin, T. S. (2014). The relationship between motivation and achievement in interdependent situations. *Journal of Applied Social Psychology*, *44*(9), 622–633.

Jones, D. E., Greenberg, M., & Crowley, M. (2015). Early social-emotional functioning and public health: The relationship between kindergarten social competence and future wellness. *American Journal of Public Health*, *105*(11), 2283–2290.

Jones, P. C., Pendergast, L. L., Schaefer, B. A., Rasheed, M., Svensen, E., Scharf, R., & MAL-ED Network Investigators. (2017). Measuring home environments across cultures: Invariance of the HOME scale across eight international sites from the MAL-ED study. *Journal of School Psychology*, *64*, 109–127.

Kaartinen, S., & Kumpulainen, K. (2002). Collaborative inquiry and the construction of explanations in the learning of science. *Learning & Instruction*, *12*(2), 189.

Kagan, J. (1989). Temperamental contributions to social behavior. *American Psychologist*, *44*(4), 668.

Kagitcibasi, C. (2012). Sociocultural change and integrative syntheses in human development: Autonomous-related self and social-cognitive competence. *Child Development Perspectives*, *6*(1), 5–11.

Kazak, S., Wegerif, R., & Fujita, T. (2015). The importance of dialogic processes to conceptual development in mathematics. *Educational Studies in Mathematics*, *90*(2), 105–120.

Kerawalla, L. (2015). Talk Factory Generic: Empowering secondary school pupils to construct and explore dialogic space during pupil-led whole-class discussions. *International Journal of Educational Research*, *70*, 57–67.

Kerawalla, L., Petrou, M., & Scanlon, E. (2013) The Talk Factory: Supporting "exploratory talk" around an Interactive Whiteboard in primary school science. *Technology, Pedagogy and Education*, *22*(1), 89–102.

Keyton, J., & Beck, S. J. (2009). The influential role of relational messages in group interaction. *Group Dynamics*, *13*(1), 14–30.

Kienbaum, J., Volland, C., & Ulich, D. (2001). Sympathy in the context of mother–child and teacher–child relationships. *International Journal of Behavioral Development*, *25*(4), 302–309.

Kim, U., Park, Y. S., & Park, D. (1999). The Korean Indigenous psychology approach: Theoretical considerations and empirical applications. *Applied Psychology*, *48*(4), 451–464.

Knauer, H. A., Ozer, E. J., Dow, W. H., & Fernald, L. C. H. (2019). Parenting quality at two developmental periods in early childhood and their association with child development. *Early Childhood Research Quarterly*, *47*, 396–404.

Kochanska, G. (1997). Mutually responsive orientation between mothers and their young children: Implications for early socialization. *Child Development*, *68*(1), 94–112.

Kozlowski, S. W. J., & Bell, B. S. (2003). Work groups and teams in organizations. In W. C. Borman, D. R. Ilgen, & R. J. Klimoski (eds.), *Handbook of psychology* (vol. 12): Industrial and organizational psychology (pp. 333–375). New York: Wiley.

Krull, D. S., Loy, M. H., Lin, J., Wang, C. F., Chen, S., & Zhao, X. (1999). The fundamental attribution error: Correspondence bias in individualistic and collectivistic cultures. *Personality and Social Psychology Bulletin, 25*(10), 1208–1219.

Krys, K., Vignoles, V. L., De Almeida, I., & Uchida, Y. (2022). Outside the "cultural binary": Understanding why Latin American collectivist societies foster independent selves. *Perspectives on Psychological Science, 17*(4), 1166–1187.

Kulkarni, T., & Sullivan, A. L. (2022). Academic achievement and relations to externalizing behavior: Much ado about nothing? *Journal of School Psychology, 94*, 1–14.

Kumar, M. (2006) Rethinking psychology in India: Debating pasts and futures. *Annual Review of Critical Psychology, 5*, 236–256.

Kumpulainen, K., & Kaartinen, S. (2003). The interpersonal dynamics of collaborative reasoning in peer interactive dyads. *Journal of Experimental Education, 71*(4), 333–370.

Latour, B. (1996). On interobjectivity. *Mind, Culture, and Activity, 3*(4), 228–245.

Lave, J., & Wenger, E. (1991). *Situated learning: Legitimate peripheral participation*. New York: Cambridge University Press.

Lee, S. Y., Kim, R., Rodgers, J., & Subramanian, S. V. (2022). Assessment of heterogeneous Head Start treatment effects on cognitive and social-emotional outcomes. *Scientific Reports, 12*(1), 6411.

Legare, C., Sobel, D., & Callanan, M. (2017). Causal learning is collaborative: Examining explanation and exploration in social contexts. *Psychonomic Bulletin & Review, 24*(5), 1548–1554.

Lemche, E., Kreppner, J. M., Joraschky, P., & Klann-Delius, G. (2007). Attachment organization and the early development of internal state language: A longitudinal perspective. *International Journal of Behavioral Development, 31*(3), 252–262.

Leontiev, A. N. (1978). *Activity, consciousness, and personality*. Englewood Cliffs, NJ: Prentice-Hall.

Li, J., & Yamamoto, Y. (2020). Western and East Asian sociocultural learning models: Evidence from cross-cultural and immigrant research. *Asian Journal of Social Psychology, 23*(2), 174–186.

Li, J., Hestenes, L. L., & Wang, Y. C. (2016). Links between preschool children's social skills and observed pretend play in outdoor childcare environments. *Early Childhood Education Journal, 44*, 61–68.

Lieber, E., Fung, H., & Leung, P. W.-L. (2006). Chinese child-rearing beliefs: Key dimensions and contributions to the development of culture-appropriate assessment. *Asian Journal of Social Psychology, 9*(2), 140–147.

Lillard, A. S., & Kavanaugh, R. D. (2014). The contribution of symbolic skills to the development of an explicit theory of mind. *Child Development, 85*(4), 1535–1551.

Lillard, A. S., Pinkham, A. M., & Smith, E. (2011). Pretend play and cognitive development. In U. Goswami (ed.), *The Wiley-Blackwell handbook of childhood cognitive development* (pp. 285–311). Hoboken, NJ: Wiley-Blackwell.

Lincoln, C., Russell, B., Donohue, E., & Racine, L. (2017). Mother–child interactions and preschoolers' emotion regulation outcomes: Nurturing autonomous emotion regulation. *Journal of Child & Family Studies, 26*(2), 559–573.

Lindsey, E. W., & Colwell, M. J. (2013). Pretend and physical play: Links to preschoolers' affective social competence. *Merrill-Palmer Quarterly, 59*(3), 330–360.

Lindsey, E. W., Cremeens, P. R., Colwell, M. J., & Caldera, Y. M. (2009). The structure of parent–child dyadic synchrony in toddlerhood and children's communication competence and self-control. *Social Development, 18*(2), 375–396.

Litowitz, B. E. (1993). Deconstruction in the zone of proximal development. In E. A. Forman, N. Minick, & C.A. Stone (eds.), *Contexts for learning: Sociocultural dynamics in children's development* (pp. 184–196). New York: Oxford University Press.

Liu, J. (2015). Globalizing Indigenous psychology: An East Asian form of hierarchical relationalism with worldwide implications. *Journal for the Theory of Social Behaviour, 45*(1), 82–94.

Liu, J., Cheng, H., & Leung, P. W. (2011). The application of the preschool child behavior checklist and the caregiver–teacher report form to mainland Chinese children: Syndrome structure, gender differences, country effects, and inter-informant agreement. *Journal of Abnormal Child Psychology, 39*, 251–264.

Lloyd, B., & Howe, N. (2003). Solitary play and convergent and divergent thinking skills in preschool children. *Early Childhood Research Quarterly, 18*, 22–41.

Lobo, F. M., & Lunkenheimer, E. (2020). Understanding the parent–child coregulation patterns shaping child self-regulation. *Developmental Psychology, 56*(6), 1121.

Löfstrand, P., & Zakrisson, I. (2014). Competitive versus non-competitive goals in group decision-making. *Small Group Research, 45*(4), 451–464.

Longobardi, C., Pasta, T., Marengo, D., Prino, L. E., & Settanni, M. (2020). Measuring quality of classroom interactions in Italian primary school: Structural validity of the CLASS K–3. *Journal of Experimental Education, 88*(1), 103–122.

Lucariello, J., Hudson, J., Fivush, R., & Bauer, P. (eds.). (2004). *The development of the mediated mind: Sociocultural context and cognitive development*. Mahwah, NJ: Erlbaum.

Luo, Z., Jose, P. E., Huntsinger, C. S., & Pigott, T. D. (2007). Fine motor skills and mathematics achievement in East Asian American and European American kindergartners and first graders. *British Journal of Developmental Psychology, 25*(4), 595–614.

Ma-Kellams, C. (2020). Cultural variation and similarities in cognitive thinking styles versus judgment biases: A review of environmental factors and evolutionary forces. *Review of General Psychology, 24*(3), 238–253.

Mantzicopoulos, P., & Neuharth-Pritchett, S. (2003). Development and validation of a measure to assess head start children's appraisals of teacher support. *Journal of school psychology, 41*(6), 431–451.

Mantzicopoulos, P., French, B. F., Patrick, H., Watson, J. S., & Ahn, I. (2018). The stability of kindergarten teachers' effectiveness: A generalizability study comparing the Framework For Teaching and the Classroom Assessment Scoring System. *Educational Assessment, 23*(1), 24–46.

Marbell, P. K. N., Grolnick, W. S., Stewart, A. L., Raftery, H. J. N., Marbell-Pierre, K. N., & Raftery-Helmer, J. N. (2019). Parental autonomy support in two cultures: The moderating effects of adolescents' self-construals. *Child Development, 90*(3), 825–845.

Markus, H., & Kitayama, S. (1991). Culture and the self: Implications for cognition, emotion, and motivation. *Psychological Review, 98*, 224–253.

Marsh, S., Dobson, R., & Maddison, R. (2020). The relationship between household chaos and child, parent, and family outcomes: A systematic scoping review. *BMC Public Health, 20*, 1–27.

Mason, B. A., Gunersel, A. B., & Ney, E. A. (2014). Cultural and ethnic bias in teacher ratings of behavior: A criterion-focused review. *Psychology in the Schools, 51*(10), 1017–1030.

Masuda, T., & Nisbett, R. E. (2001). Attending holistically vs. analytically: Comparing the context sensitivity of Japanese and Americans. *Journal of Personality and Social Psychology, 81*(5), 922–934.

Matusov, E. (1996). Intersubjectivity without agreement. *Mind, Culture, and Activity, 3*, 25–45.

Maynard, A. E., & Greenfield, P. M. (2003). Implicit cognitive development in cultural tools and children: Lessons from Maya Mexico. *Cognitive Development, 18*(4), 489.

McCord, B., & Raval, V. (2016). Asian Indian immigrant and white American maternal emotion socialization and child socio-emotional functioning. *Journal of Child & Family Studies, 25*(2), 464–474.

McCoy, D. C., Connors, M. C., Morris, P. A., Yoshikawa, H., & Friedman-Krauss, A. H. (2015). Neighborhood economic disadvantage and children's cognitive and social-emotional development: Exploring Head Start classroom quality as a mediating mechanism. *Early Childhood Research Quarterly, 32*, 150–159.

McDermott, P. A., Rovine, M. J., Gerstner, C.-C. E., Weiss, E. M., & Watkins, M. W. (2022). Latent profile analysis of classroom behavior problems in an American national sample of prekindergarten children. *Social Development, 31*, 1059–1078.

McLoyd, V. C. (1983). The effects of the structure of play objects on the pretend play of low-income preschool children. *Child Development, 54*, 626–635.

McTavish, J. R., McKee, C., Tanaka, M., & MacMillan, H. L. (2022). Child welfare reform: A scoping review. *International Journal of Environmental Research and Public Health, 19*(21), 14071.

Mejía, A. R., Rogoff, B., Dexter, A., & Najafi, B. (2007). Cultural variation in children's social organization. *Child Development, 78*(3), 1001–1014.

Mejía-Arauz, R., Rogoff, B., Dayton, A., & Henne-Ochoa, R. (2018). Collaboration or negotiation: Two ways of interacting suggest how shared thinking develops. *Current Opinion in Psychology, 23*, 117–123.

Mejía-Arauz, R., Rogoff, B., Dexter, A., & Najafi, B. (2007). Cultural variation in children's social organization. *Child Development, 78*(3), 1001–1014.

Mercier, E., Vourloumi, G., & Higgins, S. (2017). Student interactions and the development of ideas in multi-touch and paper-based collaborative mathematical problem solving. *British Journal of Educational Technology, 48*(1), 162–175.

Mishra, R. (2014). Piagetian studies of cognitive development in India. *Psychological Studies, 59*(3), 207–222.

Mistry, R. S., Benner, A. D., Biesanz, J. C., Clark, S. L., & Howes, C. (2010). Family and social risk, and parental investments during the early childhood years as predictors of low-income children's school readiness outcomes. *Early Childhood Research Quarterly, 25*(4), 432–449.

Mizuta, I., Zahn-Waxler, C., Cole, P. M., & Hiruma, N. (1996). Cross-cultural study of preschoolers' attachment: Security and sensitivity in Japanese and US dyads. *International Journal of Behavioral Development, 19*(1), 141–160.

Monette, S., Bigras, M., & Guay, M. C. (2011). The role of the executive functions in school achievement at the end of Grade 1. *Journal of Experimental Child Psychology, 109*(2), 158–173.

Morgan, B. M. (2004). Cooperative learning in higher education: Hispanic and non-Hispanic undergraduates' reflections on group grades. *Journal of Latinos and Education, 3*, 39–52.

Morss, J. R. (1996). *Growing critical: Alternatives to developmental psychology*. London: Routledge.

Morss, J. R. (2024). *Growing critical: Alternatives to developmental psychology* (2nd ed.). London: Routledge.

Mortimer, E., & Wertsch, J. (2003). The architecture and dynamics of intersubjectivity in science classrooms. *Mind, Culture and Activity, 100*, 230–244.

MSRI (2019) Inspiring Mathematics: Lessons from the Navajo Nation Math Circles. United States: Mathematical Sciences Research Institute.

Nelson, K. (1998). *Language in cognitive development: The emergence of the mediated mind*. Cambridge: Cambridge University Press.

NICHD Early Child Care Research Network. (2005). A day in third grade: A large-scale study of classroom quality and teacher and student behavior. *Elementary School Journal, 105*(3), 305–323.

Nichols, M. P. (2010). *Family therapy, concepts and methods* (9th ed.). Hoboken, NJ: Prentice Hall.

Nielsen, M., Haun, D., Kärtner, J., & Legare, C. H. (2017). The persistent sampling bias in developmental psychology: A call to action. *Journal of Experimental Child Psychology, 162*, 31–38.

Nieminen, J. H., Chan, M. C. E., & Clarke, D. (2022). What affordances do open-ended real-life tasks offer for sharing student agency in collaborative problem-solving? *Educational Studies in Mathematics, 109*(1), 115–136.

Nsamenang, A. B. (1992). *Human development in cultural context: A third world perspective*. Thousand Oaks, CA: SAGE Publications.

Nsamenang, A. B. (2004). *Cultures of human development and education: Challenge to growing up African*. New York: Nova.

Nsamenang, A. B. (2008). Culture and human development. *International Journal of Psychology, 43*(2), 73–77.

Nsamenang, A. B. (2013). Dilemmas of rights-based approaches to child well-being in an African cultural context. In D. J. Johnson, D. L. Agbényiga, & R. K. Hitchcock (eds.), *Vulnerable children: Global challenges in education, health, well-being, and child* (pp. 13–25). New York: Springer.

Nsamenang, A. B., & Tchombé, T. M. (eds.). (2012). *Handbook of African educational theories and practices: A generative teacher education curriculum*. Bamenda: HDRC.

Nwoye, A. (2006). Remapping the fabric of the African self: A synoptic theory. *Dialectical Anthropology, 30*, 119–146.

Nwoye, A. (2022). *African psychology: The emergence of a tradition*. Oxford: Oxford University Press.

Nyota, S., & Mapara, J. (2008). Shona traditional children's games and play: songs as indigenous ways of knowing. *Journal of Pan African Studies, 2*(4), 189–202.

Ogden, L. (2000). Collaborative tasks, collaborative children: An analysis of reciprocity during peer interaction at Key Stage 1. *British Educational Research Journal, 26*, 2.

Ogunnaike, O. A., & Houser, R. F., Jr (2002). Yoruba toddlers' engagement in errands and cognitive performance on the Yoruba Mental Subscale. *International Journal of Behavioral Development, 26*(2), 145–153.

Onchwari, G., & Keengwe, J. (2011). Examining the relationship of children's behavior to emotion regulation ability. *Early Childhood Education Journal, 39*(4), 279–284.

Oyserman, D. (2011) Culture as situated cognition: Cultural mindsets, cultural fluency, and meaning making. *European Review of Social Psychology, 22*(1), 164–214.

Oyserman, D., Coon, H. M., & Kemmelmeier, M. (2002). Rethinking individualism and collectivism: Evaluation of theoretical assumptions and meta-analyses. *Psychological Bulletin, 128*(1), 3.

Packer, M. J., & Cole, M. (2019). Evolution and ontogenesis: The deontic niche of human development. *Human Development, 62*(4), 175–211.

Pai, H. H., Sears, D. A., & Maeda, Y. (2015). Effects of small-group learning on transfer: A meta-analysis. *Educational Psychology Review, 27*, 79–102.

Paranjpe, A. C. (2010). Theories of self and cognition: Indian psychological perspectives. *Psychology and Developing Societies, 22*(1), 5–48.

Parten, M. B. (1932). Social participation among preschool children. *Journal of Abnormal and Social Psychology, 27*(3), 243–269.

Paterson, A. (2020). The play paradox: A systematic literature review of play-based pedagogy applied in the classroom. *Educational & Child Psychology*, *37*(4), 96–114.

Patrick, C. J., Iacono, W. G., & Venables, N. C. (2019). Incorporating neurophysiological measures into clinical assessments: Fundamental challenges and a strategy for addressing them. *Psychological Assessment*, *31*(12), 1512–1529.

Pellegrini, A. D. (2004). *Observing children in their natural worlds*. Mahwah, NJ: Lawrence Erlbaum Associates.

Peräkylä, A. (2004). Two traditions of interaction research. *British Journal of Social Psychology*, *43*(1), 1–20.

Perinat, A., & Sadumi, M. (1999). The ontogenesis of meaning: An interactional approach. *Mind, Culture, and Activity*, *6*, 53–76.

Perry, N. B., Swingler, M. M., Calkins, S. D., & Bell, M. A. (2016). Neurophysiological correlates of attention behavior in early infancy: Implications for emotion regulation during early childhood. *Journal of Experimental Child Psychology*, *142*, 245–261.

Peterson, S. S., Eisazadeh, N., Rajendram, S., & Portier, C. (2018). Young children's language uses during play and implications for classroom assessment. *Australasian Journal of Early Childhood*, *43*(2), 23–31.

Petrakos, H., & Howe, N. (1996). The influence of the physical design of the dramatic play center on children's play. *Early Childhood Research Quarterly*, *11*, 63–77.

Piaget, J. (1971). *The construction of reality in the child*. New York: Ballantine.

Pianta, R. C. (2016). Classroom processes and teacher–student interaction: Integrations with a developmental psychopathology perspective. In D. Cicchetti (ed.), *Developmental psychopathology: Risk, resilience, and intervention* (pp. 770–814). Hoboken, NJ: John Wiley & Sons.

Pianta, R. C., Downer, J., & Hamre, B. (2016). Quality in early education classrooms: Definitions, gaps, and systems. *The Future of Children*, *26*(2), 119–137.

Pianta, R. C., La Paro, K. M., & Hamre, B. K. (2008). *Classroom Assessment Scoring System (CLASS) manual, K–3*. Baltimore, MD: Brookes.

Pino-Pasternak, D., Whitebread, D., & Neale, D. (2018). The role of regulatory, social, and dialogic dynamics on young children's productive collaboration in group problem solving. *New Directions for Child and Adolescent Development*, *2018*(162), 41–66.

Portier, C., Friedrich, N., & Peterson, S. S. (2019). Play(ful) pedagogical practices for creative collaborative literacy. *Reading Teacher*, *73*(1), 17–27.

Prieto, L., Claeys, L., & González, E. L. (2015). Transnational alliances: La Clase Mágica – Nepohualtzitzin Ethnomathematics Club. *Journal of Latinos & Education*, *14*(2), 125–134.

Pursi, A. (2019). Play in adult–child interaction: Institutional multi-party interaction and pedagogical practice in a toddler classroom. *Learning, Culture and Social Interaction*, *21*, 136–150.

Pursi, A., Lipponen, L., & Sajaniemi, N. K. (2018). Emotional and playful stance taking in joint play between adults and very young children. *Learning, Culture and Social Interaction, 18,* 28–45.

Pyle, A., & Bigelow, A. (2015). Play in kindergarten: An interview and observational study in three Canadian classrooms. *Early Childhood Education Journal, 43*(5), 385–393.

Rabiner, D. L., Godwin, J., & Dodge, K. A. (2016). Predicting academic achievement and attainment: The contribution of early academic skills, attention difficulties, and social competence. *School Psychology Review, 45*(2), 250–267.

Racine, T. P., & Carpendale, J. I. (2007). The role of shared practices in joint attention. *British Journal of Developmental Psychology, 25,* 3–25

Rademeyer, V., & Jacklin, L. (2013). A study to evaluate the performance of black South African urban infants on the Bayley Scales of Infant Development III. *South African Journal of Child Health, 7*(2), 54–59.

Rakoczy, H. (2006). Pretend play and the development of collective intentionality. *Cognitive Systems Research, 7*(2/3), 113–127.

Ramani, G. B. (2012) Influence of a playful, child-directed context on preschool children's peer cooperation. *Merrill-Palmer Quarterly, 58*(2), 159–190.

Ratele, K. (2017). Four (African) psychologies. *Theory & Psychology, 27*(3), 313–327.

Reese, L., Jensen, B., & Ramirez, D. (2014). Emotionally supportive classroom contexts for young Latino children in rural California. *The Elementary School Journal, 114*(4), 501–526.

Reynolds, A. J. (2021). Child development as social action: Reflections on four underrated contributions of Edward Zigler to science and society. *Developmental Psychopathology, 33*(2), 466–482.

Ricca, B. P., Bowers, N., & Jordan, M. E. (2020). Seeking emergence through temporal analysis of collaborative-group discourse: A complex-systems approach. *Journal of Experimental Education, 88*(3), 431–447.

Roberts, A. L., & Rogoff, B. (2012). Children's reflections on two cultural ways of working together: "Talking with hands and eyes" or requiring words. *International Journal of Educational Psychology, 1*(2), 73–99.

Robinson, C. C., Anderson, G. T., Porter, C. L., Hart, C. H., & Wouden-Miller, M. (2003). Sequential transition patterns of preschoolers' social interactions during child-initiated play: Is parallel-aware play a bi-directional bridge to other play states? *Early Childhood Research Quarterly, 18,* 3–21.

Robinson, C. D., & Diamond, K. E. (2014). A quantitative study of Head Start children's strengths, families' perspectives, and teachers' ratings in the transition to kindergarten. *Early Childhood Education Journal, 42,* 77–84.

Rogat, T. K., & Adams-Wiggins, K. R. (2015). Interrelation between regulatory and socioemotional processes within collaborative groups characterized by facilitative and directive other-regulation. *Computers in Human Behavior, 52,* 589–600.

Roger Mills-Koonce, W., Willoughby, M. T., Zvara, B., Barnett, M., Gustafsson, H., & Cox, M. J. (2015). Mothers' and fathers' sensitivity and children's cognitive development in low-income, rural families. *Journal of Applied Developmental Psychology, 38*, 1–10.

Rogoff, B. (1998). Cognition as a collaborative process. In W. Damon (ed.), *Handbook of child psychology* (vol. 2, pp. 679–744). Hoboken, NJ: Wiley.

Rogoff, B. (2003). *The cultural nature of human development*. Oxford: Oxford University Press.

Rogoff, B. (2016). Culture and participation: A paradigm shift. *Current Opinion in Psychology, 8*, 182–189.

Rogoff, B., Alcalá, L., & Fraire, A. L. (2018). Sophisticated collaboration is common among Mexican-heritage US children. *Proceedings of the National Academy of Sciences of the United States of America, 115*(45), 11377–11384.

Rogoff, B., Paradise, R., Arauz, R. M., Correa-Chavez, M., & Angelillo, C. (2003). Firsthand learning through intent participation. *Annual Review of Psychology, 54* (1), 175.

Rojas-Drummond, S., Mazón, N., Littleton, K., & Vélez, M. (2014). Developing reading comprehension through collaborative learning. *Journal of Research in Reading, 37*, 138–158.

Rommetviet, R. (1979). On the architecture of inter-subjectivity. In R. Rommetviet & R. M. Blakar (eds.), *Studies of language, thought and verbal communication* (pp. 93–108). London: Academic Press.

Roncancio-Moreno, M., & Branco, A.U. (2017). Developmental trajectories of the self in children during the transition from preschool to elementary school. *Learning, Culture and Social Interaction, 14*, 38–50.

Roopnarine, J. L., & Davidson, K. L. (2015). Parent–child play across cultures: Advancing play research. *American Journal of Play, 7*(2), 228–252.

Rose, A. J., & Rudolph, K. D. (2006). A review of sex differences in peer relationship processes: Potential trade-offs for the emotional and behavioral development of girls and boys. *Psychological Bulletin, 132*(1), 98–131.

Roskos, K., & Neuman, S. B. (1998). Play as an opportunity for literacy. In O. N. Saracho & B. Spodek (eds.), *Multiple perspectives on play in early childhood education*. Albany: Sate University of New York Press.

Rubin, K. H. (2001). *The Play Observation Scale, revised (POS)*. College Park: Center for Children, Relationships and Culture, University of Maryland.

Rutter, M. (1978). Family, area and school influences in the genesis of conduct disorders In L. A. Hersov, M. Berger, & D. Shaffer (eds.), *Aggression and antisocial behavior in childhood and adolescence* (pp. 95–113). Oxford: Pergamon.

Sadurní Brugué, M., & Pérez Burriel, M. (2016). Outlining the windows of achievement of intersubjective milestones in typically developing toddlers. *Infant Mental Health Journal, 37*(4), 356–371.

Sandilos, L. E., Sims, W. A., Norwalk, K. E., & Reddy, L. A. (2019). Converging on quality: Examining multiple measures of teaching effectiveness. *Journal of School Psychology, 74*, 10–28.

Schindler, M., & Bakker, A. (2020). Affective field during collaborative problem posing and problem solving: a case study. *Educational Studies in Mathematics, 105*(3), 303–324.

Schweder, R. A., Goodnow, J. J., Hatano, G., LeVine, R. A., Markus, H. R., & Miller, P. J. (2006). The cultural psychology of development: One mind, many mentalities. In R. M. Lerner & W. Damon (eds.), *Handbook of child psychology: Theoretical models of human development* (pp. 716–792). Hoboken, NJ: John Wiley & Sons.

Scoular, C., Care, E., & Hesse, F. W. (2017). Designs for operationalizing collaborative problem solving for automated assessment. *Journal of Educational Measurement, 54*(1), 12–35.

Searle, J. R. (1995). *The construction of social reality*. New York: Simon & Schuster.

Searle, J. R. (2009). *Making the social world: The structure of human civilization.* New York: Oxford University Press.

Seay, K., & Kohl, P. (2015). The comorbid and individual impacts of maternal depression and substance dependence on parenting and child behavior problems. *Journal of Family Violence, 30*(7), 899–910.

Selby, J. M., & Bradley, B. S. (2003). Infants in groups: A paradigm for the study of early social experience. *Human Development, 46*, 197–221.

Serpell, R., Mumba, P., & Chansa-Kabali, T. (2011). Early educational foundations for the development of civic responsibility: An African experience. *New Directions for Child and Adolescent Development, 134*, 77–93.

Sheaffer, A. W., Majeika, C. E., Gilmour, A. F., & Wehby, J. H. (2021). Classroom behavior of students with or at risk of EBD: Student gender affects teacher ratings but not direct observations. *Behavioral Disorders, 46*(2), 96–107.

Shenderovich, Y., Thurston, A., & Miller, S. (2016). Cross-age tutoring in kindergarten and elementary school settings: A systematic review and meta-analysis. *International Journal of Educational Research, 76*, 190–210.

Shim, S., Herwig, J. E., & Shelley, M. (2001). Preschoolers' play behaviors with peers in classroom and playground settings. *Journal of Research in Childhood Education, 15*, 149–163.

Shwalb, D., Shwalb, B., & Murata, K. (1989). Cooperation, competition, individualism and interpersonalism in Japanese fifth and eighth grade boys. *International Journal of Psychology, 24*(5), 617.

Siekiera, N., & Białek, A. (2021). Doing things together: Development of cooperation through cultural participation. *Journal for the Theory of Social Behaviour, 51*(3), 430–448.

Sills, J., Rowse, G., & Emerson, L.-M. (2016). The role of collaboration in the cognitive development of young children: A systematic review. *Child Care, Health and Development, 42*(3), 313–324.

Silva, K. G., Correa, C. M., & Rogoff, B. (2010). Mexican-Heritage children's attention and learning from interactions directed to others. *Child Development, 81*(3), 898–912.

Siposova, B., Tomasello, M., & Carpenter, M. (2018). Communicative eye contact signals a commitment to cooperate for young children. *Cognition, 179*, 192–201.

Smilansky, S. (1968). *The effects of sociodramatic play on disadvantaged preschool children.* New York: Wiley.

Smith, J. M., & Mancy, R. (2018). Exploring the relationship between metacognitive and collaborative talk during group mathematical problem-solving – What do we mean by collaborative metacognition? *Research in Mathematics Education, 20*(1), 14–36.

Souvignier, E., & Kronenberger, J. (2007). Cooperative learning in third graders' jigsaw groups for mathematics and science with and without questioning training. *British Journal of Educational Psychology, 77*(4), 755–771.

Sperry, D. E., Sperry, L. L., & Miller, P. J. (2019). Reexamining the verbal environments of children from different socioeconomic backgrounds. *Child Development, 90*, 1303–1318.

Splett, J. W., Raborn, A., Brann, K., Smith-Millman, M. K., Halliday, C., & Weist, M. D. (2020). Between-teacher variance of students' teacher-rated risk for emotional, behavioral, and adaptive functioning. *Journal of School Psychology, 80*, 37–53.

Steele, C. (2021). A new approach to schooling in a diverse society: A research fable. *Journal of Social Issues, 77*(3), 911–916.

Stengelin, R., Hepach, R., & Haun, D. B. M. (2020). Cultural variation in young children's social motivation for peer collaboration and its relation to the ontogeny of theory of mind. *PLoS ONE, 15*(11), 1–21.

Sternberg, R. J. (2014). The development of adaptive competence: Why cultural psychology is necessary and not just nice. *Developmental Review, 34*(3), 208–224.

Stetsenko, A. (2005). Activity as object-related: Resolving the dichotomy of individual and collective types of activity. *Mind, Culture, and Activity, 12*, 70–88.

Stetsenko, A. (2016). *The transformative mind: Expanding Vygotsky's perspective on development and education.* New York: Cambridge University Press.

Stevanovic, M., & Koski, S. E. (2018). Intersubjectivity and the domains of social interaction: proposal of a cross-sectional approach. *Psychology of Language and Communication, 22*(1), 39–70.

Stevanovic, M. & Peräkylä, A. (2012). Deontic authority in interaction: The right to announce, propose and decide. *Research on Language and Social Interaction, 45*(3), 297–321.

Stipek, D., & Chiatovich, T. (2017). The effect of instructional quality on low- and high-performing students. *Psychology in the Schools, 54*(8), 773–791.

Stone, L. D., Underwood, C., & Hotchkiss, J. (2012). The relational habitus: Intersubjective processes in learning settings. *Human Development, 55*, 65–91.

Stuhlman, M. W., & Pianta, R. C. (2009). Profiles of educational quality in first grade. *Elementary School Journal, 109*(4), 323–342.

Sugland, B. W., Zaslow, M., Smith, J. R., Brooks-Gunn, J., Coates, D., Blumenthal, C., Moore, K. A., Griffin, T., & Bradley, R. (1995). The Early Childhood HOME Inventory and HOME-Short Form in differing racial/ethnic groups. *Journal of Family Issues, 16*(5), 632–663.

Super, C. M., & Harkness, S. (2002). Culture structures the environment for development. *Human Development, 45*(4), 270–274.

Sutton, E., Brown, J. L., Lowenstein, A. E., & Downer, J. T. (2021). Children's academic and social-emotional competencies and the quality of classroom interactions in high-needs urban elementary schools. *Contemporary Educational Psychology, 66*, 101975.

Talamo, A., & Pozzi, S. (2011). The tension between dialogicality and interobjectivity in cooperative activities. *Culture and Psychology, 17*, 3.

Tarchi, C., & Pinto, G. (2016). Reciprocal teaching: Analyzing interactive dynamics in the co-construction of a text's meaning. *Journal of Educational Research, 109*(5), 518–530.

Tatsis, K., & Koleza, E. (2008). Social and socio-mathematical norms in collaborative problem-solving. *European Journal of Teacher Education, 31*(1), 89–100.

Teo, T. (2015). Critical psychology: A geography of intellectual engagement and resistance. *American Psychologist, 70*(3), 243–254.

Thelen, E., & Smith, L. B. (2006). Dynamic systems theories. In R. M. Lerner (ed.), *Theoretical models of human development: Vol. 1. Handbook of child psychology* (6th ed., pp. 258–312). Hoboken, NJ: Wiley.

Thompson, B. N., & Goldstein, T. R. (2019). Disentangling pretend play measurement: Defining the essential elements and developmental progression of pretense. *Developmental Review, 52*, 24–41.

Tobin, J. J., Hsueh, Y., & Karasawa, M. (2009). *Preschool in three cultures revisited: China, Japan, and the United States.* Chicago, IL: University of Chicago Press.

Tobin, J. J., Wu, D. Y. H., & Davidson, D. H. (1989). *Preschool in three cultures: Japan, China, and the United States.* New Haven, CT: Yale University Press.

Tomasello, M. (2014). *A natural history of human thinking.* Cambridge, MA: Harvard University Press.

Tomasello, M. (2016). *A natural history of human morality.* Cambridge, MA: Harvard University Press.

Tomasello, M. (2019). *Becoming human: A theory of ontogeny.* Cambridge, MA: Harvard University Press.

Tomasello, M. (2020). The role of roles in uniquely human cognition and sociality. *Journal for the Theory of Social Behaviour, 50*(1), 2–19.

Tomasello, M., & Carpenter, M. (2007). Shared intentionality. *Developmental Science, 10*, 121–125.

Tomasello, M., & Herrmann, E. (2010). Ape and human cognition: What's the difference? *Current Directions in Psychological Science, 19*,1, 3–8.

Tomasello, M., & Vaish, A. (2013). Origins of human cooperation and morality. *Annual Review of Psychology, 64*, 231–255.

Tomasello, M., Carpenter, M., Call, J., Behne, T., & Moll, H. (2005). Understanding and sharing intentions: The origins of cultural cognition. *Behavioral & Brain Sciences, 28*(5), 675–691.

Tomes, Y. I. (2008). Ethnicity, cognitive styles, and math achievement: Variability within African-American post-secondary students. *Multicultural Perspectives, 10* (1), 17–23.

Tomicic, A., & Berardi, F. (2018). Between past and present: The sociopsychological constructs of colonialism, coloniality and postcolonialism. *Integrative Psychological & Behavioral Science, 52*(1), 152–175.

Totsika, V., & Sylva, K. (2004). The Home Observation for Measurement of the Environment revisited. *Child & Adolescent Mental Health, 9*(1), 25–35.

Trawick-Smith, J. (2010). Drawing back the lens on play: A frame analysis of young children's play in Puerto Rico. *Early Education and Development, 21*(4), 536–567.

Trevarthen, C. (2009). The intersubjective psychobiology of human meaning: Learning of culture depends on interest for co-operative practical work – And affection for the joyful art of good company. *Psychoanalytic Dialogues, 19*(5), 507–518.

Trevarthen, C., & Aitken, A. K. (2001). Infant inter-subjectivity: Research, theory and clinical applications. *Journal of Child Psychiatry and Psychology, 42*, 3–48.

Tunçgenç, B., & Cohen, E. (2018). Interpersonal movement synchrony facilitates pro-social behavior in children's peer-play. *Developmental Science, 21*(1), e12505.

Ucan, S., & Webb, M. (2015). Social regulation of learning during collaborative inquiry learning in science: How does it emerge and what are its functions? *International Journal of Science Education, 37*(15), 2503–2532.

Umemura, T., & Traphagan, J. (2015). Reviewing Japanese concepts of *amae* and *ie* to deeper understand the relevance of secure-base behavior in the context of Japanese caregiver–child interactions. *Integrative Psychological & Behavioral Science, 49*(4), 714–736.

Valsiner, J. (2017). *From methodology to methods in human psychology*. New York: Springer.

van Schaik, S. D. M., Leseman, P. P. M., & de Haan, M. (2018). Using a group-centered approach to observe interactions in early childhood education. *Child Development, 89*(3), 897–913.

Vandenbroucke, L., Spilt, J., Verschueren, K., Piccinin, C., & Baeyens, D. (2018). The classroom as a developmental context for cognitive development: A meta-analysis on the importance of teacher–student interactions for children's executive functions. *Review of Educational Research, 88*(1), 125–164.

Veiga, G., Leng, W., Cachucho, R., Ketelaar, L., Kok, J. N., Knobbe, A., Neto, C., & Rieffe, C. (2017). Social competence at the playground: Preschoolers during recess. *Infant & Child Development, 26*, e1957.

Verba, M. (1998). Tutoring interactions between young children: How symmetry can modify asymmetrical interactions. *International Journal of Behavioral Development, 22*(1), 195–216.

Voronov, M., & Singer, J. A. (2002). The myth of individualism–collectivism: A critical review. *Journal of Social Psychology, 142*(4), 461–480.

Vrikki, M., Kershner, R., Calcagni, E., Hennessy, S., Lee, L., Hernández, F., Estrada, N., & Ahmed, F. (2019). The Teacher Scheme for Educational Dialogue Analysis (T-SEDA): Developing a research-based observation tool for supporting teacher inquiry into pupils' participation in classroom dialogue. *International Journal of Research & Method in Education, 42*(2), 185–203.

Vygotsky, L. S. (1979a). *Mind and society: The development of higher mental processes*. Cambridge, MA: Harvard University Press.
Vygotsky, L. S. (1979b). *Tools of the mind*. New York: Plenum.
Vygotsky, L. S. (1987). *Thinking and speech*. New York: Plenum.
Warneken, F., Steinwender, J., Hamann, K., & Tomasello, M. (2014). Young children's planning in a collaborative problem-solving task. *Cognitive Development, 31*, 48–58.
Washington, T., Calkins, S. D., Labban, J. D., Dollar, J. M., & Keane, S. P. (2020). Family-level factors affecting social and academic competence of African American children. *Child & Youth Care Forum, 49*, 383–407.
Watts, T. W., Nguyen, T., Carr, R. C., Vernon, F. L., & Blair, C. (2021). Examining the effects of changes in classroom quality on within-child changes in achievement and behavioral outcomes. *Child Development, 92* (4), e439–e456.
Wegerif, R. (2011). Towards a dialogic theory of how children learn to think. *Thinking Skills and Creativity, 6*(3), 179–195.
Wegerif, R. (2019). Dialogic education. In G. W. Noblit (ed.), *Oxford research encyclopedia of education*. Oxford: Oxford University Press.
Weinberger, L. A., & Starkey, P. (1994). Pretend play by African American children in Head Start. *Early Childhood Research Quarterly, 9*, 327–343.
Weisberg, D. S., Zosh, J. M., Hirsh-Pasek, K., & Golinkoff, R. M. (2013). Talking it up: Play, language development, and the role of adult support. *American Journal of Play, 6*(1), 39–54.
Weldeana, H. N. (2016). Ethnomathematics in Ethiopia: Futile or fertile for mathematics education? *Momona: Ethiopian Journal of Science, 8*(2), 146–167.
Wertsch, J., & Kazak, S. (2005). Intersubjectivity through the mastery of semiotic means in student–teacher discourse. *Research and Clinical Center for Child Development, Annual Report, 27*, 1–11.
Whitington, V., & Floyd, I. (2009). Creating intersubjectivity during socio-dramatic play at an Australian kindergarten. *Early Child Development & Care, 179*(2), 143–156.
Willoughby, M., Hudson, K., Hong, Y., & Wylie, A. (2021). Improvements in motor competence skills are associated with improvements in executive function and math problem-solving skills in early childhood. *Developmental Psychology, 57*(9), 1463.
Wohlwend, K. E. (2015). One screen, many fingers: Young children's collaborative literacy play with digital puppetry apps and touchscreen technologies. *Theory into Practice, 54*(2), 154–162.
Wüsten, C., & Lincoln, T. M. (2017). The association of family functioning and psychosis proneness in five countries that differ in cultural values and family structures. *Psychiatry Research, 253*, 158–164.
Yates, T. M., & Marcelo, A. K. (2014). Through race-colored glasses: Preschoolers' pretend play and teachers' ratings of preschooler adjustment. *Early Childhood Research Quarterly, 29*, 1–11.

Young, A. G., Alibali, M. W., & Kalish, C. W. (2019). Causal learning from joint action: Collaboration helps first graders but hinders kindergartners. *Journal of Experimental Child Psychology, 177*, 166–186.

Yuill, N. (2021). *Technology to support children's collaborative interactions: Close encounters of the shared kind.* London: Palgrave Pivot.

Yuill, N., Hinske, S., Williams, S. E., & Leith, G. (2014). How getting noticed helps getting on: successful attention capture doubles children's cooperative play. *Frontiers in Psychology, 5*, 418.

Zahavi, D. & Rochat, P. (2015) Empathy-sharing: Perspectives from phenomenology and developmental psychology. *Consciousness and Cognition, 36*, 543.

Zelazo, P. D., & Lyons, K. E. (2012). The potential benefits of mindfulness training in early childhood: a developmental social cognitive neuroscience perspective. *Child Development Perspectives, 6*(2), 154–160.

Zillmer, N., & Kuhn, D. (2018). Do similar-ability peers regulate one another in a collaborative discourse activity? *Cognitive Development, 45*, 68–76.

Zulauf-McCurdy, C. A., & Loomis, A. M. (2023). Parent and teacher perceptions of the parent–teacher relationship and child self-regulation in preschool: Variations by child race. *Early Childhood Education Journal, 51*(4), 765–779.

Index

activity theory, 54, 157. *See* cultural historical activity theorists
affective social competence, 13
attunement, 50, 55, 64, 88, 114

child behavior checklists (CBCLs), 4, 9
classroom quality, 86, 87
collaborative
   cognition, 85, 93, 95, 141, 177, 179
   competence, 20–23, 24, 43
   problem-solving, 103, 118, 211, 212–214
collective subject, 71
collectivism vs. individualism, 30, 31
Confucian heritage, 38
cultural differences
   child-rearing and development, 33–42
   cognition, 38–40
   subjectivity, 29
cultural historical activity theorists, 28, 32, 40, 54, 59, 62, 65

data collection clearinghouses
   FACES, ECLS-B/K, 6
dialogic
   coding scheme, 179, 180
   education, 94, 95, 99, 177, 209
dynamic systems theory, 17

embodied, 57, 59
emotional behavior disorder, 14, 15
exploratory talk, 98, 125, 136, 181, 202

filial piety, 28

Head Start
   as research site, 11–13
HOME survey. *See* methodology
household chaos
   measurement, 7
human–computer interaction, 91, 98

Indigenous
   math practices, 41
   ontology, 29, 43
   psychology, 26–31, 33, 48
   self, 28
individualism, 26, 29, 176, 214, 224, 226
individualistic
   methods, 21, 93, 210
   research methods, 160, 175
infancy, 55, 57
interobjectivity, 175
intersubjectivity, 24, 27, 31, 43, 48
   elementary interactions, 205
   methods, 67–68
   new SAE theory, 80, 84, 114–116, 138, 228–229
   theory, 32, 54, 58, 67

joint attention, 49, 51, 57, 65, 82, 173, 175, 182, 221, 223

learning by observing and pitching in, 32, 91

metacommunication, 58, 67, 69, 72
   research, 56, 68, 72, 74
   theory, 52–53, 73
methodology
   culturally valid, 29
   for assessing collaborative competence, 62, 116–122, 142–155
   for assessing elementary interactions, 182–183
   individualistic and cultural bias, 225–228

observational measures, 86, 88, 155
ontogeny, 51, 222
outcome variable, 4, 5, 9, 10

parent–child interaction, 88–90
participatory sense-making, 54–55
perspective-taking, 31, 62, 91, 123, 222, 223
PISA, 211

play
    methods of assessment, 146
    pretend, 56, 64, 72, 101–102
    research, 139–141
    theory of, 159–161
play-based pedagogy, 93–94, 177, 220
prolepsis, 53, 56–57, 70, 75, 78

qualitative analysis, 121, 124, 131, 140, 172

risk, children placed at, 4–5, 11–20
    cumulative, 6, 8
    measurement of, 3–6, 10, 15

scaffolding, 85, 94, 212
    parent–child interactions, 57
    peer interactions, 215, 220
school readiness, 12
schooling, xiv, 12, 16, 37, 176, 218
sociolinguistic, 64, 67, 69, 75
stereotype threat, 210
subjectivity, 24, 27

synchrony, 33, 57, 75, 81, 88, 127, 178, 181, 182, 209, 213, 216
    as part of collaboration, 107
    as part of new SAE theory, 65, 69–73, 80, 104, 113, 127, 129, 130, 131, 138, 172, 216
    as part of SAE, 104–109
    dyadic, 57, 59
    fluid, 33
    research, 69–73

teacher report, 15
    bias, 7, 15, 18
teaching
    assessments of, 85–88
teaching quality
    training redesign, 218–220
technologically mediated. *See* human–computer interaction
temperament, 18
transformative activist stance, 48, 54, 229, 231

zone of proximal development, 85

For EU product safety concerns, contact us at Calle de José Abascal, 56–1°, 28003 Madrid, Spain or eugpsr@cambridge.org.

www.ingramcontent.com/pod-product-compliance
Ingram Content Group UK Ltd.
Pitfield, Milton Keynes, MK11 3LW, UK
UKHW021945070625
459283UK00021B/323